Spring 6/1983

CUBA in the 1970s

Revised Edition

CUBA
in the
1970s

Pragmatism and Institutionalization

Carmelo Mesa-Lago

UNIVERSITY OF NEW MEXICO PRESS

Albuquerque

Library of Congress Cataloging in Publication Data

Mesa-Lago, Carmelo.
    Cuba in the 1970s.

    Includes bibliographical references and index.
    1. Cuba—Economic conditions—1959-
2. Cuba—Politics and government—1959-   3. Cuba—
Social conditions—1959-   4. Cuba—Foreign
relations—1959-   I. Title.
HC157.C9M47   1978   320.9'7291'064   77-93441
ISBN 0-8263-0470-2
ISBN 0-8263-0471-0 pbk.

Library of Congress Catalog Card No. 77-93441
International Standard Book No. 8263-0471-0 (paperbound)
Second Edition, Third Printing

*To the new Cuban generations
both inside and outside of the nation
with the hope that their paths
will converge in the future.*

Contents

Preface to First Edition   ix

Note to the Second Edition   xiii

CHAPTER 1 *A New Stage of the Cuban Revolution: The 1970s*   1

Five Stages of the Revolution, 1959–77   1
Increasing Soviet Influence Since 1970   10
Idealism Bows to Pragmatism   25

CHAPTER 2 *Economics: Realism and Rationality*   30

Strengthening the Planning Apparatus   31
Improving Capital and Managerial Efficiency   33
Increasing Labor Productivity   38
Fighting "Socialist Inflation"   40
Expanding Material Incentives   44
Rationalizing the Sugar Sector   49
Recantation of Old Errors and
     Impact of New Policies   54
Evaluation and Prospectives   58

CHAPTER 3 *Government and Society: Toward
              Institutionalization*   62

The Marxist Criticism of the Political
     Structure   63
The 1970 Promises of Reform   65
Separation of Government Functions:
     The Administration, the Party, and the Army   67
The Democratization of the Labor Movement   82
The Role of the Unions: Defense of
     Workers' Rights and Participationism   87
Restructuration of Mass Organizations:
     The Small Farmers   97
Restructuration of Mass Organizations:
     The Youth   101
The Congress on Education and Culture
     and the Intellectuals   106
Institutionalization à la Soviet   112

CHAPTER 4   *Foreign Policy: Multiple Roads to Socialism*   116

Realpolitik with Latin America   117
Conflicts with Old Allies and Friends   125
Changes within the OAS   131
The Conditions for U.S.-Cuban
   Rapprochement   134
The Beginning of the Dialogue   141

CHAPTER 5   *An Analysis of the Past and a*
            Forecast of the Future   146

An Attempt at Integration and Analysis   147
A Forecast for the Remainder of the 1970s
   and Early 1980s   156

Notes   161

Index   183

Tables

Table 1. Features of Five Stages in the First Two
          Decades of the Cuban Revolution: 1959–77   2

Table 2. The Reduction of "Socialist Inflation" in
          Cuba: 1970–73   44

Table 3. Economic Growth in Cuba: 1963–75   57

Table 4. Physical Output of Selected Products in
          Cuba: 1960–75 and 1980 Goals   59

Table 5. Composition of Cuba's National Assembly
          of People's Power: 1976   81

Table 6. Trade Union Elections in Cuba: 1970   85

Table 7. OAS Members' Stand on the Cuban Issue:
          1970–75   135

Table 8. A Static Comparison of Socialist Systems
          in Mid-1968   148

Table 9. A Dynamic Comparison of the Cuban System
          at the Peak of Each Stage and with the
          Soviet System in 1973   151

Preface to First Edition

The Cuban Revolution is a phenomenon in such flux that to write about it always involves a risk: what appears as solid after some years of accumulated evidence can dramatically change in a few weeks or even days. Nineteen years after Fidel Castro's takeover, one thing at least is clear: the revolutionary process has not moved steadily and in the same direction but has been erratic, submitted to numerous changes in philosophy and policy. Five stages of the Revolution can now be distinguished: 1959–60—liquidation of the capitalist system; 1961–63—introduction of socialist institutions following the pre-reform Soviet system; 1963–65—discussion of and experimentation with alternative systems of socialist organization; 1966–70—adoption and radicalization of the idealistic Sino-Guevarist system; and, since 1970—return to pragmatism and the more conventional post-reform Soviet system.

I have already devoted considerable time and space elsewhere to describing and analyzing the first four stages of the Revolution (1959–70) and, hence, this book will not duplicate my previous writings. It will concentrate on the current stage, specifically on the four years elapsed from mid-1970 to mid-1974. Very little has been written on this stage, mostly journalistic articles which describe fragmentally specific facets of the process thus lacking an overall, cohesive analysis of it.

My contention is that the Revolution has come of age and, learning from its mistakes and under Soviet influence, has become increasingly pragmatic and institutionalized. The former personalistic-charismatic regime is being transformed by delegation of power from the "maximum leader" to technocrats, separation of functions of the administration, the party, and the armed forces, and revitalization of the party, the unions, and other mass organizations. The romanticism of the 1960s has apparently come to an end, resulting in 'disillusion for permanent revolutionaries and devoted idealists. Thus a noticeable decline of interest in Cuba is reported from university campuses in the United States and abroad. Fidel Castro is no longer a critic of the Soviet Union but its most conspicuous defender in the Third World. The days of sending armed expeditions to establish guerrilla *foci* that would transform the Andean range into the Sierra Maestra of South America are over. Today Cuba is busily working out trade, diplomatic, and anti-hijacking agreements with as many Latin American countries as possible. The appealing, quixotic attempt to skip the transitional phase of socialism and rapidly create a "New Man" in an egalitarian communistic society through the development of consciousness, the use of moral incentives, and labor mobilization has been quietly halted. The talk of the day in Cuba is economic incentives, wage differentials, and building the material base through the use of cost-benefit analysis and raising capital efficiency and labor productivity. The uniqueness of the Cuban Revolution, so much praised in the past by Sartre, has gradually dulled and the more conventional features of socialism "à la Eastern Europe" appear increasingly stronger in the island.

And yet the Revolution is there, surviving innumerable confrontations and crises. The Cubans reportedly feel that the worst is behind and that there are better days ahead. The obsessive mobilization and ascetic frugality of the 1960s have receded and life seems easier now. Instead of trying to solve all the problems of the continent at once, Cuban leaders and bureaucrats have realistically turned inward to tackle daily domestic problems with more patience, caution, and rationality. The satisfaction of basic needs like food, clothing, and housing is still the most difficult problem facing them but there have been some improvements in this area since eight years ago. The new stage, however, has negative aspects such as the tightening control over ideology, education, and culture, while the promised democratization of unions and workers' participation in decision making have to be tested in the immediate future.

Research for this book required a systematic and exhaustive review of Cuban magazines, newspapers, and radio dispatches, and of the growing specialized literature published in Cuban *ad hoc* reports and scientific journals during 1970–73. My work as editor of the *Cuban Studies Newsletter* published by the Center for Latin American Studies, University of Pittsburgh, was of great help because it gave me exposure to thousands of items that, since 1970, are annually classified by the *CSN*. In addition, through exchanges of the *CSN*, we obtain rare statistical bulletins from Cuba and technical reports most of which are not available elsewhere in the United States. I usually used *Granma Weekly Review* for the official English version of the Cuban leaders' speeches. When the latter were not reproduced in that publication or the speech had special significance, I resorted to one of the two Cuban daily newspapers (*Granma* and *Juventud Rebelde*) and did the translation myself.

Segments of this book have appeared earlier in the following articles of mine: "The Sovietization of the Cuban Revolution: Its Consequences for the Western Hemisphere," *World Affairs* 136 (Summer 1973), pp. 3–35; "Castro's Domestic Course," *Problems of Communism* 22 (September–October 1973), pp. 27–38; and "Conversion of the Cuban Economy to Soviet Orthodoxy," *Journal of Economic Issues* 8 (March 1974), pp. 41–65. I am grateful to the editors of these journals for granting permission to use materials from the cited articles in this book. My appreciation also to Professor Edward Gonzalez, from UCLA, who supplied materials for and commented on chapter 1; to Professor Lourdes Casal, from Rutgers University, who shared with me many of her impressions from a visit to Cuba in the summer of 1973; to Dr. Heinrich Brunner, from Freien Universität Berlin, who made rigorous criticisms of chapter 2 and gave me insights from his visit to Cuba in late 1972; and to Professor Nelson Valdés, from the University of New Mexico, who supplied some materials for chapter 3. The responsibility for what is said here of course is only mine. The book would not have been published without the substantial help received from: Shirley Kregar, Carolyn Wilson, and Donna Bobin from the University of Pittsburgh's Center for Latin American Studies who edited and/or typed the manuscript several times; Eduardo Lozano, the Latin American bibliographer of the University of Pittsburgh who was, as always, generous with his time and extremely helpful with his knowledge of the Cuban collection; and to Carl Mora from the University of New Mexico Press who encouraged me to put together this book and did the final editing.

Each of my last three books on Cuba has been preceded by the birth of a new daughter, this one by Helenita. She, as well as Elizabeth and Ingrid, and my always cheerful wife Elena have filled with love the time that the book robbed from them. In return I offer this book to them, with my love increased for their precious contribution.

Pittsburgh, June 1974   C. M. L.

Note to the Second Edition

The success of this book produced a second printing in 1976. Faced with the alternative of having a third printing in 1977 or a revised, updated second edition I chose the latter. The reason was the significant events that have taken place since mid-1974 both within Cuba and in the island's foreign policy: the first congress of the Communist party (1975), the enactment of the first socialist constitution (1976), the establishment and expansion of the Organs of People's Power (1974–76), the complete reorganization of the government structure (1976–77), the sugar-pushed economic boom (1974–75), and subsequent decline (1976–77), the introduction of the five-year plan (1976–80) and the Economic Management System, the OAS decision to free member countries to reestablish trade and diplomatic relations with Cuba (1975), the successful military intervention of Cuba in Angola (1975–76), and the direct U.S.-Cuban negotiations and agreements which have improved relations between the two countries (1977).

In opening the Preface to the first edition of this book, I emphasized the risks involved in writing and making predictions on the Cuban Revolution. Some of my forecasts in that edition proved to be wrong but, in general, I think that the analysis is still valid and the trends detected were remarkably accurate.

One personal hope that has not materialized in the last three years in spite of considerable efforts has been to return to Cuba in order to conduct field research in my native country. At the time I finished writing the first edition of this book, the Cuban government informed me through its mission in the United Nations that it had granted me a visa to stay in Cuba for three weeks in September 1974. One week prior to departure, however, I was notified that the visa had been suspended. Since then I have been told several times that the possibility of my visit is not closed but waiting for a better atmosphere. In the meantime, a good number of U.S. social scientists of divergent ideological coloration have been allowed to enter the island and U.S.-Cuban relations have improved considerably. It is still my hope that I will be allowed to enter Cuba in the near future and personally check many of my views and analyses conducted in the United States throughout more than fifteen years of research.

Oxford, England, October 1977   C. M. L.

Abbreviations of Cuban Institutions Referred to in this Book
with Date of Founding

ANAP	National Association of Small Farmers, 1961
CDR	Committees for the Defense of the Revolution, 1960
CTC	Confederation of Cuban Workers, 1939
EJT	Youth Army of Work, 1973
FAR	Revolutionary Armed Forces, 1961
FMC	Federation of Cuban Women, 1960
ICAIC	Cuban Institute of Cinema Arts, 1959–76
INRA	National Institute of Agrarian Reform, 1959–76
JUCEPLAN	Central Planning Board, 1960
MININ	Ministry of Interior, 1961
OLAS	Organization of Latin American Solidarity, 1967
OPP	Organs of People's Power, 1974
ORI	Integrated Revolutionary Organizations, 1961–63
PCC	Communist party of Cuba, 1965
PSP	Socialist Popular party, 1925–61
PURS	United Party of the Socialist Revolution, 1963–65
SDE	Economic Management System, 1977
SMO	Compulsory Military Service, 1963
SS	Compulsory Social Service, 1973
UMAP	Military Units to Aid Production, 1964–73
UNEAC	National Union of Writers and Artists of Cuba, 1961
UJC	Young Communist League, 1962

1

A New Stage of the
Cuban Revolution: The 1970s

Since the triumph of the insurrection against the Batista regime in 1959, the Cuban Revolution has passed through five distinct phases. In the 1970s the Soviet Union has been increasing its influence over Cuba through personal and institutional channels of both a political and economic nature.

Table 1 presents a concise but global picture of the principal features of each of the five stages of the Revolution from 1959 to 1977. The following sections will not review all of these features but will attempt to pinpoint the currents of thought that promoted changes and shaped the various stages.[1]

Five Stages of the Revolution, 1959–77

The first stage of the Revolution (1959–60) lacked a defined ideology, but there were statist, populist, antimarket, con-

1

TABLE 1

Features of Five Stages in the First Two Decades of the Cuban Revolution: 1959–77

Features	Liquidation of Pre-revolutionary Institutions 1959–60	Attempt to Introduce the Soviet System 1961–63	Debate of and Experimentation with Alternative Systems 1963–66	Adoption and Radicalization of the Sino-Guevarist System 1966–70	Return to Pragmatism and the Soviet System 1970–77
Development Strategy	Industrialization, anti-sugar bias	Ibid; sharp decline in sugar output, delays in industrial development	Return to sugar, heavy industrialization postponed	Emphasis on sugar reaches climax in 1970; record crop but target is not fulfilled and output declines in rest of economy	Deemphasis on sugar; targets set at levels that can be reached without affecting other sectors
Ownership of Means of Production	Increasing collectivization with momentum in late 1960; agriculture is exception with predominance of private farms and cooperatives	Agricultural cooperatives transformed into state farms in 1962; reduction in private farm sector in 1963 and procurement quotas ("acopio") imposed upon farmers	No significant changes	State ownership is completed (except for 1/3 of agriculture) in 1968 during the "Revolutionary Offensive"	Pressure on private farmers to expand their sales to and work for the state
Planning Model	Economic disorganization and lack of controls; gradual reduction of market	Attempt to introduce highly centralized, physical planning with the aid of Soviet and Czech technicians	Change in development strategy and problems with central planning induce experimentation with decentralization techniques	Long-run, central "macro" plan substituted by short-run, loose "micro" (sectorial) plans	Return to long-run central planning with aid of computer techniques
Financing Method	Mixture of private (rapidly declining) and budgetary (in state sector)	Mainly budgetary, but problems with capital efficiency	Experiments with self-financing in 1/3 of state enterprises, particularly in agriculture and foreign trade	Budgetary throughout the economy, except private farms	Gradual return to self-financing
Consumption and Capital Accumulation	Emphasis on consumption (wage increases, free social services); capital accumulation declines sharply	Individual consumption restricted, rationing begins in 1962; recuperation of pre-revolutionary investment rate	Emphasis on capital accumulation continues	Capital accumulation is escalated reaching a peak in 1968; but there is considerable waste of investment due to inefficient allocation and use of capital	Moderate reduction in capital accumulation and increase in consumption; emphasis on capital efficiency
Incentives and Egalitarianism	Material incentives, mainly of an individual nature, reduction in extreme inequalities	Decline in material-individual incentives, emphasis on collective incentives, mostly material; rationing is an equalizer	Limited experimentation with individual-material incentives, e.g. wage differentials, awards in kind, production bonuses	Drastic reduction of individual-material incentives; enormous emphasis on moral stimuli and egalitarianism to forge the unselfish "New Man"	Previous excesses on moral incentives and egalitarianism are criticized; return to individual-material incentives

Criteria for Manager Selection	Alienated managers and technicians who fled the country or were fired are replaced by loyal but incompetent revolutionaries	Attempt to train managerial personnel in Cuba or abroad—principally in Eastern Europe and U.S.S.R.	Increased emphasis on raising managerial and technical skills	Antibureaucracy campaign reaches climax; revolutionary zeal takes predominance over expertise	Emphasis in training returns; loyal but incompetent managers have to acquire skills or will be fired
Employment and Labor Productivity	Expansion of employment in agriculture and services; labor productivity stagnant	Full employment practically achieved but largely through artificial job creation; labor productivity declines	Attempt to transfer labor surplus to agriculture and to increase labor productivity by introducing Soviet system of work quotas and wage scales	Work-quota system is neglected; labor productivity reaches lowest ebb; manpower deficit is aggravated by labor absenteeism	Reintroduction of work quotas, increase in labor productivity, reduction of labor absenteeism, a few unemployment pockets appear
Financial Equilibrium (inflation)	Consumption increases faster than production and imports; depletion of stocks; balance of payments deficit grows	Prices are frozen, rationing is introduced and gradually expanded to cover most consumer goods; the black market appears	The disequilibrium between monetary supply and available consumer goods increases and the black market grows rapidly; this operates as a disincentive for labor	The disequilibrium reaches a record in 1970 when the monetary surplus is almost equal to the population income; labor absenteeism increases to a record	The monetary surplus is reduced to less than half the population income, through price increases and expanded supply of consumer goods
Army and Para-military Bodies	Rebel Army systematically destroys remnants of old army and plays crucial role in implementing agrarian reform; militia founded in late 1959	Ministry of Armed Forces established; army is trained and equipped by the U.S.S.R.; militia is vital in defeating Bay of Pigs invasion	Increasing professionalization of the army; compulsory military service is established in 1963; weapons are taken away from militia and its role declines	Military men take top positions in the party, administration, management; increased militarization of labor through brigades	New ranks introduced in the army which becomes more specialized and reduced in size; militia is being phased out and labor brigades merged into separate agency
Party Development	Only a few political organizations are allowed to function: 26th of July Movement, Student Directorate, and PSP	ORI is integrated by the three political organizations but largely controlled by PSP; purge against sectarianism results in substitution of ORI by PURS, controlled by Castroites	PCC is established in 1965 with top positions in Castroite hands; membership is very small, seldom holds meetings and lacks program	Functions of the administration and the party are fused in practice; a new purge against the "microfaction" (some members of former PSP) is launched in 1968	Separation of administration and party functions; the latter is reorganized, its membership expanded and its first congress held in 1975
Unions and Other Mass Organizations	Pressures upon unions begin in 1959 and control measures surface in 1960; the Committees for the Defense of the Revolution are founded in 1960	Unions become "transmission belts" of administration; in 1961 private farmers are integrated into ANAP, and in 1962 youth associations into UJC	No significant changes	National congress of unions adheres to the new line; unions are practically substituted by vanguard-worker movement	Elections are held in local unions in 1971 and a national congress in 1973; ANAP and UJC are also reorganized

TABLE 1 continued

Features of Five Stages in the First Two Decades of the Cuban Revolution: 1959–77

Features	***Liquidation of Prerevolutionary Institutions 1959–60***	***Attempt to Introduce the Soviet System 1961–63***	***Debate of and Experimentation with Alternative Systems 1963–66***	***Adoption and Radicalization of the Sino-Guevarist System 1966–70***	***Return to Pragmatism and the Soviet System 1970–77***
Mobilization Techniques	Big rallies in support of government decisions and policies; mobilization is basically political	Labor mobilization begins in 1962 ("voluntary labor") to help in sugar harvest and other crops due to manpower deficit	Labor mobilization increases but more sophisticated techniques are used to increase its productivity	Labor mobilization increases dramatically, both for economic and educational reasons (development of consciousness) reaching a peak in 1968–70; productivity is neglected	Labor mobilization is gradually reduced; voluntary labor is only allowed when its productivity is assured beforehand
Control Over Education and Culture	General freedom in spite of numerous incidents and controversies	Private schools and universities are closed; government policy is defined as: within the Revolution everything, outside of it nothing; UNEAC is founded	Many "deviant" writers and intellectuals are sent to labor camps, but the measure is later reversed	Increased militancy is required from writers; several of them are officially critized by army and government officials	The Cultural and Educational Congress of 1971 introduces a more rigid and dogmatic line; conflict with foreign intellectuals
Relations with The U.S.S.R.	Reestablishment of relations; the U.S.S.R. grants credits and takes part of the former U.S. sugar quota	The U.S.S.R. becomes Cuba's main trade partner and creditor; influx of Soviet technicians; first confrontation in 1962 due to Missile Crisis	New accommodation; Castro travels twice to the U.S.S.R.; Guevara steps out; long-term economic and trade agreement between the two countries for 1965–70	New confrontation due to divergent ideologies, economic practices and foreign policy; U.S.S.R reduces oil supply and Castro purges former PSP members; beginning of new accommodation with Cuba supporting Soviet invasion of Czechoslovakia	Improvement of relations climaxes with four visits of Castro to the U.S.S.R. and Brezhnev's visit to Cuba; Soviet-Cuban Commission established, Cuba enters COMECON; long-term economic agreements signed for 1973–75 and 1976–80
Exportation of Revolution to Latin America	Ill-prepared expeditions that fail, lack of a clear ideology and strategy	Cuba ousted from OAS and isolated from Western Hemisphere; Cuban support to guerrillas increases; conflicts with communist parties	Compromising attitude with communist parties in Latin America; agreement on a few countries to which the revolution should be exported	Tricontinental conference and OLAS established; theory of the guerrilla foco as the only way to revolution officially accepted; Guevara tries it in Bolivia and is killed	The exportation of the Revolution practically ends; non-guerrilla roads to revolution are accepted; relations are reestablished with several Latin American countries

sumptionist, and nationalistic tendencies. The new revolutionary elite undertook the systematic liquidation or control of the most powerful prerevolutionary pressure groups: the army, political parties, unions, and farmers' and professional associations. These were substituted in many cases by new institutions which strongly supported the Revolution such as the Rebel Army, the militia, and the Committees for the Defense of the Revolution. In this stage a few of the political organizations that were active during the insurrection (e.g., the 26th of July Movement, the Student Directorate) plus the prerevolutionary Communist party (Popular Socialist party: PSP) and had accepted Castro's leadership were allowed to function. All important decisions, however, were made by the new government elite who mobilized huge political rallies in their support. There was expanding collectivization of the means of production and a concomitant reduction in market forces. The latter were not substituted by planning and central orders, partly because of the lack of a clear economic program and due to the alienation of former managers and technicians usually replaced by enthusiastic but unskilled revolutionaries. The net result of this situation was widespread economic disorganization. The leaders, however, had a firm commitment to expand employment and raise the living standards of the low-income strata of the population. This goal was achieved at the cost of a drastic curtailment of capital accumulation which in turn affected the viability of other goals such as the elimination of sugar monoculture through rapid industrialization and agricultural diversification. Profoundly nationalistic, the Revolution confronted U.S. interests while reestablishing diplomatic relations and expanding trade with the U.S.S.R. and other socialist countries. The prevailing spirit of continental solidarity combined with the absence of a well thought out strategy induced ill-conceived, futile efforts to promote revolution in Latin America.

After the declaration of socialist faith in early 1961, a second stage began (1961–63) in which an attempt was made to mechanistically apply the system of politico-economic organization and development prevalent at the time in the U.S.S.R. to Cuba. The few revolutionary organizations allowed to operate merged into the ORI (Integrated Revolutionary Organizations), later transformed into

PURS (United Party of the Socialist Revolution), the germ of the future Communist party. The vacuum of the market was intended to be filled by a centralized system of planning and technical aid from the Soviet Union. Emphasis was placed on the training of managerial personnel, and the unions became conduits for the orders of the central administration. Curtailment of consumption to increase investment began with the hope of accelerating the industrialization process and generating high rates of economic growth. It was during this stage that Cuba defeated the U.S.-sponsored invasion at the Bay of Pigs, became almost isolated in the Western Hemisphere, increased its efforts to export the Revolution, and moved closer to the U.S.S.R. This warm relationship was suddenly shaken by the Soviet-American understanding in the Missile Crisis of 1962 which, in the official Cuban view, was a Soviet retreat aggravated by the lack of consultation with Cuba. Failures in planning and the development strategy made now skeptical Cuban leaders question the universality of the Soviet system and its applicability to an island plantation economy. Thus the Revolution moved into a third stage (1963–66) dominated by a lively debate on alternative systems of organization and development strategies.[2]

In that controversy, Ernesto "Che" Guevara and his followers, influenced by the system of the Maoist "Great Leap Forward," endorsed an idealistic line of thought (departing from more conventional Soviet thought of the 1960s) which presented three main objectives. First was the total elimination of the market or "commodity production" through full collectivization of the means of production, a highly centralized-computerized planning system, central financing of all state enterprises through budgetary appropriations (i.e., nonrepayable, interest-free grants, with transfer of all enterprise profits back to the state budget), and the gradual eradication of money and "material incentives." To be successful, the first action had to be paralleled by the creation of an unselfish, self-sacrificing, frugal, fully-socialized, egalitarian human being—the "New Man." This would be attained by raising mass consciousness through education, mobilization, unpaid voluntary labor, and "moral incentives" (e.g., banners, medals, and free social services provided by the state). Such steps, in turn, would facilitate the process of capital accumulation and economic development. The third goal was the exportation of the Cuban revolutionary model to Latin America. This action was urged on by the premise that continental revolution was indispensable for the survival of socialism in Cuba; it was assumed that the rural guerrilla *foco* was the only way to generate this revolution. The Guevarists were openly critical of the U.S.S.R because, according to their criteria, this nation's domestic and foreign policies did not conform with what socialism should be. They were in favor of the principle of permanent revolution, had a distaste for institutionalization, did not elaborate on the role that the party should play, and proclaimed that trade unions were unnecessary.

Confronting Guevara was a moderate pragmatist group led by the economist Carlos Rafael Rodríguez and composed mostly of pro-Soviet members of the prerevolutionary Communist party (PSP). This group, under the influence of Libermanism (publicized and experimented within the U.S.S.R. by Khrushchev and moderately implemented by Brezhnev and Kosygin), advocated three different positions. One was that central planning should also be based in cybernetic and input-output techniques but with some autonomy at the enterprise level and with partial use of market mechanisms. Against the budgetary technique, they introduced self-financing in about one-third of the state enterprises. These received loans from the central bank, loans which earned interest and had to be repaid; in turn, the enterprise could retain a good part of its profits for reinvestment and expansion. A second goal of the group was economic institutionalization based upon an efficient bureaucracy, high labor productivity through the Soviet system of work quotas, and material incentives (e.g., wage differentials, bonuses for overfulfillment of work quotas, overtime payments, and awards in kind). Thirdly, the group also favored a strong Communist party, Soviet-style unions, close links with the U.S.S.R., and more flexibility in Cuba's foreign relations with Latin America.

For four years, Castro abstained from openly participating in the controversy but cleverly dismissed or sent abroad the leaders of the two opposing groups. Once his path was cleared of potential opponents, he started the fourth stage of the Revolution (mid-1966 to mid-1970) by endorsing Sino-Guevarism although embellished with personalistic Castroite features. For instance, the most important economic decisions were not concentrated in a "scientific and objective" central planning apparatus, but were made by the prime minister and his inner circle of loyalists and implemented through "mini" or sectorial plans. Emphasis on capital accumulation, mobilization, moral incentives, egalitarianism, and abolition of money was heavier than in Guevara's scheme. Grandiose output targets were set for the years ahead, including ten million tons of sugar for the harvest of 1970. The army's influence increased enormously and pervaded many facets of society while the party stagnated. (In 1965, still under Soviet influence, the Communist party of Cuba [PCC] was established but under Castroite control.) In the meantime, Guevara was fighting in Bolivia to transform the Andean mountain range into a Latin American Sierra Maestra, and Cuban-Soviet relations reached their lowest ebb when Castro denounced the U.S.S.R. for limiting the supply of oil to Cuba and imprisoned a group of PSP leaders ("the microfaction") for their alleged antigovernment activities. The radicalization movement reached a climax in the spring of 1968 with the "Revolutionary Offensive" (in some aspects similar to the Chinese Cultural Revolution), under which the remainder of the private sector was nationalized, mobilization was accentuated, and a record was established in capital accumulation at the cost of sacrificing consumption. Cuba then claimed that it was building communism and was ahead of the U.S.S.R. in communist ownership, the development of consciousness, and egalitarian distribution. Disaster on both the internal and external fronts (Cuba's deteriorating economy and Guevara's death in Bolivia) forced a reconsideration of some of the previous policies, and the Soviet invasion of Czechoslovakia offered the golden opportunity for it.

Castro's endorsement of the invasion, although qualified, facilitated a steady improvement in Cuban-Soviet relations. This accommodation, together with the realization that continental revolution was not possible for the moment, was pivotal in shaping a less idealistic, more compromising foreign policy vis-à-vis Latin America. Hence other roads to revolutionary change—besides that of the guerrilla *foco*—were accepted, such as peaceful elections and military coups. Both exportation of the Revolution and aid to revolutionary groups in Latin America declined. Although externally the revolutionary policy became increasingly moderate, internally Sino-Guevarism continued in operation as the gigantic mobilization for the 1970 sugar crop gained momentum. The Soviet leaders had accurate information on the poor chances for achieving this goal but they abstained from obstructing Castro's chosen strategy. Probably the gains in Cuban foreign policy were enough reward for them at that point, and to exert pressure in internal matters could have once again generated friction. The sugar harvest eventually produced a record 8.5 million tons; this, however, was below the 10 million-ton target and was achieved at the cost of a sharp decline of production in the nonsugar sector and overall economic dislocation. As a result, the Sino-Guevarist model suffered a mortal blow, Castro's prestige and strength were eroded, and the Soviet Union increased its bargaining power.

Since mid-1970, Soviet influence in Cuba has increased considerably, shaping a fifth stage of the Revolution with the following features.[3] Externally Cuba has moved closer than ever to the U.S.S.R. and become its chief defender in the Third World against criticism from more revolutionary leftist positions. Diplomatic and/or trade relations have been reestablished with a dozen Latin American countries with divergent socio-politico-economic systems. Internally there is a process of institutionalization characterized by delegation of power from the previously quasi-omnipotent Castro, strengthening of the Communist party, specialization of the army, and reorganization of the unions and other mass organizations. This has been paralleled by the tightening of central controls in ideology, education, and culture. In economics there has been an acknowledgment that the previous policy was too idealistic and that a more realistic, conventional approach is necessary. New policies include the strengthening of the central planning apparatus, the more rational use of capital and manpower to increase productivity, the expansion of material incentives, the drastic reduction in labor mobilization, and the setting of realistic output targets (particularly in sugar).

Increasing Soviet Influence Since 1970

Most specialists on Cuban affairs believe, regardless of their ideological coloration, that since Prime Minister Fidel Castro endorsed the Soviet invasion of Czechoslovakia, the U.S.S.R. has played an increasing role in Cuban affairs, particularly since 1970.[4] Soviet control has been achieved in various ways. Castro has delegated most economic powers to President Osvaldo Dorticós, a moderate whom the Soviets trust, and to Carlos Rafael Rodríguez, chief economist, planner, and former member of the PSP who is in charge of foreign relations. The prime minister seems to have turned his energies outside of the country. From the end of 1971 to the end of 1977, he spent a total of seven months traveling abroad. Through an intergovernmental Cuban-Soviet Commission, controlled from the Cuban side by Rodríguez, the U.S.S.R. has institutionalized its supervision over the use of its economic and military aid to the island. A new wave of Soviet technicians has flooded into Cuba, and native personnel in charge of plants built with Soviet aid are being trained in the U.S.S.R. The Cuban economy and its planning have become even more integrated into the Soviet bloc through the former's entrance into Comecon (or CMEA: Council for Mutual Economic Assistance). Numerous agreements and joint communiqués have been signed by the two countries concerning trade, technical aid, repayment of debts, credits, planning, satellite communication, and foreign policy.

In December 1970, Carlos Rafael Rodríguez led a Cuban delegation to Moscow where meetings were held with a team of Soviet economists headed by Nikolai Baibakov, director of the Soviet Central Planning Board (GOSPLAN). As a result of such conversations, the Cuban-Soviet Commission of Economic, Scientific, and Technical Collaboration was established. In February 1971, the Cuban-Soviet long-term trade and payments agreement for 1965–70 was temporarily extended until 1975.[5] The signing of a permanent trade agreement was delayed until the Commission had carefully studied the situation. To complete the basic details for the Commission's organization, Baibakov visited Cuba in April and May, and Cuban chancellor Raúl Roa went to Moscow in June 1971. Roa's delegation, which included the President of the Central Bank and the Minister of Foreign Trade, met with Brezhnev, Kosygin, and Gromyko.[6]

The first meeting of the Commission was held in Havana early in September 1971. The Soviet delegation was led by the vice president of the U.S.S.R. Council of Ministers, Vladimir Novikov, and was composed of top officials from the ministries of foreign trade, merchant marine, construction of agricultural and industrial machinery, electricity and civil aviation, as well as the Soviet ambassador in Havana. The Cuban delegation was led by Rodríguez, who also presided over the meetings, and was composed of top officials from the Central Planning Board (JUCEPLAN), the ministries of foreign trade, merchant marine, basic industry, mining-fuel-metallurgy, the state agencies of agricultural mechanization and development, fishing, electricity and aviation, and the Cuban ambassador in Moscow. Rodríguez opened the meetings praising the Soviet role in the birth and support of the Cuban Revolution. In the same line, Novikov reported that Soviet-Cuban trade in 1970 had increased by 60 percent over 1966, reaching more than one billion rubles per year (about three million dollars daily); he also stressed the pivotal importance of Soviet oil, steel, and machinery for the island's economy and listed the factories and plants built with Soviet aid as well as the repairs made in seventy-eight sugar mills (more than half of those in existence).[7]

The agenda for the meeting included the establishment of a more efficient system of training the Cuban personnel in charge of the Soviet-made plants; Cuban reports on the measures adopted to make up for the delays caused by the 1970 sugar-harvest mobilization in the Soviet-aid construction of one electrical plant and two fertilizer plants; and the possibility of future Soviet cooperation in mechanizing the sugar harvest, expanding electrical capacity, and establishing a pharmaceutical industry in Cuba. Premier Castro

attended the signing of the agreements but, unaccustomedly, did
not say a word; in the official picture he was standing behind
Rodríguez, who was signing the document. The latter thanked the
Soviet delegates "for their efforts in organizing and making more
effective use of the aid provided by the U.S.S.R." In the protocol,
the Cubans agreed to speed up the operation of loading and
unloading Soviet vessels in Cuban ports, to accelerate the work at
plants being built with Soviet aid, and to send to the U.S.S.R. the
technicians who would direct such plants. The Soviet Union
promised to send Cuba a new sugar-cane harvester jointly designed
by engineers from both countries (the KTP-1) and to provide
technical aid for Cuba's attempt to locally produce its own
harvesters ("Libertadora" and "Henderson") on a large scale. Tests
to be supervised by Soviet experts would be conducted on both
machines during the 1972 harvest. Nothing concrete was agreed
upon regarding new electrical and pharmaceutical plants.[8] Upon his
return to Moscow, Novikov announced that the Commission had
also reviewed the fulfillment of trade agreements in 1969–71.[9]

At the end of October 1971, Premier Alexei Kosygin visited
Cuba. He had previously been in Havana in June 1967, on his
return to Moscow from his Glassboro meeting with President
Johnson. This was at a time when Soviet-Cuban relations were
deteriorating, and the important dignitary received a cool official
reception and little attention from the Cuban press. In contrast, his
second visit was heralded with great fanfare, newspapers devoted
almost entire issues to reporting the event, and Kosygin held talks
with both Castro brothers, President Dorticós and, of course,
Rodríguez. More cordial relations were evident when in a meeting
with Castro the Soviet premier said: "We have lost no time in
getting together with comrade Fidel. . . . It isn't only on this
meeting but also in other matters that we came to a quick
understanding with him." Castro replied: "One way to express our
gratitude to the U.S.S.R. for their great aid is to extract the
maximum out of the Soviet equipment, to use it efficiently, and to
keep it in running condition."[10] There was a communiqué signed by
both premiers stressing the "complete mutual understanding"
reached on the strengthening of politico-economic links between

the two nations. In the document, Castro fully endorsed Soviet foreign policy while Kosygin condemned the United States' "illegal holding" of the Guantánamo base and invited Castro to visit the U.S.S.R.[11]

In November 1971, Castro partly accepted responsibility for Cuba's previous conflicts with the Soviet Union; one month later, in Moscow, Dorticós acknowledged that the U.S.S.R. was the leading socialist country in the world. Once the frictions between the two countries had been overcome, Kosygin announced in Moscow that conversations had begun on the signing of a trade agreement for 1972–75 that would replace the old 1965–70 agreement which had been provisionally extended.[12] (In the meantime, the old trade agreement was hurting Cuba economically: in 1972 the international price of sugar was above the 6.11 cents per pound paid to Cuba by the U.S.S.R. In December 1971, the latter paid 7.14 cents per pound for 270,000 tons of sugar bought from Brazil, the archenemy of Cuba.)[13]

The extent to which Cuba had departed from Sino-Guevarism and sided with the Soviets became evident in the treatment given by the Cuban press to Nixon's visit to China and his visits to Moscow and Warsaw in 1972. Reports of Nixon's visit to China were cleverly manipulated by the Cuban press to criticize the Chinese. In one issue of the party newspaper *Granma*, the front page was divided into halves: the top half contained news and photographs of the U.S. bombing of Vietnam, while the bottom half had photographs of Nixon shaking hands with Mao and Chou En-lai. The newspaper also reproduced excerpts of the friendly toasts exchanged between Nixon and Chou, and its last page was full of well-selected, embarrassing photographs with ironic comments.[14] In contrast, Nixon's visits to Moscow and Warsaw were reported factually (taken from TASS), although very briefly, not in prominent places, and without evaluation or comment.[15]

The second meeting of the Cuban-Soviet Commission was held in Moscow on April 10–15, 1972, but scanty information is available about it. Rodríguez was the head of the Cuban delegation, and Novikov presided over the meeting. The composition of the delegations was similar to that of the first meeting. At this meeting, mechanization of the sugar harvest was discussed, and the results of the tests done during the 1972 sugar crop on the various types of cane-harvesters were probably evaluated. (Significantly, in June, the U.S.S.R. announced that a factory to build the KPT-1 model— sponsored by the Soviets—would be sent to Cuba.) The Commission also agreed to supply Cuba with an electronic computer to help in economic planning, thus strengthening Rodríguez's position in favor of a more technical and powerful central planning apparatus. (At the same time that the Commission was holding its sessions, representatives of the central planning boards of both countries, the Soviet GOSPLAN and the Cuban JUCEPLAN, were discussing collaboration in planning.) Other topics discussed were the mechanization and modernization of ports (the inefficiency of loading and unloading Soviet ships had been a matter of discussion in the first meeting), civil aviation, irrigation, hydroelectric energy, a pharmaceutical industry, education, and communications. Rodríguez decorated Novikov with the medal of the Cuban Academy of Sciences, met with Kosygin, and traveled to Berlin.[16]

Although the subject of military aid was not included in either of the two agreements of the Commission, events in 1972 showed that this was on the agenda. Early in January the Cuban Navy received several Soviet missile-carrying launches that doubled its missile and anti-aircraft equipment.[17] In April, the air force, in turn, received a flotilla of MIG-23s, the most technologically advanced Soviet aircraft, which modernized the Cuban stock of MIG-15s, MIG-17s, MIG-19s, and MIG-21s. For several months a team consisting of hundreds of Soviet military experts led by Lt. General Dimitri Krutskikn had been training Cuban personnel in the use of this equipment. The ceremony to present the airplanes received wide publicity; it was opened by Krutskikn, who was followed by the Soviet ambassador in Cuba, Nikita Tulubeev, and it was closed by Minister of the Armed Forces Raúl Castro, who said that the military aid was proof of Soviet confidence.[18]

In May 1972, Castro began a trip to Africa and Eastern Europe, which lasted sixty-three days (May 2–July 6), longer than all of his previous trips abroad put together. Before taking off, the premier said: "Only a few years ago none of us would even dream of being outside of our country for too long, considering the way the imperialists were acting, with all their threats. Fortunately things are different now."[19] Castro was no longer afraid of the possibility of an invasion, either directly by or sponsored by the United States. He was concerned, however, about the Soviet commitment to detente with the United States, which was manifested by the fact that Nixon's decision to blockade North Vietnamese ports and escalate the bombing of the North did not impede his visit to Moscow. Probably the announcement of this visit precipitated Castro's trip to Eastern Europe. In Castro's mind, Cuba and Vietnam were in a similar position; thus, he devoted a large portion of his speeches in Eastern Europe to attacking the United States and pledging solidarity with the Vietnamese. In his speech on arriving in Poland—Nixon had just left——Castro pointed out that Cuba was not part of any security pact or military alliance (an obvious reference to the Warsaw Pact) but depended only on its own power. He was evidently attempting to apply pressure on the Soviets before his arrival in Moscow.

Brezhnev rhetorically responded to this strategy by condemning the U.S. blockade and bombing of North Vietnam as well as the U.S. occupation of the Guantánamo base in Cuba. He assured Castro that the policy of peaceful coexistence would not weaken the ideological struggle, that the confrontation between capitalism and communism would become more acute rather than weaker, and that small socialist nations would be defended and treated equally by the Soviet superpower. Apparently satisfied, Castro said that for twelve years the United States had exerted pressure on Cuba to break its ties with the U.S.S.R. but that, instead, the relations between the two countries had consolidated, reaching a level never attained before, and that Cuban confidence in the U.S.S.R. had been strengthened. Then he pledged that Cuba would never accept "opportunism, neutralism, revisionism, liberalism, or capitalist ideological penetration." One wonders whether this statement was a betrayal of his subconscious hope that the Soviet Union would abstain from such vicious practices.

In addition to showing his concern about the Soviet rapprochement with the United States, Castro's trip also made evident his new, more compromising attitude toward other countries. Four or five years earlier when Houari Boumédienne overthrew Ben Bella, who had supported Castro and whom Castro had supported, the Cuban press was strongly critical of Boumédienne. However, Castro began his long trip with a stay in Algeria of nine days, equal to the time he later spent in the U.S.S.R. (The nine days in Algeria were followed by six days in revolutionary Guinea and one day in traditional Sierra Leone.) Castro had also earlier sorted friend from foe by the country's prevailing antagonism toward the U.S.S.R.; hence, Rumania had been very high in his esteem several years ago. Now the length of stay in each of the Eastern European countries was positively correlated to their orthodoxy and good standing with Moscow: nine days in the U.S.S.R., eight in East Germany and Bulgaria, seven in Poland and Hungary, five in Czechoslovakia, and four in Rumania.

Rodríguez joined Castro for the Eastern European stage of his trip, replacing Major Juan Almeida, a black who had been an asset during the African stage of the trip. (Some members of the Cuban delegation who were ideologically unacceptable to the U.S.S.R. also returned to Havana.) Both the Cuban and the Eastern European news media ranked Rodríguez second in the Cuban delegation. He was decorated in several countries and in the Moscow meetings he, Castro, Brezhnev, Kosygin, and Podgorny met alone. Photographs of Rodríguez at important meetings were frequently shown; he apparently was taking care of the serious business. During the trip, Castro did all that he could to build up his own image. He submitted to unaccustomed formalties such as wearing a necktie to receive the Dimitrov Order in Bulgaria and the Lenin Order in Moscow, and wearing a cap and gown in his investment as Doctor Honoris Cause at Charles University in Prague. On the other hand, he played his old role of a populist, charismatic leader, visiting dozens of factories and farms even in remote areas, playing football with Bulgarians and basketball with Poles, and often mixing with the population. Castro's visit to the U.S.S.R. was originally scheduled for three weeks but lasted only nine days. When leaving the country, the prime minister said that he would return in 1973 or 1974 "for a more extended unofficial visit." Rodríguez stayed in Moscow for a few days after Castro left, preparing a significant announcement.

On July 11, 1972, at Comecon's twenty-sixth meeting, Rodríguez officially requested Cuba's entrance into the organization, and its eight members unanimously accepted.[20] Rodríguez promised to eliminate "once and for all" the instability of the Cuban supply of sugar to the socialist camp, asked Comecon's support in developing Cuba's nickel industry and derivates of sugar-cane bagasse, and requested entry into the Intergovernmental Commission of Socialist Countries for the Development of Electronic Computation. In turn, Kosygin stated that the needs of the Cuban economy should be coordinated with the 1976–80 plans of Comecon members.[21]

In the West, there was the impression before Castro's trip that neither he nor the Soviet leaders were eager for Cuba's entrance into Comecon.[22] After the step was taken, it was speculated that Cuba's admission could be a Soviet concession to give guarantees to Castro that Moscow's improved ties with Washington would not be detrimental to the remote Caribbean island.[23] But if this was the case and Castro had a vested interest in getting such a "concession," why did he not stay in Moscow for five more days to make the request himself? What he probably wanted was Cuba's admittance into the Warsaw Pact, but this was too much to ask of the Soviets because it might have jeopardized their delicate new detente with the United States. It is doubtful that Cuba's entrance into Comecon would bring any significant advantage to the island; and, conversely, it may result in less flexibility in Cuban economic plans, now to be coordinated with those of the seven Eastern European nations (and Mongolia!). This step will personally reduce Castro's power in economics even more and strengthen that of Rodríguez. On the other hand, it may be advantageous to the U.S.S.R. Since it dominates Comecon, the U.S.S.R. may try to distribute the Cuban economic burden more equally among Comecon members. The Soviets also hope that through more "scientific and sound economic collaboration" Cuba will fulfill its sugar supply commitments with Comecon members. Soviet sugar output is ten million tons, enough to satisfy domestic consumption and export commitments with some Comecon members. But production of the Soviet sugar beet is very costly, and it would be more efficient to use this land for other crops with higher yield and value. Thus if Cuba is capable of becoming the steady supplier of sugar to Comecon, the U.S.S.R. would be able to cut its sugar output and exports. Furthermore, the Soviets would be able to fully utilize their sugar refineries, increasing their productivity by refining Cuban sugar. The Soviet sugar harvest takes place during a different season than Cuba's and hence their refineries would be operating most of the year.[24]

Cuban dependence on the U.S.S.R. seemed to have reached a point of no return in 1972. Some 60 percent of Cuban trade was with the Soviets (70 percent with Comecon), approximately the same proportion it had been with the United States in the 1950s.[25] Cuba had also systematically failed to meet its sugar export commitments with the Soviets, thereby building in 1965–72 a cumulative deficit of 20 million tons of sugar, the equivalent of three good sugar crops.[26] According to Soviet sources, the island's cumulative trade deficit with the U.S.S.R. for 1960–70 amounted to $1.5 billion; but Cuban statistics for the same period gave a figure above $2 billion.[27] Due to the bad sugar crops of 1971–72 (and a bad tobacco crop in 1971), Cuba's cumulative trade deficit with the U.S.S.R. increased to $3 billion by 1972.[28] Cuba's total debt to the Soviet Union in 1972 was probably close to $4 billion if the annual repayment of loans ($130–150 million) plus interest, shipping costs, and the cost of maintaining Soviet technical and military advisors were added. It has been reported that the National Bank of Cuba estimates that half of this debt could have been saved if Cuba traded with market economies.[29] Cuba's merchant marine, despite its remarkable growth in the last decade, carried only 7–8 percent of the island trade, most of which was handled by Soviet vessels.[30] The U.S.S.R. gave Cuba $1.5 billion in military aid until 1971; and although apparently not charging for it, the U.S.S.R. has gained substantial control in the supervision of such equipment. Diplomatic sources in Havana conservatively estimated that in the summer of 1971 there were some 3,000 Soviet technicians and military advisors in Cuba.[31] Some 1,500 Cubans who will be in key positions (85 percent of them engineers and technicians) were being trained in the U.S.S.R. in 1973, a number similar to all the Cubans that studied there in 1961–71.[32]

In the 1960s, conflicts between the U.S.S.R. and Cuba were generated by several causes. Cuba often felt treated in a neo-

colonial manner by a big power. The first serious crisis between the
two nations occurred in 1962 when the Soviet Union agreed with
the United States (without consulting Cuba) to withdraw the
missiles that had created the October crisis. Six years later, Castro
accused the "developed socialist countries" of using commercial
practices similar to those employed by the capitalist countries and
specifically denounced the U.S.S.R. for restricting its oil supplies to
Cuba, thus obstructing the latter's development. Other points of
friction resulted from divergent doctrinal stands; thus, in 1966–68
(the Sino-Guevarist stage) Castro imputed the Soviets with neglecting ideological consciousness and political awareness for the development of the material base and with introducing economic reforms
that pushed them back to capitalism.[33]

In his speech of July 26, 1972, the Cuban prime minister showed
how his dependence on the Soviets had forced him to retreat from
his previous critical positions. He said that Cuban-Soviet relations
were "based on principles and doctrine" and that "the success of the
Revolution [and] its principled policy" had been made possible and
was guaranteed by the U.S.S.R. He reported that since his 1964
visit to the U.S.S.R. impressive Soviet progress had occurred in
technology, economics, science, and in the cities, and stated that
this development of the material base had been paralleled by the
achievement of a "tremendous political awareness": "It is an
unquestionable fact that imperialist ideology, propaganda and
corruption have not succeeded in gaining a toehold anywhere in the
Soviet Union. . . . Marxism-Leninism lives on there, [it] is the daily
bread of the Soviet people." Finally Castro stated that the Soviet
leadership had "deep feelings of solidarity, affection, and respect"
for the Cuban people and that they, in turn, were "proud to have
the priceless, disinterested, and revolutionary" friendship of the
U.S.S.R.: "The economic relations between Cuba and the Soviet
Union have been the most generous and the most revolutionary
possible. . . . Relations of this kind used to be unknown in the
history of relations among nations. . . . Though the world of
tomorrow will change, our friendship with the Soviet people will
remain a constant and our gratitude will be eternal."[34]

In November 1972, there was an important reorganization of the top Cuban government apparatus: an Executive Committee with power above the Council of Ministers was established, composed of ten deputy prime ministers with direct control over sectors of the economy and administration, each one grouping several central ministries and agencies. Castro became the president of the New Executive Committee and retained the premiership of the Council of Ministries and his control over several ministries and agencies, principally the armed forces and internal security. But, obviously, there was some delegation of his previous omnipotence. Rodríguez was appointed deputy minister of foreign policy with control over the Cuban-Soviet Commission and foreign relations. President Dorticós was given control over JUCEPLAN, the Ministries of Foreign Trade and Labor, the National Bank, and other minor agencies.[35] Nevertheless, Rodríguez's control over the foreign sector gives him enormous power in foreign trade (in addition, this ministry is headed by Marcelo Fernández, a follower of Rodríguez's economic thought) and his expertise on planning a *de facto* control over JUCEPLAN.

The Cuban-Soviet Commission, Cuba's entrance into Comecon, the strengthening of the former's planning apparatus, and the increasing influence of Rodríguez and other technocrats trusted by the U.S.S.R. assured the latter that the island would use Soviet aid more efficiently, follow a more conventional and rational economic policy, and do its best to honor its export commitments in the future. And yet Cuba's accumulated debt was so colossal that it jeopardized the new economic strategy. Important concessions were necessary to allow such a strategy to consolidate, bear fruit, and eradicate the negative image of Cuba's poor economic performance which had been so embarrassing for the Soviets all over the world, particularly in Latin America.

In December 1972, Castro and Rodríguez returned to Moscow to participate in the festivities surrounding the fiftieth anniversary of the founding of the U.S.S.R. As part of the celebrations a plenary meeting of all the participants was held; Castro, in a final political concession, proposed at this meeting that the Soviet "single multinational state" become a model for a "Latin American socialist community."[36] The next day he and Brezhnev signed five economic agreements through which the U.S.S.R. made the following important commitments: 1) a stipulation for higher prices in 1973–75 for Cuba's two main export items—sugar (an increase from 6.11 to 11 cents per pound) and nickel; 2) technical aid in 1973–75 (at a value of 300 million rubles) to mechanize the sugar harvest, to repair, modernize and/or expand nickel, electricity, oil-refining, textile, and metallurgic installations, and to help in planning and electronic computation (this credit will be paid in 1976–2000); 3) deferment for thirteen years of the payment of the Cuban debt to the U.S.S.R. (both principal and interest) accrued in 1960–72 (payments will be made in 1986–2011); 4) granting of the necessary credit to compensate for the expected Cuban deficit in the balance of payments in 1973–75 with the Soviets (probably about one billion rubles) under the same payment conditions as in the third commitment above; and, 5) a three-year (1973–75) trade agreement (details were not given).[37] The numerous concessions made by Cuba since 1970 had finally paid off economically, but the island's dependency on the U.S.S.R. was greater than ever before and extended into the twenty-first century.

The third meeting of the Cuban-Soviet Commission was held in Havana from February to March 1973, to implement the new economic agreements signed in Moscow. Rodríguez, the head of the meeting, opened it with praise of the U.S.S.R. for the concessions made.[38] After the meeting was over, two significant events took place. On March 13, 1973, Rodríguez gave the closing speech of the act commemorating the sixteenth anniversary of the attack on the Presidential Palace by the Student Directorate.[39] This speech had been traditionally pronounced by Fidel Castro or a representative of the Student Directorate. The assignment of the speech to Rodríguez was a symbolic "cleaning" of responsibility of the PSP. In 1964 several members of the PSP had been accused by Castroites of revealing to Batista's police the hiding place of various members of the Directorate who had attacked the Palace in 1957 resulting in their deaths at the hands of the police.[40] In April 1973, Joaquín Ordoqui, one of the former PSP members who was involved in the accusation and held in home confinement since 1964, was freed without being brought to trial because "his collaboration had not been established." These were two significant political concessions granted by Castro to the U.S.S.R., probably in reciprocity for the economic agreements.

Cuba's relations with Eastern Europe were strengthened even more in 1973 with official visits of important dignitaries from the latter to the former. In April, Gustav Husak, first secretary general of the Czechoslovak Communist party heard Castro praise his country for being the first to send weapons to Cuba in the early 1960s and for the numerous factories sold to the island.[41] This was a significant rectification of Castro's accusations at the time of the Soviet invasion of Czechoslovakia in the sense that the latter had sold obsolete weapons and factories to Cuba.[42] In May, it was the Poles' turn: Henryk Jablonsky, chairman of the Council of State, and Wojciech Jaruzelski, minister of defense. In June, Castro accepted an invitation, made by an official delegation of the League of Communists of Yugoslavia touring Cuba, to visit Yugoslavia.[43] This would have been inconceivable five years before when that party had been publicly denounced by Castro as an imperialist agent and Titoism as a rightist tendency.[44] In August, Nicolae Ceausescu, general secretary of the party and chairman of the State Council of Rumania, visited Cuba and granted it a $65 million loan for a new cement factory.

In September 1973, Castro attended the Fourth Conference of Nonaligned Nations in Algiers. His trip took more than two weeks because the Cuban prime minister paid short visits to Guyana, Trinidad and Tobago, Guinea, Baghdad, New Delhi, Prague, Hanoi, and the areas controlled by the Provisional Revolutionary Government in South Vietnam.[45] In Algiers, Castro rejected the theory of "two imperialisms" (the United States and the U.S.S.R.) "encouraged by theoreticians from the capitalist world and echoed by leaders of nonaligned countries" who hence had "betrayed the cause of internationalism from supposedly revolutionary positions." He reminded the audience of the "glorious, heroic, and extraordinary services rendered to the human race" by the U.S.S.R. and labeled as counterrevolutionary any criticism against it: "Inventing a false enemy [the U.S.S.R.] can have only one aim, to evade the real enemy [the United States]."[46] This speech created a split in the conference, provoked an irate interruption by Cambodia's Prince Norodom Sihanouk, and a strong attack by Libya's President Muammar el-Qaddafi who said: "We are against Cuba's presence in this Conference of Nonaligned Nations. There is no difference between Cuba and any East European country, or for that matter Uzbekistan and the Soviet Union itself."[47] Reportedly the affair upset Houari Boumédienne, the host of the conference, and precipitated the Cuban break in relations with Israel to please the Arab nations. The Cuban press only gave coverage to Castro's interventions, disregarded the incidents in the conference, and neither published Boumédienne's speech nor the conclusions of the conference. Scarcely one year after the economic agreements were signed in Moscow, they were producing an excellent political payoff: Castro had not only become "safe" but was the staunchest, most unconditional defender of the U.S.S.R. both at home and abroad. This series of events was to culminate in 1974 with Brezhnev's visit to Cuba.

The visit of the secretary of the Soviet Communist party had been a matter of long negotiation. In his trips to the U.S.S.R. in July and December of 1972, Castro had personally invited Brezhnev to visit Cuba. In June 1973, when the Soviet leader met Nixon in the United States, the Cubans hoped that Brezhnev would stop in Havana on his way back to Moscow. But he did not, concerned that such a visit could have been seen by the United States as an unfriendly gesture. Instead he announced, upon his return to Moscow, that he had accepted Castro's invitation to visit Cuba by the end of the year. Early in December, Rodríguez went to Moscow to discuss the travel plans but the Soviet leader—probably worried that his presence in the festivities of the fifteenth anniversary of the Revolution in Havana would embarrass the United States—postponed the trip again, this time until the end of January.[48] Still cautious, Brezhnev addressed greetings to President Nixon from aboard the plane carrying him to Cuba, only one hour from Havana, and said: "I am confident that relations between the Soviet Union and the United States will be developing further to the benefit of the peoples of our two countries and in the interest of international security and universal peace."[49]

Cuba prepared a great reception for the first visit of Brezhnev to a Latin American country and "the most important ever" in Cuban history. A week before the trip, the Cuban media gave wide biographical coverage to Brezhnev. The day of his arrival the newspaper *Granma* devoted the whole first page to a closeup of the Soviet dignitary, topped by "welcome" in Russian. Cuban and Soviet flags adorned Havana, the Ministry of Labor declared a national holiday, the traffic routing in Havana was modified to facilitate the visit, and the Cubans shouted words of welcome in Russian. The population was exhorted to attend a mass rally after the airport reception and maps were published to that effect.[50] Brezhnev's arrival, the airport reception, and the mass rally were transmitted live and in color to an estimated 170 million viewers in the U.S.S.R.[51] One million Cubans gathered in the mass rally for what was considered "the most grandiose, gigantic, and extraordinary ever held in the nation."

In his welcoming speech at the rally, Castro reviewed fifteen years of revolution and the role played in it by the United States. He made an important concession by acknowledging for the first time that in the 1962 Missile Crisis the U.S.S.R. played a crucial role in avoiding Cuba's invasion by U.S. forces and guaranteeing the security of the island. In spite of his criticism of the United States, Castro indirectly supported the Soviet-U.S. detente to reduce international tension and stop the arms race. The Cuban prime minister ended his speech defending the Soviet Union from attacks of "pseudo leftists" and promised: "We will never be disloyal or ungrateful to the U.S.S.R."[52] Brezhnev opened his speech praising the Cubans for having "reached a stage of development" in which they were building the foundations of socialism "in a positive and systematic manner." The thrust of the speech was peaceful coexistence. He stated that the normalization of Soviet-American relations was an indisputable step forward in achieving world peace and that they would continue in that path. Referring to Latin America, Brezhnev said: "The Soviet Union considers inadmissible and criminal any attempt to export the counterrevolution. . . . By the same token we Communists are not partisans of the exportation of the revolution. This should ripen in the soil of each country. How and when it emerges, what forms and methods it uses is only the business of the people in each country." As if this had not been sufficiently clear to the Cubans, he ended the speech saying: "Soviet weapons in Cuban hands are neither to attack anybody nor a tool to aggravate international tension. They serve the fair cause of [domestic Cuban] defense."[53]

In the Cuban-Soviet communiqué signed by Brezhnev and Castro at the end of the visit, both countries declared a "total unity" in their ideas and positions in world affairs, in favor of cohesion of the international communist movement, and against any attempt to split it (an indirect reference to China). They also condemned revisionism from either the right or the left, renounced the use of force, and agreed that the normalization of Soviet-American relations was an important step towards world peace.[54] Brezhnev's visit consolidated the new stage of the Cuban Revolution and showed how Soviet influence had contributed to shape that stage.

Idealism Bows to Pragmatism

In Sino-Guevarist thought, "subjective conditions" (ideas, consciousness, willingness; all belonging to the superstructure in Marxist terms) can decisively influence "objective conditions," that is, the material base, the forces of production, the structure which in the orthodox interpretation of Marxism determines the superstructure. (Thus a socialist revolution took place in Cuba, although the material base was not ripe for it, because of the consciousness of the guerrilla *foco*.) The successful development of consciousness (ahead of the material-base development) can enable a country to skip the transitional stage of development between capitalism and communism (i.e., socialism) or, as the Cubans put it, to build socialism and communism simultaneously. The U.S.S.R. rejects this interpretation of Marxism, arguing that a socialist country cannot go further than the development of its material base allows it to. Here lies the Soviet emphasis on building the material base first. Soviet ideologists have transformed the original two-step development ladder into four: "building the foundations of

socialism," "full socialism," "building the foundations of communism," and "full communism," and placed the U.S.S.R. at the
third step as the most advanced country in the socialist world.

In August 1970, Castro announced: "The Revolution is now
entering a new phase; a much more serious, mature, profound
phase."[55] He explained that at the beginning of the Revolution
there were many people who thought that its triumph "was the
result of some sort of magic," and others who minimized the
difficulties faced by the revolutionary government, alleging that
these difficulties "could be whisked away very easily." In order to be
successful, Castro warned, Cubans had to be carefully realistic in
the future:

> Let's not do as we have done so often, when we get an idea . . .
> putting it into practice without further ado, only to discredit
> the idea later because . . . it was taken directly from the brain
> to the world of reality where it died for lack of minimal
> [objective] conditions. . . . Some [unrealistic theorists] try to
> impose their ideas on reality rather than reality on their
> ideas.[56]

In September, Castro put in doubt the possibility of skipping or
accelerating the stages of development: "Perhaps our major idealism
has been to believe that a society which has scarcely left the shell of
capitalism could enter, in one bound, into a society in which
everyone would behave in an ethical and moral manner."[57] Three
months later, he recommended going "slowly to arrive quickly;
slowly to arrive well; and slowly to be sure to arrive!"[58] On May Day
1971, the premier stated:

> The way to communism is not a question of consciousness
> alone. It also has to do with the development of the forces of
> production. . . . We cannot fall into the idealism of thinking
> that . . . consciousness has been developed and that we
> already have the necessary material base. . . . This really is
> not the case . . . ["our consciousness has a long way to go in
> the matter of development"]. . . . We must understand that
> we are in a transitional stage . . . that we cannot just act as if

we were already in communism. . . . If in the pursuit of
communism we idealistically go further ahead than is possible,
we will have to retreat sooner or later.[59]

During his visit to Chile in November 1971, he sadly acknowledged: "Let us not forget one thing, and that is that spontaneity
does not solve any problems. . . . It is easier to change the structure
than to change the conscientiousness of man." Answering a
newspaperman who asked him whether there were contradictions in
the relations between Cuba and the socialist countries, he said: "We
have had contradictions at times. On occasion those contradictions
were due to a certain idealism [from our side] . . . we expected
things to develop the way our imagination pictured them."[60]

At the end of 1971, the Cuban newspaper *Granma* reported on its
front page that in a meeting held in Moscow between Secretary
General Brezhnev and visiting Cuban president Dorticós, the latter
spoke of the efforts aimed at "creating the foundations of socialism"
in Cuba while the former reported on "the progress made in the
construction of communism" in the U.S.S.R.[61] Thus Cuba acknowledged being at the bottom of the Soviet-invented, four-step ladder
to full communism, two steps below its protectors. Dorticós also
expressed his gratitude "for the public recognition by the Soviet
Union of the significance of the Cuban Revolution with respect to
the liberation movements in Latin America." This subservient attitude would have been inconceivable during the 1960s when the
Cubans attempted to lead the Third World revolutionary movement, thus challenging the Soviets. The new mood was for coexistence and moderation; hence, in another meeting, Kosygin warmly
welcomed the increasing number of Latin American states in favor
of reestablishing commercial and diplomatic relations with Cuba.

In November 1972, Carlos Rafael Rodríguez in his official speech
commemorating the fifty-fifth anniversary of the Bolshevik Revolution, made a clever manipulation of Cuban history to adapt it to
the current circumstances. First he pointed out that Guevara, at the
beginning of the Revolution, was a great admirer of the U.S.S.R.
recalling that when Che visited Moscow in 1960 he was "deeply
impressed" not only with the great material transformation that was

going on there but also with the "Soviet man," the one who was going to create the communist society. Second, Rodríguez quoted Castro during his 1972 visit to the U.S.S.R. when the latter praised the impressive development of the Soviet material base and said that it had been paralleled by an increase in the degree of awareness of the Soviet man in the ideological field, political culture, and revolutionary firmness and asserted that there were no traces of "ideological penetration" by capitalism in the U.S.S.R. Rodríguez then reached the corollary (skipping almost a decade of Cuban history, from 1962 to 1970) that Castro, together with the PCC, had "carried out throughout the Cuban Revolution" Marxism-Leninism as interpreted by the Soviets.[62]

Materials being used in the 1972–73 "Course on Political Education" taken by party members criticized idealism and spontaneous development of social consciousness as unscientific while giving full support to the Soviet standard interpretation that the mode of production (or material base) is the generator of social consciousness and never vice versa.[63]

In his 1973 speech commemorating the twentieth anniversary of the attack on the Moncada Barracks, the beginning of his Revolution, Fidel Castro stated: "Marx said that rights can never be more advanced than the economic structure and the cultural [consciousness] development determined by it." He then accepted that in the current stage of Cuban development, distribution should not be done according to needs but according to work and that excessive use of moral incentives would lead to idealism. He concluded: "If we think and act as if [the attitude of the minority of conscious leaders] was the conduct of every member of society, we would be guilty of idealism and the results would be negative on the economy."[64] Insisting on the same topic, Castro said a few months later:

> In certain cases we tried to make more headway than we were prepared for . . . if you try to go farther than you can, you are forced to retreat. . . . A series of measures and principles of a certain communist character have been put into effect since the triumph of the Revolution. . . . There are many examples to show us we are not yet prepared to live in communism. . . .

We should have the courage to correct idealistic mistakes we have made [in the past].[65]

While the painful denunciation of past idealism and the acceptance of reality was being manifested, the Cubans were reintroducing the post-reform Soviet system in the island, slowly, prudently, and without fanfare.

2

Economics:
Realism and Rationality

The revolutionary economic policy of the second half of the 1960s gave predominance to the development of the "New Man" while ignoring many basic economic laws. Such a policy was characterized by extreme idealism, labor mobilization, egalitarianism, moral incentives, and gigantic sugar production harvest while negligent of central planning, capital and labor productivity, and financial stability. The failure to reach the grandiose targets, the economic dislocation of 1970, and the increasing Soviet pressure for economic rationalization were the main determinants in the policy shift. The new, pragmatic economic policy, more conventional by Soviet standards, emphasizes central planning and computer development, efficient allocation and use of capital, improved managerial organization, labor productivity, reduction in the financial disequilibrium ("socialist inflation"), material incentives, and a more balanced economy with less emphasis on sugar. The economic results of this policy are positive in terms of industrial output, overall economic growth, and increased consumer satisfaction. Conversely, such policy may induce selfishness, some stratification, and unemployment pockets. The goal of the "New Man" in an egalitarian and mobilized society has been postponed, but for the man in the street this pragmatic decision probably does not look too bad after all.

Strengthening the Planning Apparatus

In the Cuban debate of 1963–65, both sides advocated a rational, efficient, centralized planning system with the use of mathematical techniques and computers but with one significant difference: Guevara dreamed of a perfect plant that would completely replace market mechanisms—the cybernetic solution supported in the U.S.S.R. by the conservative politicians and old-style planners. Conversely, Rodríguez, more pragmatic and knowledgeable, sponsored centralized planning with the limited aid of market mechanisms—following the timid economic reform introduced in the U.S.S.R. in 1962–65. Castro did not buy either of the two variants. In 1966 he drastically reduced the power and functions of the Central Planning Board (JUCEPLAN), discarded the medium-range plan (only partially tried in 1962–65), probably discontinued the annual plans (in 1965–70), assumed a number of the decisions formerly made by the planners, seriously neglected computation and statistical gathering, and launched a series of "mini," "extra," or "special" plans. These plans, designed to tackle a particular aspect of the economy, received priority and were entrusted to loyal *fidelistas* who had to report only to the prime minister. Frequently, capital and human resources were transferred from a project in operation (which was left uncompleted or badly functioning) to start new "mini" plans, which in many cases ended in failure.[1]

In 1965 Rodríguez was removed by Castro from his job as president of the National Institute of Agrarian Reform (INRA) and given a ministry "without portfolio." Displaced from one of the most important centers of economic activity, Rodríguez put all his energies into planning research. He organized a team of eleven statisticians and economists, which by 1968 had computerized the first (although rudimentary and incomplete) input-output table of the industrial sector of the Cuban economy. When Leontief, the inventor of input-output, visited Cuba in 1969, he was impressed by the expertise of Rodríguez's team and reported that it had moved its headquarters to JUCEPLAN.[2]

In 1970 when the new stage of the Revolution began, Rodríguez combined two key attributes: he headed Cuba's leading team of experts on central planning and computer techniques and—being a former member of the prerevolutionary PSP—had the confidence of the Soviets. The desperate internal need for economic rationalization and Soviet pressure for a technical approach in planning pushed Rodríguez back to the fore. In a rapid sequence of successes, he became the founder and chairman (on the Cuban side) of the Cuban-Soviet Commission of Economic, Scientific, and Technical Collaboration; the deputy prime minister of foreign policy; the chief negotiator of foreign-trade agreements; the Cuban delegate to several socialist transnational committees on planning, trade, and electronic computation; and the man with *de facto* control of domestic planning.

The acceptance of the Soviet "model" and the rise of the technocrats resulted in two clear changes: "mini" plans were substituted by short- and medium-range central plans, and computation (particularly for application to planning and management) was rapidly developed. Certain market tools were also introduced to improve the allocation and use of investment as well as managerial performance—this aspect will be discussed below.

It seems that the year 1971 was one of transition and preparation for the dramatic changes in planning. Probably in this year, the ground work to improve the system of statistical collection—which had been neglected in 1966–70—was also done. By the end of the year, JUCEPLAN had published its biannual statistical bulletin; this publication subsequently would be considerably improved, after the global economic indicators that were discontinued in 1966 had been added.[3] By early 1972, JUCEPLAN was preparing a global economic model for 1973–75.[4] This would encompass the Cuban economy during the last three years of the 1971–75 plan, already being implemented by Comecon members. In mid-1972 it was reported that annual economic plans for 1973, 1974, and 1975 were being drawn. (This was the first news released on annual plans since 1964.) Nothing further was published on the 1973 plan, but in late 1973 it was reported that the Council of Ministers and the PCC Political Bureau had discussed the 1974 plan. The study for the five-year plan (1976–80) started in 1972 and it was approved at the first congress of the Communist party of Cuba at the end of 1975. (This is the first Cuban five-year plan; there was a four-year plan—1962–65—that was discarded in 1964.) The congress resolution stated that the macro national economic plan was reinstated as the main tool in the economy and that all lower-level plans (e.g., micro, sectorial) would be subordinated to the former.[5] The Cuban plan has been coordinated with similar plans of other Comecon members.[6]

A Center for National Computation and Applied Mathematics (CEMACC) was functioning in Cuba by the end of 1970 and it seems that substantial resources have been invested in it.[7] In 1972, the U.S.S.R. promised to send Cuba a gigantic electronic computer and, in 1973, a technical team to aid in the application of electronic computation to the 1973–75 plans. Cuba has been a member of the Intergovernmental Commission of Socialist Countries for the Development of Electronic Computation since 1972.[8] In the 1970s there has been an impressive development of computer science in Cuba: 15 million pesos were invested in new computers in 1971, seventy computers were operating in 1973, two computer centers were established, numerous Cuban specialists were sent to the U.S.S.R for training, Cuba began manufacturing small digital computers, and a first meeting on computer sciences took place in 1972.[9]

Improving Capital and Managerial Efficiency

During 1962–70, Cuba saved, with great sacrifices in consumption, an increasingly large proportion of GNP (as much as 31 percent in 1968) for investment purposes. Part of this accumulated capital did not pay off as expected because, largely through the "mini" plans, it was arbitrarily allocated to projects that failed or were left uncompleted, or it was wasted through inefficiency and lack of proper maintenance. Inefficient use of capital was accentuated in 1966–70 by the Sino-Guevarist neglect of objective conditions, the setting up of overambitious projects, the emphasis on fixing output targets in physical terms, and the distaste for monetary accounting and cost analysis, on the one hand, and excessive reliance on spontaneity, on the other. President Dorticós has said: "In the late 1960s some people assumed a distorted ["*deformada*"] position disregarding costs as an element of bourgeois economies, as if costs did not play a pivotal role in socialist economies."[10]

The year 1971 was symbolically named the "Year of Productivity," marking a clear departure from previous policies and leading toward a more efficient allocation and use of capital. In November, Castro stated: "Frequently, the desire to accomplish a great deal in a short time led us to gather together a large amount of resources. And the result was that we didn't make the most effective use of them—we squandered them." For instance, some fifty thousand tractors imported since 1959 were used for all sorts of nonproductive functions such as driving to baseball games, to the beach, to parties, and to visit relatives and friends. Individuals who became tractor operators overnight did not know how to handle and maintain the equipment properly. The result, Castro said, was that "the former owner of a private business had a tractor and it lasted twenty years, but later, when the ownership of that production center passed to the state, a tractor lasted only two, three, or maybe four years."[11] In terms of years of service, the fifty thousand tractors were reduced to about seven thousand.

One month later, Castro pointed out other investment misuses, partly caused by the dropping of the central plan and the proliferation of mini plans. Imported equipment lay unutilized for years (sometimes rusting on the docks) because the building to house it had not been constructed. A large thermoelectric plant and some factories were nearly completed but could not be put into operation because of a vital missing part. Light cranes broke down as a result of lifting excessively heavy loads. Frequent electric blackouts and water scarcity were caused by neglect of maintenance of electrical installations and the waterpipe system. (In 1971, 120 million cubic yards of water were lost in the city of Havana alone.) Lack of care and maintenance of housing by owner and renters was also common—in the modern housing complex at East of Havana, dwellers took out the toilets and sold them or used doors for firewood.[12] In agriculture, the construction of small dams was not matched by the development of irrigation systems; hence much of the accumulated water could not be used or was wasted. President Dorticós reported in early 1972 that there was a serious crisis in railroad transportation because out of 300 locomotives only 134 were working, the rest being wrecked by careless workers. He also said that Cuba had the world's highest per capita consumption of spare parts due to poor treatment of equipment. On another occasion Dorticós referred to 145 oil tanks imported from the U.S.S.R. in 1970 which had not been installed by 1972.[13]

The Cuban leadership has announced various measures to correct this situation: future projects will be more realistic according to the nation's level of development; incompleted projects will be finished before new ones are started; maintenance and repair of equipment and adequate training of maintenance personnel will receive priority; quality standards will be strictly enforced in all enterprises; and cost accounting and analysis will be an indispensable tool to increase efficiency.[14] Three concrete measures merit special consideration: training of technical personnel, introduction of a new Economic Management System, and elaboration of a device to improve the efficiency of investment allocation.

Since late 1970 there has been a revival in Cuba of economic and accounting studies which had suffered a serious setback in 1966–70. Furthermore, two new careers have been introduced: "systems analyst" and "economic comptroller." The curricula of these careers include mathematical analysis, calculus, statistics, economic theory, planning, systems analysis, informational techniques, accounting, management, and production processes.[15] Graduates are a mixture of accountant, economist, and business administrator. In August 1972, Rodríguez lamented the loss of valuable technicians who fled at the beginning of the Revolution due to excessive radicalism and other errors of the leadership. He promised that currently employed technicians convinced of capitalist advantages but with a "national conscience" would continue to work for the Revolution and acknowledged that the substitution of political cadres for technocrats was an error which led to the failure of the 1970 harvest.[16] One year later President Dorticós warned managers of state enterprises that they had to acquire the necessary qualifications for their jobs or else would be fired regardless of their revolutionary credentials.[17] By the end of 1973, the following stimuli were introduced to raise the technical levels of the labor force: promotion to a higher post must be based on the acquisition of the required skills; enrollment in higher education conveys a right to a paid leave of absence which increases from one to four hours according to the level of study reached; and completion of training is automatically rewarded with a salary increase. There were sanctions too: those who drop out without justification or change their specialization after the training is completed ought to return to the state wages paid during their study leaves.[18] In 1976, a National School of Management and fourteen Provincial Management Schools were established. At the inauguration of the National School, Raúl Castro said: "[In the 1960s] we deprived our cadres of handling the budget, the overall financial plan, charges and payments [among enterprises], profits and taxes, all of which are essential for controlling and directing the economy and encouraging greater efficiency. . . . Moreover we taught [cadres] to look down on [these key economic tools] as running counter to communist morale and awareness, because in our ignorance of economic matters we viewed them as overly capitalist."[19]

The congress of the party approved, in 1975, the establishment of an Economic Management System (SGE) "in accordance with the wide experience gained by other socialist countries in the course of several decades." The SGE will be based on "objective economic laws" (e.g., law of value or supply and demand) and will take into account "existing monetary-mercantile relations in the socialist stage." As indicators of managerial performance and to improve efficiency in the utilization of capital, human, and financial resources, the SGE will use market instruments such as profit, credit and interest, rational prices, budget, "economic calculation" (in relation to self-financing), taxes and purchase-and-sale relations among state enterprises. The latter will enjoy relative independence (e.g., to hire labor, request loans, make investment decisions) but also will be held responsible to balance revenue with expenses and generate a profit. As in the U.S.S.R., the efficiency of Cuban enterprises will be measured by a set of indicators including output, quality, cost, productivity, and profit. Repayable loans with interest will be granted to state enterprises and farms by the National Bank. The price fixed for enterprises and wholesalers will include production costs (labor, capital amortization and interest, depreciation) and a profit out of which the enterprise has to pay to the state a profit tax and a social security tax and develop an "incentive fund" which will be used partly to develop the production-technical facilities of the enterprise (to be discussed below). Retail prices will include, in addition, a "turnover" (sale) tax which will be aimed at balancing supply and demand as well as generating revenue for the state (private farmers and the self-employed are to be taxed too). The timetable for introduction of the SGE is as follows: in 1977, the national "economic calculation" system, the national budget, and purchase-and-sale relations among enterprises; in 1978, the new systems of prices, taxation, and banking-credit-interest, as well as a pilot plan of self-financing in selected enterprises; and in 1978–80, the extension of the pilot plan to all enterprises.[20]

The debate on alternative systems of economic organization, lively in 1963–65 and stopped in 1966–70, timidly reappeared in 1971 limited to technical and narrow subjects. For example, an article written by a foreign economist criticizing the use of profit as the main indicator of managerial performance in socialist economies (in use in the U.S.S.R. since 1965) was translated in the Cuban official economic journal, *Economía y Desarrollo*. It was followed by a cautious defense of such a system written by a Cuban economist.[21] The discussion was largely concentrated around the question of which was the best technique to evaluate investment alternatives in order to select the most efficient one. A Cuban specialist said that the old Soviet technique of the "coefficient of relative effectiveness" (practiced in the 1950s and early 1960s) had been superseded in socialist countries by more sophisticated techniques (one of which is the use of the interest rate). The party congress decided in 1975 to reintroduce self-financing and, in 1976, nine hundred enterprise managers were learning the system. Although in 1977 practically all enterprises were still under budgetary financing, the "economic calculation" system (a necessary basis for self-financing) was introduced. A pilot plan for self-financing is to be tested in 1978. Two Soviet specialists have acknowledged that in 1966–70 the Cubans had tried to eliminate self-financing but that the reality of the socialist stage forced them to reintroduce the former. Another Soviet expert has said that Cuba's ultimate goal is to eradicate budgetary financing, replacing it with self-financing.[22]

Increasing Labor Productivity

A time-loss study conducted in 1968 on more than two hundred enterprises (but not published until mid-1970) revealed that from one-fourth to one-half of the workday was wasted.[23] The causes of this phenomenon were overstaffing of enterprises and the poor enforcement, since 1966 (under the Sino-Guevarist belief in self-consciousness), of the Soviet-style work quota system introduced in Cuba in 1963–65. Work quotas (or labor norms) assigned to each worker fix how much he should produce in a given time schedule (month, week, day, hour) and are a managerial tool for control of labor productivity.[24]

In July 1970, a newspaperman asked the Minister of Labor whether it was true that work quotas would be reintroduced and if this action was not in contradiction with moral incentives. The minister confirmed the reintroduction of the quotas but avoided the delicate second question, saying that the quotas were indispensable to measure the workers' effort.[25] President Dorticós was more explicit later: "We have lost the levels we had reached on [both] the establishment and control of the labor norms and the technicians on norms who are now working on less important jobs. [In the past] there was excessive confidence placed on spontaneity, in the belief that without labor norms everybody would have worked willingly in an efficient manner. . . . We must develop a serious and continuous labor-norm policy and get the technicians back."[26]

From October to November, commissions integrated by managerial personnel, party members, technicians, and skilled workers discussed the reintroduction of the labor norms, which actually began in December. By May 1971, almost 600 enterprises had been normed, and by the end of the year the number had increased to 1,500, including part of the sugar industry. The year 1972 was called the "Year of Emulation," and by May Day more than 3,000 enterprises and 700,000 workers (one-third of state employment) were under the work-quota system. By the end of 1973, some 53,000 enterprises employing 70 percent of all state workers were normed. In early 1976, 68,091 enterprises hiring 1,602,900 workers were normed.[27]

Other measures taken to increase labor productivity, besides labor norms, are the recently introduced stimuli for workers to raise their skills, mechanization of certain operations, and improvements in labor organization and conditions. A success story that received considerable publicity refers to the reduction of long delays in unloading and loading Soviet merchant vessels in Cuban ports. The average time assigned for this job was eleven days but the longshoremen usually took as many as twenty days (each extra day costing an indemnification to the Cubans). Labor norms were tightened, the U.S.S.R. sent technicians, a new mechanized dock was built in Havana harbor, ship arrivals were coordinated, and job conditions (even using music in the docks!) were greatly improved. The delays were cut by 50 percent in 1972.[28]

The above measures generated in 1972 an overall increase of 21 percent in labor productivity.[29] Such advances, however, were concentrated in industry and in those service activities which are especially important to the economy, but agriculture is still plagued by low labor productivity. In late 1973 Raúl Castro asserted that it was common in state farms that labor costs alone exceeded the value of production. As a significant case, he gave figures from a state farm in which the annual wage bill was 48,000 pesos while the value of output was 8,000 pesos, thus resulting in a loss of 40,000 pesos without taking other costs of production into account. Raúl's conclusion was that a large number of workers were unnecessary and that such labor surplus should be eliminated.[30]

In fact, superfluous manpower has been already released mostly in the nonagricultural sector and the government has restricted the hiring of unnecessary workers. In 1971 it was initially estimated that the country needed 300,000 additional workers, but the figure was reduced to only 48,000. Samples taken nationally in 1972 showed that employment had been cut by one percent.[31] According to President Dorticós in mid-1972, although the manpower deficit was still the main problem in the country, there were two provinces (Oriente and Las Villas) in which the opposite was true, resulting in some unemployment.[32] By the end of 1973, Fidel Castro acknowledged that the employment pendulum was swinging the other way and that the manpower deficit was rapidly being filled by a greater demand for jobs: "The time may come when we will have a headache finding jobs for all those who want to work." He promised, however, that solutions would be found to avoid the return of an "army of the unemployed."[33] Apparently, as a first step to cope with the problem, the Confederation of Cuban workers (CTC) requested in its 13th congress a modification of regulations passed when the manpower deficit was acute. (For a detailed discussion of the congress, see chapter 3.) Such regulations reserved certain types of service jobs for females to force males into fields in which their physical strength was more necessary. Now that conditions have changed, such service jobs should be reopened to male workers.[34]

Fighting "Socialist Inflation"

Since 1961, there has been spiraling inflation in Cuba generated by a widening gap between the demand for and the supply of consumer goods. Demand rose steadily because the population's disposable income was enlarged by full employment; a guaranteed annual salary for sugar workers even if they did not have work to do in the dead season; the increase in minimum wages and pensions; the expansion of free social services (i.e., education, medical care, social security, burials, public telephone calls, water, sports, and, in part, housing); and a reduction in the cost of other services (i.e., electricity, gas, and public transportation). Demand for many of these services (e.g., electricity, water, phones) increased additionally due to consumer waste, and use was not controlled because of the free or very cheap supply of such services. On the other hand, the supply of consumer goods was negatively affected by stagnation or the small increase in domestic output, reduction of imports, and exportation of goods that were previously assigned to internal consumption.

In a market economy this disequilibrium would have resulted in a steady increase of prices. Taking an egalitarian approach, the Cuban leadership instead decided to introduce rationing in 1962 and to expand it thereafter to all consumer goods. Most families, however, received a total income that far exceeded the cost of the monthly-ration basket of goods. Excess money in circulation began to grow. In 1970, there were 3,478 million pesos in excess, and the total income of the population exceeded by almost twofold the value of available supply. Hence the population could have lived one year without working.[35] As a result of this situation, the black market (where goods were sold from five to ten times the official price) flourished in spite of government restrictions.[36]

At the end of 1970, Castro said: "Abundance isn't created by decree or law. By decree you can distribute what there is; no decree can distribute what isn't there. [We have to] reduce the money in circulation [otherwise] the black market price will rise."[37] Cigarettes were a good example of this situation. In 1971, 40 percent of the tobacco crop was lost due to drought; but even before this there was a problem in meeting both domestic consumption and export demands for this product. Hence the price of cigarettes in the black market skyrocketed—smokers paid from 12 to 15 pesos per pack, that is, 60 to 75 times the official price. Nonsmokers used their cigarette ration to trade for other things in the black market.[38]

In order to reduce the money in circulation, the decision was made to decrease demand and increase supply. To avoid a further increase in demand, the abolition of house rents (scheduled for 1970 and which would have put from 70 to 80 million pesos into circulation) and the raising of bottom wages (promised by Castro in

1968) were postponed indefinitely.[39] Measures to decrease demand included increases in the price of cigarettes, beer, and rum; in rates paid on water and electricity by those who had a high consumption of such utilities; and in the cost of services, such as long-distance transportation and restaurant meals (worker-canteen meals now charge 10 pesos monthly for lunch). In mid-1973, the price of unrationed cigarettes was 2.40 pesos a pack, compared with twenty cents a rationed pack. The price of consumer durables also seemed to have been increased, for instance, 850 pesos for a black and white television set, 550 pesos for a small refrigerator, 700 pesos for a portable record player, 125-500 pesos for a Soviet camera, and 125 pesos for a portable radio.[40] To cut demand even further, in late 1973, the government reversed some of its previous generous policies. Thus the granting of 100 percent salary to workers in vanguard factories who were sick or retired was eliminated with an estimated annual savings of 140 million pesos. The guaranteed annual wage for sugar workers—which resulted in a subsidy to idle workers during four or five months of the dead season—was being subjected to drastic modification.[41] In the fall of 1976 free calls from public phones were terminated; there is now a charge of five cents.[42] In 1977 there were rumors that admission would be charged at sports events and that the price of cinema tickets would be increased.

Probably the first step to increase the supply of consumer goods was the reduction of the rate of capital accumulation in 1971 to some 28 percent, and in 1974 to 22 percent, thus allocating more resources for consumption.[43] In 1972, official sources and foreign press agencies reported that there were more consumer goods available. Although most of the new monthly rations which started in July were unchanged (sugar had been cut from 6 to 4 pounds in February and was cut to 3.5 pounds in December), there was an increase in the butter ration. The supply of fish, milk, some tubers (potatoes, yucca), some fruits (bananas), and both alcoholic and soft beverages was more regular; and there was an apparent increase in the supply of clothing, shoes, and cosmetics. Some 30,000 refrigerators, 31,000 radios, and 350,000 pressure cookers were domestically produced and a large number of nonessential items imported (e.g., transistor radios) or domestically produced (e.g., perfumes, sunglasses). In 1974 production of domestic appliances increased as follows: 42,000 refrigerators and radios, and 450,000 pressure cookers. The 1976–80 plan calls for the production of 100,000 black-and-white television sets and the introduction of color television. The government also intended to buy a large number of motorcycles, air conditioners, and cars from Japan. Restaurants and workers' canteens have improved their menus somewhat, there are plans to build hotels and vacation resorts for workers, and even the carnivals are more sophisticated and luxurious.[44]

The new rationing booklet distributed in the second half of 1973 remained unchanged as far as food was concerned, but introduced significant modifications in manufactured goods. Many of the latter were freed from rationing ("*liberados*") and could be bought even when traveling to the interior; among them: film, still and motion-picture cameras, projectors, record players, parts for bicycles and kitchen appliances, coffee sets and crystal cups, silver wedding rings, stationery, plastic shoes and slippers, deodorants, and some cosmetics and perfumes (including brands with such exotic names as "Red Moscow" and "Bulgarian Rose"). A number of goods were put on limited distribution. Two or three times a year each consumer has the option to one or more of the following: toothbrushes, handkerchiefs, socks and stockings, underwear, slacks, pajamas, rubber shoes, raincoats, swimsuits, threads, cream cleansers, pots and pans, irons, meat grinders, hoses, and selected furniture. Hotel and vacation resorts were provided with convenient, freed goods such as swimsuits, lifesavers, sunglasses, cosmetics, and stationery. Some twenty manufactured goods remained strictly rationed such as pants, shirts, dresses, skirts, blouses, leather shoes, and fabrics. To facilitate buying, each member of the family received a booklet allowing direct purchases, certain goods (such as toys at Christmas time) were to be sold by appointment to avoid long queues, and specialized stores (e.g., for infants) were opened.[45]

As a result of these measures, in the second half of 1971 the amount of money in circulation began to drop. According to Castro, the extraction of money from circulation, in the first quarter of 1972, was due to price increases (13 percent) and to increases in goods and services (87 percent). [46] A total of 1,230 million pesos was taken out of circulation from mid-1971 to the end of 1973: 150 million in 1971, 680 million in 1972, and an estimated 400 million in 1973. The ratio of monetary surplus over total population income was reduced from .87 in 1970 to .47 in 1973. (See table 2.) The current five-year plan predicts a balance between population income and value of available goods and services for 1980.

By the end of 1973, Castro exclaimed: "Money has started to have

TABLE 2

The Reduction of "Socialist Inflation" in Cuba: 1970–73
(In millions of pesos)

	Income				
	Total Wage Bill	Other payments to farmers, students, and for pensions	Total (Population Income)	Accumulated Monetary Surplus	Ratio M. Surplus over P. Income
1970	3,111	895[a]	4,006[a]	3,478	.87
1971	3,187	948[a]	4,135[a]	3,328	.80
1972	3,367	1,005[a]	4,372[a]	2,648	.61
1973	3,690	1,060	4,750	2,248	.47

[a]Estimates by the author.

Sources: F. Castro, "Discurso en el acto de clausura del XIII Congreso de la CTC," *Juventud Rebelde,* November 16, 1973, pp. 6–7.

some value!"[47] People had less money to spend and hence felt the incentive to work more in order to increase their income and buy the new consumer goods available. This partly explains the increase in the labor supply discussed in the previous section.

Expanding Material Incentives

The apparent rise in the rate of GNP devoted to consumption, the postponement in the granting of new free social services, the partial

functioning of market prices, and the increase in the availability of
consumer goods are clear indications of a shift away from moral
incentives. The excessive emphasis between 1966 and 1970 on
moral incentives was not necessarily motivated by ideological
reasons but perhaps induced by an excessively high rate of capital
accumulation, too much money in circulation, and the acute scarcity
of consumer goods. Thus, the sudden stress on wage differentials, a
typical material incentive strongly opposed before by the egalitarian
trend, is not surprising. Certainly in 1966–70, under the conditions
pointed out above, wage differentials did not make sense as
economic stimuli; thus, the emphasis on egalitarianism was logical.
In this sense Fidel Castro has said:

> . . . the application of material incentives is useless and
> ineffective in a situation of tremendous inflation. . . . When
> everybody has his pockets bulging with money, none of these
> things [wage differentials, material incentives] is effective.
> . . . A superabundance of money becomes a disincentive to
> work for many people. [48]

On May Day 1971, Castro explained that salaries could not be
equal for all and that wage differences would be significant in the
future as a means of motivating those with labor skills or heavy
responsibilities, and those who worked at hard jobs or in places
devoid of minimum facilities. If wage differentials were abolished,
Castro argued, then those who made an extra effort to acquire skills
or had physically hard jobs would be discouraged. [49] The main thesis
of the 13th congress of the CTC was the reinforcement of the
socialist system of distribution according to work instead of the
communist system of distribution according to need. Castro stated
that distribution according to need, as practiced in 1966–70 could no
longer be applied: "Paying the same wage for the same type of work
but without taking into account the productive effort required to do
it is an egalitarian principle we must correct." Furthermore, the
"effort" would not only be measured in physical terms but in the
complexity of the job. Hence in 1974, Castro announced, 132 million pesos would be allocated to raise wage rates for technical and
managerial personnel to provide a more adequate recompense for

their skills. He also announced that cars would be imported to be sold to technicians "in order to increase their productivity."[50]

Other theses approved by the 13th congress of the CTC dealt with the reintroduction of material incentives (e.g., production bonuses, overtime pay), the elimination of "historical wages," and the new system of socialist emulation. Wages were linked again with the work quotas (as in 1963–66). If the worker fulfills his quota, he will receive his entire fixed wage; if he doesn't fulfill it, his wage will be reduced in the same proportion of underfulfillment. Finally, if he overfulfills the quota, his wage will be increased proportionally with a bonus. (Not only are bonuses back, but they are paid at a higher proportion than before: 50 percent of overfulfillment in 1963–66, 100 percent of overfulfillment now). In 1976, the new salary system was introduced in 9,860 enterprises employing 600,000 workers.[51]

Overtime pay was massively renounced by the workers in the campaigns of 1968–70. This is now considered a mistake: "In many cases unpaid overtime turned out to be more costly than regular paid hours of work [because unnecessary overtime was imposed upon the workers who performed poorly while other operating costs were fixed] reducing real production and yield per man hour." The congress agreed that overtime should be worked only when it is really necessary and then should be paid. Overtime due to the worker's fault should not be paid but entered in his labor record as a "demerit."[52]

"Historical wage" is the difference between the wage that a worker had been assigned prior to the introduction of wage scales in 1963–65 (and the revision of the 1970s) and the new wage rate assigned to him by the corresponding scale. This addition operates as a disincentive to new workers who joined the labor force after the introduction of the wage-scale system, because they are paid less than workers doing the same job who were hired earlier. The CTC congress decided to eradicate the "historical wage" through a joint review of each case by the administration and the union. If a worker is found to have the proper skills, he may be offered a higher job; if he doesn't have such skills, an opportunity will be given him for training. If the worker refuses the transfer or retraining, the "historical wage" paid to him will be eliminated.[53]

The new system of socialist emulation approved by the congress (the fifth in force since 1961) combines material and moral rewards for winners in individual and collectively productive competition. Material rewards for individuals consist of priority to enjoy vacations and recreational programs, and for collectives (e.g., enterprises) to receive allocations for the establishment or improvement of day-care centers and sports and cultural facilities. Moral rewards consist of diplomas, buttons, banners, and honorary titles such as "National Hero of Labor" or "Enterprise of Heroic Effort." Indices to evaluate emulation should be "objective" such as fulfillment of the plan without overtime, cost reductions, proper maintenance, and quality improvements.[54]

The government is making an effort to link the new material incentives closely with workers' productivity. One of the difficulties that moral incentives faced in motivating the workers' efforts was that they were mostly of a communal nature (i.e., free social services) and not directly connected with individual labor performance. In order to cope with this problem, in 1971 the government introduced the "Plan CTC-CI." Under this plan, consumer durables (such as television sets, refrigerators, washing machines, radios, bicycles, sewing machines, pressure cookers, watches) are not available in stores but allocated by the Ministry of Domestic Trade to enterprises. A list of available goods is put on a bulletin board of the enterprise and workers who are interested fill out forms. A committee of workers ranks the applicants mainly by their attitudes and merits (e.g., fulfillment of work quotas, productivity) and, to a lesser extent, by their need.[55]

The above policy is also applicable to vacations in beach resorts and, particularly, to the distribution of housing. The acute shortage of housing, especially in Havana and other cities, has been generated by the disappearance of all private construction in 1960 and the drastic curtailment of state housing construction *circa* 1962. To put a halt to the growing housing gap, at least 100,000 new homes are needed annually, but only a few were built in the 1960s. According to Castro, nine out of every ten people who approach him have housing problems; there are as many as ten people living in one room, couples who get divorces cannot move, and many couples cannot get married because they have no place to live. The distribution of houses, Castro has reported, has caused disorders, irregularities, and discontent. People have moved into houses without permission, and, in other cases, the distribution was unfair.[56] The exodus of Cubans to the United States helped to ease the problem, but in 1971 the Cuban government restricted the exit. It was suspended for six months in 1972, reestablished at lower levels by the end of that year, and stopped in mid-1973, thus closing the safety valve.

In mid-1971, Castro proposed a plan to reduce the housing shortage. The state would supply construction materials, and industrial workers would provide the manpower in two ways: regular workers would donate two or three daily hours of overtime plus Saturdays and Sundays; and surplus labor released in enterprises through "norming" could permanently work in housing construction while the rest of the workers would donate extra labor, if necessary, to maintain the production level. Apparently, the second system has been the most used, but the government has been careful to avoid depleting workers whose absence could harm production. By August 1971, 100 "minibrigades" enrolling 3,000 workers were organized. Minibrigades increased gradually to reach 1,068 in number enrolling 35,000 workers two years later. Each minibrigade is integrated by some 33 members who work from 10 to 15 hours daily. By mid-1973 the minibrigades had built 6,385 homes and had 37,500 more under construction (others built schools, day-care centers, and clinics). At the beginning of the program, ten minibrigades claimed a right to the houses built by them. Thereafter it was established that the homes would belong to the work centers so that "a close link will be established between the productive unit [enterprise] and the homes in which its workers live." Houses are distributed (for rent, not ownership, at 6 percent of wages) according to the merits (mainly productivity) of the workers and, to a lesser extent, according to their need. The government expects that under this program from 70,000 to 80,000 homes will be built annually beginning in 1975.[57]

Finally, the new SGE regulates an "economic incentive fund" that will attempt to strengthen the connection between enterprise performance and material incentives for its workers. The size of the fund is determined by enterprise profitability and it is used, among other things, to provide material-individual rewards for its workers, and for the construction of enterprise restaurants, day-care centers, and recreational facilities.[58]

Rationalizing the Sugar Sector

The economic dislocation of 1970 was caused by the excessive emphasis placed on the sugar sector at the cost of sacrificing the rest of the economy. The nation's infrastructure and resources (sugar-mill equipment, harvest combines, transportation, skilled manpower) were obviously insufficient to reach the ten-million-ton target; even more, they were incapable of producing much more than six million tons without a harmful depletion of resources from other sectors. The too-ambitious goal wrecked part of the mills, and they were not repaired or replaced in 1971–72.[59] Facing reality, sugar production targets have been gradually reduced, labor mobilization has sharply declined, and emphasis has been placed on finding adequate alternatives (such as the Australian system for burning the cane) and improving and expanding the mechanization.

The 1965–70 sugar plan called for an investment of more than 1 billion pesos in expansion and modernization of the sugar mills, but by 1970 only 400 million pesos had materialized. Modernization was apparently postponed in 1971–72 due to delays in the supply of machinery. In 1959, there were 161 sugar mills (mostly built before the end of the 1920s); but ten years later due to deterioration, lack of spare parts, and "cannibalization," the number of mills declined to 152. The strenuous effort to which the old equipment was subjected in the 1970 harvest put four other mills out of operation, and in the 1971 harvest frequent breakdowns were reported in the active mills. At the beginning of the 1972 harvest, it was announced that 144 mills would be in operation; but by the end of February only 136 were functioning and two months later only 115 mills were active.

The number of professional canecutters declined from 350,000 in

1958 to less than 73,000 in 1971. Mobilization of urban workers ("volunteers") could not adequately substitute for the professional canecutters due to the lack of the volunteers' expertise and their low productivity. In addition, the excessive depletion of urban manpower for use in the 1970 crop (some 170,000 men) precipitated an acute fall in industrial output. Some 60,000 fewer volunteers were mobilized in the 1971 harvest, another 35,000 less in the 1972 harvest, 25,000 less in the 1973 harvest, and 28,000 less in the 1974 harvest. (The government expects to reduce total manpower in the 1980 harvest to 50,000 workers.) The number of days of the harvest declined from 334 in 1970 to 230 in 1972. (The participation of thousands of university students in the 1969–70 sugar harvests for periods of from two to four months was quietly but drastically cut in the 1971–72 harvests because their time was more usefully spent in studying.)[60]

Unpaid voluntary labor, in general, was limited in 1973 by the CTC congress to tasks which are proven necessary; specifically, for the sugar harvest. Unions should select the most productive canecutters so as to reduce the number of volunteers. Often in the past the cost of mobilizing volunteers (transportation, food, electric power, inputs) was higher than the value of the product created by them.[61] Now such costs must be calculated in advance because if "what is accomplished does not compensate for the material and human resources invested, the mobilization would be uneconomical and wasteful." Unions that decide to use voluntary labor must carefully quantify the factors in the mobilization: number of workers, tools, transportation, food, shelter, inputs, and work quotas. On the basis of all these factors, an analysis must be done of the efficiency of the work performed. In the new SGE, enterprises ought to pay the "net value" of voluntary labor (i.e., gross value of output less mobilization costs) to the mobilization agency which, in turn, transfers this revenue to the state. The news media should abstain from publicizing volunteer-labor activities unless enough data are provided to measure their productivity.[62]

Mechanization of the sugar harvest, the rational alternative to massive labor mobilization, has been "a very difficult nut to crack" as Castro has acknowledged. (On the other hand, the total

mechanization of harvesting rice and potatoes is almost complete.)
In 1967 a National Direction of Mechanization (DINAME) was
created in the National Institute of Agrarian Reform (INRA); this
agency was to be in charge of mechanization, importation of
equipment, and repairs. The easiest task has been plowing; in 1970,
there were 2,000 Cuban-made sugar plowers ("Herrera") in operation and half of the planting was mechanized. But some 1,000
Soviet-made cutting machines sent to Cuba in 1963–65 were too
heavy and complicated and broke easily; hence, they were discarded in 1967. (There was a futile attempt to put them back in
operation for the 1970 harvest. The irregularity of the terrain
presented a problem to the cutting machines. In 1972 work began to
level large sugar plantations in Camagüey province—the flattest and
the one with the highest manpower deficit.) Cuban-made cutting
machines ("Henderson" and "Libertadora") were tested with fair
results in 1967–68, but they had to be mounted on imported
bulldozers, and only a few could be built (e.g., 150 in 1969, while
some 3,000 to 4,000 were needed). By the end of 1970, Castro
complained that it was "one thing to make one machine by hand and
quite another to turn them out in quantity and running perfectly."[63]
In September 1971, Cuba bought 100 cutting machines from the
Australian firm, Massey Ferguson, which were used in the 1972
crop (it was reported that a total of 250 machines were in operation
in that harvest). Almost at the same time, at the first meeting of
the Cuban-Soviet Commission, the U.S.S.R. agreed to help Cuba
in manufacturing improved versions of the "Libertadora" and
"Henderson" canecutting machines and to supply a new type of
machine (called KTP-1) designed by Soviet and Cuban engineers
based on the experience of the 1971 harvest. In mid-1972 the
U.S.S.R. announced that a new factory to build KTP-1 machines
would be sent to Cuba; fifty of these machines built in the Soviet
Union were tested in the 1973 sugar harvest. Early in 1973 it was
reported that the construction of the KTP-1 factory in Cuba would
begin in Holguín (Oriente province) during that year. The defects
observed in the KTP-1 machine have apparently been eliminated
and a better machine, the KTP-2, developed. The factory was finally
inaugurated in mid-1977; it is expected to produce 250 KTP-1 and

50 KTP-2 machines in 1978 and to reach a total of 600 machines by 1980. The mechanization of the sugar harvest has increased as follows: 7 percent (1972), 12 percent (1973), 19 percent (1974), 26 percent (1975), 33 percent (1976), and 42 percent (1977). The goal for 1980 is 60 percent.[64]

The small number of cutting machines currently in operation is compounded by their incapacity to clean the cane of leaves and trash (only the "Libertadora" allegedly does this work), which amounts to half the volume of the cane cut. Cane-cleaning centers (which mechanically strip the cane of leaves) were tested in 1966; by the end of 1971 some 200 had been built and 300 other centers were scheduled to be built for the 1972 harvest. If these had been built, they could have cleaned half of the whole cut cane, but it was reported that only 20 percent of the cane was actually processed through the centers. By 1977 only 500 centers were in operation. Loading of the cut cane (into carts, railroad wagons) was mechanized by 80–90 percent in 1973, with some 4,000 lifters mounted on old American tractors and imported Soviet cranes made for this purpose. In 1977 mechanized loading had reached 98 percent. In late 1971, the U.S.S.R. agreed to send Cuba 1,600 carts (2-PTT-6) to be used for transporting sugar in the 1972 harvest, and a factory to produce these carts began to be built in early 1973 increasing motorized transportation to 60 percent.

Trying to ease some of the above problems, in the 1970 harvest the Center for Research on Sugar Cane conducted an investigation of the Australian system of burning and cutting cane.[65] (Besides Australia, the system has also been used in the last twenty or thirty years in Hawaii, Mexico, Peru, and South Africa.) The Australian system was tested on a minor scale in January–February 1971; thereafter, 60 percent of the cane was burned.[66] The system apparently saved considerable manpower, as much as 62 percent. The burned cane did not have to be cleaned of leaves and dirt, it was not recut into two pieces, it weighed less, and did not have to be piled.

Conversely, the Australian system created new complications. In order to have the system work properly, the terrain had to be prepared, a special variety of cane was needed (to have stalks of equal size), replanting had to be done more frequently, the seed had to be planted at a given depth and separation, and special fertilizer had to be used. The burning process had to be carefully planned: a schedule had to be prepared based on the degree of maturity of the cane, the burning had to take place at sunset, and excessive burning which provokes losses in sugar and incomplete burning which leaves the trash in the plant had to be avoided. There was also always the risk of fire expansion and losses resulting from leaving the burned cane in the fields too long before being ground. Since the cane was neither recut into two pieces (as done manually) nor piled up, there were problems with the traditional equipment in use. Cranes faced difficulties in picking up the unpiled cane. The long cane stalks stuck in the too-narrow railroad cars which transported 70 percent of the cane to the mills. In the canecutting centers, the engines overheated and, in some cases, burned. The machete, the most popular Cuban tool for cutting cane, which is used in 58 percent of the harvest, was too long and narrow; and the Australian tool (shorter and wider) was disliked by the canecutters. Finally, special clothing and safety devices (steel padding to protect the legs and reinforced gloves) had to be introduced; the workers rejected the gloves because they reduced their movements and hurt their hands.

In late 1971, several measures were tested to cope with some of these difficulties. For instance, a "pusher" was attached to the crane machines to pile up the cane; the cane was cut into two pieces in the cleaning centers; to avoid engines overheating in the centers, the speed of the feeder belts was reduced; Chinese cutters (smaller and wider than the machete, similar to the "mochas" traditionally used in 32 percent of the Cuban harvest) were tried, and gloves were eliminated. This resulted in a modified Australian system which is claimed to be twice as productive as the traditional methods used in Cuba although only one-third as productive as the pure Australian system.

No information is available on the results of the application of the modified Australian system in the 1972 sugar harvest, but there are data on the industrial yield which suggest that things did not go as well as expected. (The industrial yield is the percentage of sugar obtained in the mills in relation to the weight of the cut cane. Out of every 100 tones of cane cut, from 8 to 14 tons of raw sugar are squeezed, depending on the cleansing of the leaves from the cane, the sugar content of the cane, and the efficiency of the mill equipment.) The prerevolutionary yield was systematically above 12 percent, but it went down to 11.8 percent in 1965–69. The yield in the 1970 harvest was a very low one, 10.9 percent, mainly attributed to the excessively large crop. In the 1971 harvest, the yield rose to 11.5 percent, but it went down to 10.5 percent in the 1972 harvest.[67] Drought could not be held responsible for the difference because it affected both crops; in fact, there was less rain during the period of cane maturation of the 1971 crop than in that of the 1972 crop. The deteriorating equipment could have been a cause, but not an important one if we assume that those mills that had functioning difficulties were not in operation in 1972. (This probably affected the total amount of the crop but not necessarily its yield.) There was a significant difference in the two crops: the Australian system applied in less than one-third of the 1971 harvest but throughout the 1972 harvest. Probably improper burning, bottlenecks caused by the insufficient number of cane-conditioning centers, and difficulties generated by the use of the new technique resulted in loss in the sugar content of the cane. These problems led to the elimination of the Australian system in 1973.

On July 1, 1972, President Dorticós announced that beginning in 1973 Cuba would not attempt to produce large sugar crops but only the amount of sugar that the country could rationally turn out.[68] The Ministry of Sugar reported at the same time that repairs and maintenance of the sugar mills would receive priority in 1973. Later it was stated that fertilizers would increase by 30 percent in 1974.[69] And the president of the National Academy of Sciences announced that in 1973–77 electronic calculation would be used in sugar production.[70] The trend toward rationality seems to continue.

Recantation of Old Errors and Impact of New Policies

In his major address to the first congress of the Communist party at the end of 1975, Castro passed review over the economic "mistakes" committed by the Cuban leadership in 1966–70. His speech is a shocking confirmation of the Sino-Guevarist flaws that I had analyzed in several of my works of the late 1960s and in the first edition of this book. Castro began his painful exercise on self-criticism by stating:

> It is necessary to speak about [idealistic] mistakes. Revolutions usually have utopian periods in which their protagonists . . . assume that historical goals are much nearer and that men's wills, wishes, and intentions, towering over objective facts can accomplish anything. . . . Sometimes the utopian attitude is accompanied by a certain contempt for the experiences of other processes. . . . From the very beginning the Cuban Revolution did not take advantage of the rich experience of other peoples that had undertaken the construction of socialism long before we had. Had we been humbler we would have been able to understand that revolutionary theory was not sufficiently developed in our country and that we actually lacked profound economists and scientists of Marxism to make really significant contributions to the theory and practice of building socialism. . . . Even though our conditions were highly difficult, due to the economic blockade and to underdevelopment, the intelligent utilization of those experiences would have helped us a great deal. [71]

Then Castro discussed, in a more concrete manner, some of the mistakes committed: "The budgetary financing system [was] fostered by Che" but "it turned out to be highly centralized and used economic levers, mercantile relations, and material incentives in a very restricted way." The self-financing system did operate only partially and in a limited way; it "seemed to be too capitalistic" to us. The two systems coexisted for a while, then "we took the less correct decision—to invent a new procedure." Interpreting Marxism "idealistically and breaking away from the practical experience of other socialist countries we established our own methods." The Castroite "invention" was neither self-financing nor truly budgetary financing because the state budget and bookkeeping were eliminated. The connection between salaries and output was severed, fulfillment and unfulfillment of quotas lost importance, work-hour schedules on the basis of consciousness were stimulated, renunciation of pay for extra hours was encouraged, interest on loans and taxes from farmers were eliminated, and the universities abolished courses on political economy and public accounting. "Failure to take account of remuneration according to work [together with the need to eliminate unemployment] markedly increased the excess currency in circulation against a background of shortages in goods and services, which . . . stimulated absenteeism and caused disciplinary problems with labor: when it might have seemed as though we were drawing nearer to communist forms of production and distribution, we were actually pulling away from the correct methods for the previous construction of socialism."[72]

Let us now discuss the impact of old and new policies on production. Table 3 summarizes Cuba's global economic performance in three periods: 1963–65 (debate on alternative systems), 1966–70 (Sino-Guevarism), and 1971–75 (pragmatism à la U.S.S.R.). Data refer to gross material product (GMP) which excludes the value of productive and nonproductive services (e.g., transportation, commerce, education, health care). There are no data for 1959–61; the figures in the table have as a base the years 1962–63, the trough of economic performance throughout the Revolution, hence giving the illusion of growth in 1964; and 1967–75 figures do not correct for inflation, thus growth rates are higher than if given at constant prices (for instance, real GMP declined by 9.3 percent in 1967 but according to the table increased by 2.4 percent.)[73] In spite of these problems, table 3 can be taken as a fair illustration of growth patterns throughout the Revolution. It shows that there were consistent although low economic growth rates in 1963–65: an average 3.8 percent in absolute terms and 1.2 percent per capita. But in 1966–70 the economy deteriorated badly with average absolute rates declining to 0.4 percent and per-capita rates to –1.3 percent. In 1971–75 there was a rapid economic recuperation and the record growth rates of the Revolution: 14.1 and 13 percent. This impressive growth was partly the result of the new economic policies (particularly in 1971–72) but also an effect of the record-breaking sugar prices in the international market (an increase from 4 cents per pound in 1970 to 65 cents in November 1974.) Unfortunately the impact of these two causes is impossible to separate.[74]

TABLE 3

Economic Growth in Cuba: 1963–75

| Years | Annual | Gross Material Product[a] | |
| | | Average in the Period | |
		Absolute	Per-capita
1963	1.0		
1964	9.0	3.8%	1.2%
1965	1.5		
1966	−3.7		
1967	2.4		
1968	7.2	0.4%	−1.3%
1969	−4.5		
1970	0.6		
1971	14.7		
1972	25.3		
1973	11.1	14.7%	13.0%
1974	10.5		
1975	12.1[b]		

[a] 1962–66 in constant prices; 1967–75 in current prices.
[b] Global Social Product.

Sources: República de Cuba, Junta Central de Planificación, Dirección Central de Estadística, *BE Boletín Estadístico 1966* (Havana, 1969), p. 20; *BE Boletín Estadístico 1971* (Havana, 1973), pp. 44–45; *Anuario Estadístico de Cuba 1972* (Havana, 1974), pp. 30–31; *Anuario Estadístico de Cuba 1973* (Havana, 1975), p. 35; *Anuario Estadístico de Cuba 1974* (Havana, 1976), p. 35; and *La economía cubana, 1975* (Havana, n.d.), pp. I-3.

Table 4 summarizes production trends in twenty-six major agricultural, mining, and manufacturing products by comparing four points in time: before the economy was collectivized (1960), on the eve of the introduction of Sino-Guevarism (1965), at the end of Sino-Guevarism (1970), and after the economic recuperation (1975).

With a few exceptions to be discussed below, production in both agriculture and traditional industries either (1) increased in the first half of the 1960s, declined in 1966–70 and recuperated thereafter (e.g., refrigerators, cigars, textiles, salt, gas ranges, radios, liquor, sodas, canned fruits, soap, tomatoes), or (2) declined throughout most of the 1960s but recuperated by 1975 (e.g., tobacco, coffee, yucca, malanga, potatoes, cement, textiles, beer). In the few modern, capital intensive, mechanized sectors (e.g., eggs, fishing, nickel, electricity) production steadily increased throughout the 1960s and 1970s. Sugar shows an erratic performance with output reaching a record high of 8.5 million tons in 1970 but declining in the 1970s. Rice plantations were considerably reduced in the first half of the 1960s but the 1966 Cuban quarrel with China (Cuba's main supplier of rice) forced the expansion of rice fields again; and yet, the 1960 level was not recuperated until 1975. With few exceptions the level of output in 1970 was below the 1965 level, but also in most cases output recuperated in 1975 surpassing the 1965 level.

Tables 3 and 4, therefore, vividly show the catastrophic failure of the Sino-Guevarist experiment. The economic loss in the quinquennium could be estimated between 20 percent (if the 1963–65 average rate of growth is used) and 70 percent (if the 1970–75 average rate of growth is used). The tables also demonstrate the substantial payoff of the pragmatic economic policies of the first half of the 1970s. In 1976–77, however, there was a significant slowdown of economic growth due to the sharp decline in sugar prices (which reached a low of 7 cents per pound in early 1977) and possibly the economic side effects of the Cuban military operations in Angola.[75]

Evaluation and Prospectives

The new economic policy toward pragmatism, inaugurated in 1970, has been followed by good performance in industry and fishing but with bad performance in sugar and not-too-impressive performance in non-sugar agriculture. A factor that may largely

TABLE 4

Physical Output of Selected Products in Cuba:
1960–75 and 1980 Goals
(In thousand metric tons unless specified)

Products	1960	1965	1970	1975	1980
Sugar	5,943	6,156	8,538	6,200	8–8,700
Tobacco	45	43	32	43	60
Citrus fruits	73	160[d]	155[e]	199	350–400
Coffee	42	24	20	29[f]	—
Eggs (million units)	430	920	1,509	1,770	2,000
Rice	323	50	291	338	—
Yucca	255	62	22	83	—
Malanga	257	47	12	32	—
Potatoes	97	84	77	88	—
Tomatoes	116	120	62	184	—
Fish	31	40	106	144	350
Nickel	13	28	37	37	100
Salt	92[c]	106	89	138[f]	—
Electricity (million kwh)	2,981	3,387	4,888	6,583	9,000
Cement	813	801	742	2,083	4,000
Textiles (million m²)	116[c]	96	78	140	260–80
Tires (thousand units)	364[c]	197	202	391[f]	—
Soap	34[c]	37	33	40[f]	—
Refrigerators (thousand units)	0	12	5	50	100
Gas ranges (thousand units)	9[c]	10	6	45[f]	—
Radios (thousand units)	0	82	19	42[f]	300
Beer (thousand hectolitres)	1,394[b]	993	659[e]	1,808[f]	—
Liquor (thousand hectolitres)	154[c]	170	170	198[f]	—
Sodas (thousand hectolitres)	2,372[c]	2,406	871	1,710[f]	—
Canned fruits and vegetables	64[c]	80	39	84[f]	—
Cigars (million units)	591[a]	657	277	378[f]	—

[a] 1959   [b] 1961   [c] 1963   [d] 1966   [e] 1969   [f] 1974

Sources: C. Mesa-Lago, "Availability and Reliability of Statistics in Socialist Cuba," *Latin American Research Review* 4 (Spring and Summer 1969): 53–91 and 47–81; *Anuario Estadístico de Cuba 1971* and *1974; La economía cubana, 1975;* and Comité Central del Partido Comunista de Cuba, Departamento de Orientación Revolucionaria, *Directivas para el desarrollo económico y social del país en el quinquenio 1976–1980: Tesis y resolución* (Havana, 1976).

explain the different outcome is the drought, one of the worst in the century, which reduced water in dams from one-fourth to one-half their average level.[76] Illnesses that affected livestock could have been significant also. Another reason is that in order to restore output in an economy seriously dislocated by the 1970 sugar-harvest mobilization, it was necessary to drastically cut the depletion of manpower from industry and this had to affect the sugar sector. The application in large scale of the Australian system in the 1972 sugar harvest and the deteriorating equipment may have affected output also. Still a third reason is that industrial output and productivity, especially in modern, concentrated factories, can be easily and rapidly increased with Soviet aid, repairs and maintenance, improved organization and control of labor output (e.g., work quotas), but this is not so easy in the dispersed, backward, unpredictable agricultural sector. Most of the economic incentives introduced in the 1970s (e.g., more consumer goods available, the housing program) appeal fundamentally to the urban worker but not to rural workers and private farmers. Last but not least is the fact that the shift toward pragmatism will not be fully completed until 1980.

Assuming that the current pragmatist trend continues un-changed, prospectives in terms of overall economic growth should be positive although not spectacular. The prime minister has said in this respect: "The objectives of our people in the material field cannot be very ambitious. . . . We should work in the next ten years to advance our economy at an average annual growth rate of six percent."[77] With declining sugar prices, however, real economic growth may be below the target of 6 percent. The performance of Cuban production in the next three or four years can be prudently predicted as follows: in the sugar sector, fair-sized crops of from five to six million tons (mechanization should expand in the late 1970s and crops may reach seven million tons); in non-sugar agriculture, recuperation of previous output (e.g., in tobacco) and possibly more advances in mechanized harvests (e.g., rice, potatoes, tomatoes) or modern enterprises (e.g., poultry, eggs); in livestock, stagnant out-put of meat but increases in milk; in fishing, continous steady increases in output; and in industry, steady and moderate increases especially in the dynamic sector (basic industry, mining—particularly nickel—fuel, metallurgy, and electricity). Production of steel will not be initiated until the 1980s. Tourism could significantly expand by 1980 (particularly if U.S.-Cuban relations are fully normalized) becoming again a significant source of revenue for the island.

Most output targets set for 1980 by the current five-year plan and shown in table 4 are too optimistic in view of historical trends and the economic slowdown of 1976–77 (e.g., in sugar, citrus, nickel, fish). A few targets are attainable if the necessary premises materialize (e.g., eggs, electricity, refrigerators).

3

Government and Society:
Toward Institutionalization

At the end of the 1960s, the political structure of Cuba became the target of criticism from several Marxist and leftist sympathizers of the Revolution. They claimed that decision making was done by Fidel Castro and a small group of followers and that he was reluctant to delegate his power. The party and the unions had almost withered away, the government elite imposed its will upon the masses without consultation, and Cuban society had gradually become militarized. Therefore it was urgent to reform the system and develop socialist democratic institutions. Be it the result of this criticism or the effect of other causes, in the second half of 1970 Fidel Castro acknowledged some of the flaws pinpointed by his critics and promised dramatic reforms to decentralize the state administration, revitalize and democratize the labor movement and other mass organizations, and allow mass participation in decision making and the supervision of state functions.

This chapter begins with a summary of both the Marxist criticism and Castro's promises of reform. This is followed by a thorough description of the reforms undertaken in the 1970s aimed at the separation of governmental functions, the strengthening of socialist legality and the party, the reorganization and democratization of the unions and other mass organizations, and the introduction of participatory types of institutions. In addition, there is a discussion of measures, taken simultaneously, that have strengthened government control over the workers, small farmers, the youth, and the intellectuals. The chapter ends with an analysis of the type of institutionalization that is taking place in Cuba, confronting two opposite trends: one toward decentralization and democratization and another toward centralization and rigidity in ideology, culture, and education.

The Marxist Criticism of the Political Structure

In the midst of Cuba's "Revolutionary Offensive" (1968–69), several Marxist scholars visited the island, the majority of them invited by Prime Minister Fidel Castro.[1] The visitors, internationally known in various specialties and from Europe and the United States, had all previously been in Cuba—some as consultants of the government—and had thereafter published sympathetic accounts of the revolutionary accomplishments. They had something else in common: their endorsement of a more democratic, participatory type of socialism. If they originally expected to find in Cuba the kind of socialism that they dreamed of, their books and articles published in 1969 and 1970, although supportive of the Cuban Revolution in general, showed their disappointment in this respect.

The American economists Paul Sweezy and the late Leo Huberman were the first to state that the Cuban Revolution was moving close to autocracy and to recommend, as an alternative, the participation of the people in decisions and responsibilities.[2] In a controversy with Sweezy, the French planner and ideologist Charles Bettelheim criticized the Cuban leaders as a section of the petty bourgeoisie that had concentrated all powers unto itself, thus becoming a class. He further charged that it had imposed its political domination upon the masses, curtailing their independent movements; and that it had done nothing to create the necessary conditions—ideological, political, and organizational—for the democratic exercise of proletarian power.[3]

The American sociologist, Maurice Zeitlin, found that the Cuban Communist party (PCC) did not have real power and that trade unions seemed to have withered away. He also stated: "The Cuban revolutionaries have so far done little to establish institutions to guarantee that competing points of view can be heard within the revolutionary socialist consensus; that meaningful alternatives are debated; that policies are initiated, as well as implemented by the citizenry at large." Zeitlin concluded that the Cubans had to choose between autocracy and the establishment of socialist democratic political forms.[4]

In his third visit to Cuba, René Dumont, the French agronomist, observed that the lack of confidence in the base, Castro's reluctance to delegate responsibility, and the making of all important decisions at the top of the administrative hierarchy had resulted in increasing personalism, paternalism, and authoritarianism. Central controls had been imposed on the population, the universities, and the press; and there was expanding militarization of education, manpower, agriculture, the economy, and society in general. Dumont suggested that Castro give up some of his powers or otherwise be induced to do so by his responsible colleagues; that the administration be simplified and that more autonomy and initiative be given to local units; and that fundamental issues be publicly discussed and the party and state agencies controlled by the worker.[5]

The Polish-British journalist and writer, K. S. Karol, asserted that by 1968 all mass organizations in Cuba had ceased to exist except on paper, that the unions were neither autonomous nor had the right to express and defend the claims of their members, and that the Cuban rulers believed that they knew best how to interpret the thoughts and needs of the working class. According to Karol, Castro disagreed with both China's Cultural Revolution and the Czech Spring of 1968 because he was afraid of changes initiated by uncontrolled and spontaneous forces and suspicious of rank-and-file independent action.[6]

In mid-1970, in the midst of the economic dislocation, widespread labor absenteeism, and popular disenchantment that followed the sugar crop failure, the Cuban leadership seemed to reconsider its previous attitudes. On July 26, Castro acknowledged his own errors; in August he announced the "new phase" of the Revolution; and in the fall he proposed several measures that, deliberately or not, were addressed to the correction of most of the defects indicated by his Marxist critics.

The 1970 Promises of Reform

From May through December 1970, Castro made numerous speeches in which he strongly criticized the excessive centralization of the administration and its bureaucratization, the absorption of administrative functions by the PCC, the exaggerated role of the state in all national affairs (which killed the initiative of the masses), the one-manager system of state enterprises (which did not allow the workers to express their opinions), and the weak and nondemocratic state of mass organizations. He proposed several measures to decentralize the administration, assign separate roles to key state agencies, allow the workers to participate in enterprise management, democratize and strengthen mass organizations, and establish channels for a more active role of such organizations in national affairs.

First Castro proclaimed that in the future the PCC's role would be restricted to the coordination and supervision of the administrative function.[7] To separate political and administrative functions within the PCC, Castro proposed that in the Central Committee, besides the Political Bureau, there be a "bureau of social production" to coordinate the activities of the administration. In another move, Castro acknowledged that it was no longer possible to direct all national production through the Council of Ministers alone and announced the clustering of various central ministries with connected functions into groups that would help in the planning and coordination of such functions. Thus a group would deal with capital (or intermediate) goods production (the Ministry of Basic Industry; and the Ministry of Mining, Fuel, and Metallurgy); another group with consumer-goods production and distribution (Ministries of Food Industry, Light Industry, and Domestic Trade); and another with manpower (Ministries of Labor, Education, and Armed Forces). At a third level, Castro said that the administration of the enterprise would not be the task of the manager alone but of a "collective body" presided over by the manager and integrated by representatives of the workers, the party, and youth and female organizations.[8] A few days later Minister of Labor Jorge Risquet stated: "The administrator may be making one mistake after the other, and this happens every day, everywhere. . . . The workers cannot do anything about it. . . . How can the worker be made to feel more involved with his place of employment, with his production goal if he is only a producer who never has any opinion, who cannot make any decisions, who is never consulted about factory management?" Risquet also said that forms of participation were under discussion so that output plans and long-term decisions in the enterprise could be discussed with the workers.[9]

Mass participation would not be limited to the enterprise alone, Castro proclaimed: "We must begin to substitute democratic methods for the administrative methods that run the risk of becoming bureaucratic."[10] The democratization process would be the basis for the participation of the masses in decision making, and all mass organizations would go through such a process.[11] He acknowledged that the trade union movement was in poor shape and should be revitalized through democratization (free elections); it should also be allowed to defend the workers' rights. Other mass organizations (e.g., youth, farmers, women) would follow the democratization of the unions. Castro went further: "Starting with our mass organizations [we will] create other organizations in which the workers, the women, the young people will be represented so that they carry out close supervision and control of all activities [including those of the party] on a territorial level."[12]

At the end of the year, Castro elaborated on his participatory scheme: "[Why has everything] to be administered directly by the state? . . . Immediately the need arises for the superorganization [which makes the citizen indifferent]. . . . We believe that this is wrong. . . . And it is up to us to create the links and the mechanisms through which the citizen will be made to feel his duty and to take an interest in these matters." The central agencies should handle only those functions that, because of their national character, had to be centralized, while other functions should be transferred to city-district bodies integrated by representatives of the workers and of youth, women's and student organizations. Castro gave an example of how this could be accomplished: "[The Ministry of Domestic Trade] should continue running the wholesale distribution and laying down the guidelines for the distribution of goods, but it should be relieved of the job of running a grocery store. . . . It is the representatives of the mass organizations who should handle the things that pertain to the community." He reported an experiment developed in the small town of Peñalver, east of Havana, in which some eight neighbors working every day until 11:00 P.M., with construction equipment and material supplied by the state, built a baseball field and a communal garage and repaired some roads. But he warned that before mobilizing the energy of the masses the necessary time had to be taken to carefully study the proposed undertaking.[13]

Separation of Government Functions: The Administration, the Party, and the Army

When in 1970 Castro acknowledged the need to separate the functions of the administration and the party, he was only referring to part of the problem. The main feature of the Cuban political structure in the 1960s was extreme diffusion; there was no clear separation among the following three main institutions and their functions: the central administration, the party, and the army. Castro exerted a charismatic, personalistic type of government characterized by the concentration of power in the "Maximum Leader" and his inner circle of loyalists and by the lack of institutionalization. The Council of Ministers, headed by Castro and composed of his closest associates, controlled the administration which performed executive, legislative, and judicial functions. Most ministers and directors of central agencies, nevertheless, came from the Rebel Army. The party, except in its brief period of inception (1961 to early 1962 when PSP members had strong influence), was in Castroite hands. In 1965, two-thirds of the PCC Central Committee members were from military ranks. In practice, Castro and his small circle occupied the top positions in the administration, the party, and the army; he was the best example combining the jobs of prime minister, first secretary of the party, and commander-in-chief of the armed forces (figure 1). The latter was probably the only body that, in spite of constant changes and crises, grew increasingly professionalized, institutionalized, and efficient. Thus the army absorbed more and more nonmilitary functions (e.g., organization of production, criticism of rebel intellectuals, cane cutting) and by the end of the decade pervaded many facets of Cuban society.[14] The changes being introduced in the 1970s indicate that the announced separation of functions within the government is not only limited to the administration and the party but to the army as well. In addition, each of the three institutions is going through a reorganization process whose main traits are: delegation of power but central coordination in the administration, revitalization in the party and specialization in the army. The general trend in the 1970s appears to be toward institutionalization following the Soviet model.

The creation of the Executive Committee of the Council of Ministers at the end of 1972 seemed to be a step forward in the delegation of power from the prime minister and central coordination (see chapter 1). The Committee was composed of the prime minister as chairman and nine "deputy prime ministers," a post typical of the Soviet hierarchy that did not previously exist in Cuba. Each of the deputies coordinated several ministries and state agencies which were clustered by sectors, i.e., basic industry and energy; consumer-goods industries and domestic trade; sugar industry; non-sugar agriculture; construction; transportation and communication; labor, planning, and foreign trade; foreign relations; and education and culture.[15] This measure had been announced by Castro in 1970 to better coordinate planning and production.

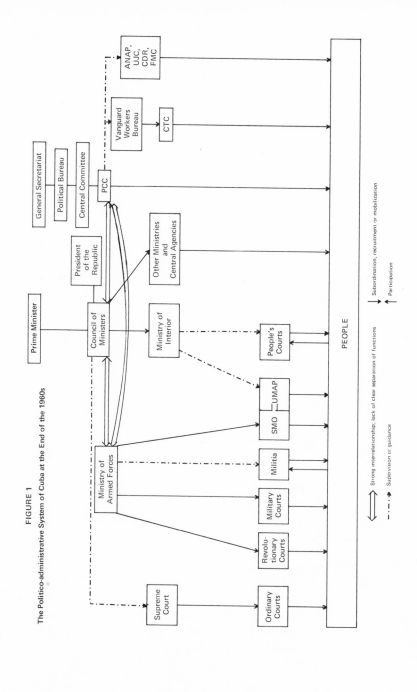

FIGURE 1

The Politico-administrative System of Cuba at the End of the 1960s

General Secretariat

Political Bureau

Central Committee

PCC

Prime Minister

President of the Republic

Council of Ministers

Ministry of Interior

Ministry of Armed Forces

Other Ministries and Central Agencies

Vanguard Workers Bureau

CTC

ANAP, UJC, CDR, FMC

Supreme Court

Revolutionary Courts

Military Courts

Militia

SMO

UMAP

People's Courts

Ordinary Courts

PEOPLE

⟹ Strong interrelationship, lack of clear separation of functions

⟶ Subordination, recruitment or mobilization

⟵ Participation

–·–·→ Supervision or guidance

The reorganization of executive powers was followed, in mid-1973, by the reform of both the judicial system and the criminal and procedural codes. The study of the reform, initiated in 1970 as part of the "new phase of the Revolution," was led by Blas Roca, a layman but former president of the PSP and, since 1965, chief of the Commission on Juridical Studies of the PCC.[16] The Commission was also working on a new political constitution and the reform of the Civil Code. The 1973 reform rejected the division of state powers into three branches—executive, legislative and judiciary—as a bourgeois institution and confirmed the Council of Ministers as "the supreme, the sole organ of power" embracing the three branches plus constitutional functions. The reform placed the judicial system hierarchically subordinated to the executive. At the top of the former, there was a "Council of Government of the People's Supreme Court," which, instead of following the system of judicial independence for interpretation of the law, "transmits [to the lower judicial echelons] the instructions received from the leadership of the Revolution whose fulfillment is compulsory." The new judicial system unified the four branches of justice: ordinary, military, revolutionary (political crimes), and people's courts (minor offenses of a social nature).[17] Exempted from the jurisdiction of the unified courts were the president of the republic, the prime minister and other ministers, and the members of the PCC Political Bureau who can be tried only by special party courts.[18] Private law practice was to be abolished, and all lawyers were to abide by and promote the revolutionary ideology in their political and juridical relations. It was also expected that lawyers would "improve themselves ideologically" and be militantly behind revolutionary causes. Defendants in trials would only have a state lawyer, even in those cases in which the state was a party.[19]

The PCC has two executive branches at the national level: the Political Bureau and the General Secretariat, initially integrated by eight and six members and both headed by Castro. The party's deliberative body is the Central Committee, initially integrated by some one hundred members. It should, theoretically, elect the members of the political bureau and the secretariat but these were appointed in 1965 and new appointments (to fill vacancies caused by deaths and purges) were not made for almost a decade. At the time of its inception the composition of the Central Committee was as follows: 67 percent military (including 57 majors), 26 percent professionals, and 7 percent workers. The executive and deliberative bodies of the PCC seldom met in the 1960s. There were also party secretariats in each of the six Cuban provinces, which in turn supervised smaller secretariats in districts and municipalities. Party cells were organized in most important enterprises, state farms, government offices, and military units. Until 1975, the party did not have a congress, lacked both a program and statutes, and had a tiny membership.[20]

In 1973 the General Secretariat was increased to ten members and the four new posts were filled (one of the new secretaries was the Cuban ambassador to the U.S.S.R.).[21] Meetings of the PCC executive bodies became regular: the secretariat met weekly and the Political Bureau bimonthly. There was no information on Central Committee meetings. In the same year, besides the 6 secretariats in the provinces, 60 were reported in districts, and 401 in municipalities, plus 14,360 in local cells.[22]

In 1969 there were only 55,000 party members; in the subsequent six years, quiet efforts began to increase party membership through selection of candidates, political education, and recruitment. The number of members increased to 101,000 in 1971, 122,000 in 1972, 153,000 in 1973, 186,995 in 1974, and 202,807 in 1975.[23] The PCC membership was still small in 1975 (equivalent to 2 percent of the population and 7 percent of the labor force) but had increased almost fourfold in six years. Reportedly there was also an effort to expand the proletariat segment of the membership.[24] Both party members and candidates were taking political education courses which closely followed the Soviet interpretation of Marxism.[25]

The first congress of the party was announced by Castro in 1966 for the following year but it did not take place. The congress was then rescheduled for 1969 but later cancelled on the allegation that all the nation's efforts had to be concentrated on the 1970 sugar harvest. In late 1973, Castro promised that the congress finally would take place in 1975.[26] Prior to the congress, drafts were elaborated on the platform of the party as well as on resolutions to be adopted by the congress. These were sent for discussion to provincial, district, and municipal secretariats and to local cells.[27] Elections held at local, provincial and national levels turned out 3,116 delegates to the congress as well as nominations of candidates for the new Central Committee.

The congress, finally held on December 17–22, 1975, resulted, as a leading Cuban scholar has asserted, in "the full incorporation of orthodox Soviet-style institutions and practices [making the PCC] resemble its Soviet counterpart in both style and substance."[28] Approved by the congress were: (1) the draft of the socialist constitution; (2) the five-year economic plan; (3) the geographic-politico-administrative reorganization of the country; (4) the new system of economic management; and (5) the party platform (which will serve until the definite party program is approved by the second congress scheduled for 1980). Other resolutions were passed by the congress on ideological struggle, education and culture, mass media, religion, women, and peasants. In addition, the congress elected: (1) the new General Secretariat, expanded to 9 members, with Fidel as first secretary and Raúl as second secretary, excluding former President Dorticós and including for the first time 3 "old" communists (Rodríguez and Roca among them); (2) the new Political Bureau, expanded to 13 members including 3 "old" communists; and (3) the new membership of the Central Committee, expanded to 112 members including 26 old communists. The party executive bodies now have the presence of old communists and the latter still make up about one-fourth of the Central Committee; the composition of the three bodies also shows increased representation of technocratic-bureaucratic ranks. Although the ruling party elite has been considerably broadened, Fidel and his close associates are still in firm control.[29]

The socialist constitution, approved by the PCC congress without any significant modification, was in turn ratified by a national referendum on February 15, 1976, and enacted nine days later. The new Cuban constitution is shaped by its Soviet counterpart: 32 percent of the articles of Cuba's 1976 constitution come from the Soviet constitution of 1936, 36 percent from Cuba's constitution of 1940, 18 percent are influenced by both sources but with Soviet predominance, and only 13 percent of articles are at least partially innovative.[30] The U.S.S.R. is mentioned by name in the preamble of the Cuban constitution—perhaps the only instance in recent history where a foreign country appears in the constitution of another. And the fundamental political bodies introduced in the new constitution closely resemble their Soviet counterparts; thus Cuba's National Assembly of Peoples' Power is equivalent to the Supreme Soviet, the Council of State corresponds to the Presidium of the Supreme Soviet, and the Council of Ministers, the judiciary, and the Organs of Peoples' Power can also be paired with similar institutions in the U.S.S.R. And yet there is an important difference between the two politico-administrative systems: a more significant concentration of power in the Cuban model. Within the spirit of institutionalization, the constitution clearly differentiates the functional roles of the party, state, government, armed forces, and mass organizations. But, as a Cuban scholar has pointed out, by unifying the direction of several bodies (state, government, armed forces) into a single officeholder, in practice Fidel's central role has been constitutionally confirmed.[31] Or as another scholar has concluded: the constitution has been a compromise between those who wanted to fully institutionalize the Cuban revolutionary process and those wanting to maintain its charismatic features.[32]

Let us now describe the principal bodies in Cuba's new politico-administrative structure: the Organs of People's Power (OPP), the Council of State, and the Council of Ministers (figure 2). In 1970, Fidel promised the creation of city-district bodies composed of representatives of mass organizations to closely supervise, at the local level, the state administration and the party. In early 1974, however, Raúl announced a different scheme: from mid-1974 to mid-1975 a pilot project would be tested in Matanzas province to set up the OPP.[33] In May 1974 two amendments to the *Ley Fundamental* of 1959 (transitional revolutionary constitution in force until 1976) were passed. One granted all Cuban citizens sixteen years of age and over (including the armed forces) the right to vote by secret ballot, and those eighteen years and over to be elected for public office. The other amendment introduced a commission—to be headed by Blas Roca—to regulate and conduct the election of the OPP.[34] The elections were held and the OPP operated in Matanzas

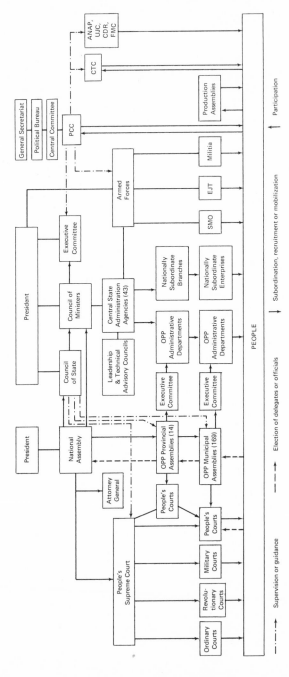

FIGURE 2
The Politico-Administrative System of Cuba at the End of the 1970s

until the end of 1975. The new constitution and a resolution passed at the PCC congress further regulated the OPP and its operation throughout the island. There are OPP at three levels: municipal, provincial, and national. The first two are entrusted with the municipal and provincial management (through "administrative departments") of services such as schools, day-care centers, hospitals, stores, hotels, restaurants, cinemas, night clubs, transport, retail trade, housing, public utilities, and sports, as well as "some local industries" (unspecified). The municipal and provincial OPP also select the judges for the corresponding peoples' courts. The national OPP is the National Assembly, "the supreme organ of state power": it combines constitutional and legislative powers; elects the Council of State from among the Assembly members; appoints the People's Supreme Court magistrates and the attorney general; approves the general outlines of domestic and foreign policy, economic plans, state budget, and monetary-credit-management systems; can modify or revoke decree laws, decrees, or resolutions enacted by any state body; and exercises the highest supervision over the organs of state and government. In July 1976, the island's politicogeographic division was modified: the previous six provinces were subdivided into fourteen, and the existing 407 municipalities clustered into 169. In elections conducted in October of the same year, 10,725 delegates to municipal OPP were elected to serve two-and-one-half-year terms; these, in turn, elected 1,084 deputies to the provincial OPP to serve similar terms, and 481 deputies to the National Assembly for five-year terms. Blas Roca was elected president of the National Assembly which was constituted on December 2, 1976. (The municipal and provincial OPP also elected—in consultation with the party and mass organization—from among their members, the officials in charge of the OPP Executive Committees which manage the "administrative departments" discussed above.)[35]

The Council of State made up of thirty-one members represents the National Assembly (in between the two regular sessions that it should hold annually), implements its decisions, enacts decree-laws between sessions of the Assembly, and supervises the Council of Ministers, the judiciary, the OPP, and the diplomatic corps. The president of the Council of State also presides over the Council of Ministers, is the supreme commander of the armed forces (and empowered to reorganize it), can assume the direction of any central state agency, and oversees the judiciary system and the OPP. Fidel was elected for that position thus becoming head of state (a post formerly held by Dorticós) and government; while Raúl was elected first vice-president.

The Council of Ministers is the "foremost executive and administrative body" of the land. Its members are formally appointed by the National Assembly at the initiative of the head of state and government. The law regulating the functions of the Council of Ministers and the central administrative agencies was enacted at the end of 1976.[36] The Council of Ministers is in charge of socioeconomic development, administration, monetary and fiscal policies, foreign trade, defense and internal security, foreign policy and international treaties, and so forth. The Executive Committee of the Council of Ministers is made up of the president, first vice-president, and vice-presidents of the Council and decides on urgent matters. Forty-three central state administration agencies, of three types, are under the Council's jurisdiction: (1) state committees, which deal with all state agencies (e.g., JUCEPLAN, the National Bank, committees on prices, labor, construction, and finance); (2) ministries, which are in charge of one or more branches of the administration (e.g., agriculture, domestic trade, foreign trade, education, defense), and (3) institutes, which also deal with an administrative branch but whose heads are not a part of the Council of Ministers (e.g., Academy of Sciences, radio and television, and tourism).[37]

The armed forces have also undergone an important reorganization in the 1970s.[38] Its ranks have been reduced but in concentrating on purely military activities have become increasingly specialized and hierarchical. Former army labor squads such as the remnants of the "Military Units to Aid Production" (UMAP) and the "Divisions of Permanent Infantry" (DIP) have been merged with civilian (although militarily organized) labor brigades as the "Youth Centennial Column" and the "Followers of Camilo and Che," into the new "Youth Army of Work" (EJT). This has been structured as a paramilitary agency of the Ministry of the Armed Forces (FAR) but completely separate from the regular army. One reason for this reorganization was the need for centralization to avoid "the proliferation of minicolumns that disperse and divert efforts, developing a structure parallel to that of the administrative leadership." Another was to institutionalize a selective process to strengthen the increasing professionalization of the army. The regular army will not be involved in production while the EJT will draft youngsters who are neither fit for the army nor for study into a three-year program of disciplinary training and work in agriculture.[39]

Another step in the direction of centralization of military activities has been the absorption and programmed phasing out of the militia. This paramilitary organization integrated by armed workers and peasants played a crucial role in consolidating the Revolution in its early years. Its fate was marked in 1963 when the compulsory military service was established; the following year the militia's arms were taken away by the army. Ten years later, in April 1973, all militiamen were put on military "reserve," given the honorary rank of sublieutenants of the FAR, received ID cards, and were ordered to change their grey uniforms for the traditional olive-green fatigues of the army. They may use the army uniforms only when performing official activities and while on active reserve. Once the latter expires, the militiamen's services will no longer be required.[40]

In the 1970s the trend toward modernization and professionalization of the army has reached its highest point so far. The Soviet Union has supplied Cuba with the most modern weapons and trained Cuban military personnel in their use (see chapter 1). The ministers of defense or army chiefs of the U.S.S.R., Czechoslovakia, and Poland have visited Cuba and participated in military exercises. Raúl Castro has reciprocated these visits by traveling through Eastern Europe.

As an outcome of this process, in 1973 and 1976 the officer corps of the Cuban armed forces had their ranking system reorganized into a more conventional hierarchy according to their growing complexity and status. To avoid and repudiate the escalation of military ranks under Batista during the insurrection, Castro decided that the highest rank in the Rebel Army would be that of major. Theoretically, he and his brother, as well as Guevara, were equal in rank to the most obscure major; obviously then, some majors had more power than others. This *de facto* situation was formalized with the first hierarchical reform introduced in 1973. In the army, three types of officers were created, each one with three or four ranks: superior, first, and subaltern. The superior officers' category included four ranks from "army commander" (four-star general granted only to Commander-in-Chief Fidel Castro) down to "brigade commander" (one-star general). Raúl Castro became a "division commander" (two-star general) leaving two ranks vacant between him and his brother. The first officers' category included three ranks from colonel to major (formerly the highest rank); and the subaltern officers' category included four ranks from captain to sublieutenant. The navy also had three categories (including ten ranks), going from admiral to rear admiral, from commodore to commander, and from lieutenant commander to ensign.[41] Explaining the reasons for the new hierarchy, Fidel Castro said that the armed forces had been distinguished in the past for "their modesty in uniform and rank" but that the Revolution had become more mature and so had the armed forces. Other official reasons were the increasing complexity of the armed forces and the need to provide ranks equivalent with those of other countries (e.g., U.S.S.R., Peru) that had a different hierarchy.[42] The new hierarchy was probably accompanied by salary increases for the top ranks and could be seen also as an economic incentive for the new military elite.

The 1973 hierarchy was probably conceived as a transitional step between the chaotic ranks of the Rebel Army and the ultimate ranking of the Revolutionary Armed Forces. Technically, the transitional hierarchy kept the title "commander" for the superior officers in the army and some first and subaltern offices in the navy. In practice, however, equivalencies were established (and publicized in the media) between the Cuban ranks and the more universal ranks; for instance, Raúl Castro, a "division commander" was also called a "lieutenant general." To eliminate this confusion and establish the internal military ranks in Cuba (and probably also to reward the military for its victory in Angola) a second hierarchy was introduced at the end of 1976. The new hierarchy has a similar structure to the previous one but the word "commander" has been replaced by "general." Both Fidel and Raúl are now "generals of the army," each one with four stars, but although the ranking gap has been closed, Fidel is still at the top as "Commander in Chief of the Armed Forces." The law introducing the new rankings justified them by noting that similar ranks were used by the Cuban *Mambís* (independence fighters) during the wars against Spain.[43] More candidly, Fidel stated the need for clear and universally accepted ranks, criticized the Chinese for attempting to eliminate military ranks during the Cultural Revolution, and acknowledged that the previous ranking system had not worked and hence they had decided to call a general by that name.[44]

At the end of 1976, Fidel Castro stated that after eighteen years of revolution the process of institutionalization was basically concluded and, symbolically, the year 1977 was called the Year of Institutionalization.[45] Two questions still remain: one is whether the political system of the late 1970s (figure 2) is substantially different from the system of the 1960s (figure 1), and the other is whether such a system is truly democratic and representative of the masses, allowing for their real participation in decision making. Unfortunately these questions cannot be accurately answered at this time because the new system has been in operation for only a few months and there is no detailed information on its workings. But we can, however, provide educated guesses based on the legislation in force, the speeches of the leaders, and the scanty data published in the Cuban press.

First, there is no doubt that the process of institutionalization of the political system has produced positive effects: the various organs of the state now have their legal functions delineated, the top posts have been assigned specific duties and boundaries, the military and civilian sectors now appear fairly separated, there have been elections for the first time since the Revolution, and there are channels opened to the people that enable them to have some input into the administration.

Second, the center of decision making in Cuba continues to be highly concentrated (although somewhat broadened) in the same clique. Fidel is now president of the Council of State (thus he has taken some of the functions that Dorticós used to perform), president of the Council of Ministers, first secretary of the PCC, commander-in-chief of the Armed Forces, General of the Army, chairman of the National Commission for the Implementation of the SGE, and can assume at any time the leadership of any central state administrative agency. Raúl is first vice-president of the Council of State, first vice-president of the Council of Ministers, second secretary of the PCC, minister of the Armed Forces and General of the Army. The only state organ which is not directly controlled by the two brothers is the National Assembly, but it holds sessions only twice a year and it is difficult to foresee the Assembly confronting or curtailing the Castros' power. Thus it is ironic that in his speeches closing the first congress of the PCC and inaugurating the National Assembly, Fidel strongly criticized the concentration of political power in one person, family favoritism, and revolutionary cliques, making China the target of his attacks.[46]

Third, the composition of the National Assembly (table 5) vividly illustrates its elitist character: the typical deputy is male, either an executive, a technician or a military man, above forty years of age, educated, and a member of the party. Although workers and peasants make up at least two-thirds of the labor force, they are only represented by 31 percent of the deputies; females constitute about half the population but have 22 percent of the deputies; more than 80 percent of the population are neither members of the PCC nor of the UJC but they are represented by only 3 percent of the deputies; more than 60 percent of the population is below thirty years of age but share only 10 percent of the deputies; and the majority of the population, which does not have intermediate and higher education, is represented by 12 percent of the deputies.

Fourth, the powers and functions of the provincial and municipal OPP are significantly limited: (1) the party decides in practice who is eligible to sit in and chair the OPP Executive Committees which are the decision-making and managerial bodies of *poder popular;* (2) the OPP manage the least important sectors of the economy (basically services) while the central state agencies administer the key industries, all agriculture, mining, and finance; (3) the size and distribution of resources allocated to the services administered by the OPP are also centrally decided; (4) the Council of State

TABLE 5

Composition of Cuba's National Assembly of People's Power: 1976

Occupation	Number	Percent	
Leaders in politics, economics, culture and science*	199	41.4	
Technicians in industry, agriculture, and services	38	7.9	56.6
Military men (who don't have another occupation)	35	7.3	
Workers in production, services, and education	144	29.9	
Peasants	7	1.5	
Others (occupations not listed above)	58	12.0	
TOTAL	481	100.0	
Sex			
Male	374	77.8	
Female	107	22.2	
TOTAL	481	100.0	
Political Affiliations			
Communist party members or candidates	441	91.7	
Young Communist League members	24	5.0	
Nonaffiliated	16	3.3	
TOTAL	481	100.0	
Education			
Higher	137	28.5	
Intermediate	287	59.7	
Elementary	57	11.8	
TOTAL	481	100.0	
Age			
18 to 30 years	51	10.6	
31 to 40	196	40.8	
41 to 50	158	32.8	
51 and over	76	15.8	
TOTAL	481	100.0	

*National leaders 12.3%; local leaders 29.1%.
Source: *Granma Weekly Review,* December 12, 1976, p. 4.

supervises the OPP, and the Council of Ministers (through the state central agencies) exerts direction and supervision over the OPP administrative departments; and (5) the OPP decisions can be annulled, modified, or revoked by other organs of the state and the government.

The Democratization of the Labor Movement

From 1959 to 1970, the trade union movement went—as an official Cuban publication states—through a period of decline "which almost ended in total dissolution," due to the alleged "total identity between the government and the workers' interest." Economic demands, the crucial activity of the unions before, ceased to be a matter of struggle "because the government was expected to take care of them." The unions were assigned new tasks such as "to win the workers for the Revolution, fight the counterrevolution, and push production forward." But, since these were also government and party tasks, the unions "became ancillary instruments" in the pursuit of such goals. "Trade union democracy was limited and formal . . . it was neither encouraged nor practiced." The absence of institutional channels, such as the holding of periodic meetings, impeded the workers in manifesting their opinions. "A common question in the decade of the 1960s was: which is the role of the trade unions? Many thought that the unions could be eliminated without the nation losing anything, because the government, the administration, and the party were apparently capable of doing whatever the union could do." Beginning in 1967, the problem was aggravated by the launching of the movement of vanguard workers, composed of the most productive and revolutionary workers in an enterprise. "In theory and practice, in many enterprises, the movement [composed by a selected minority] substituted for the union [which embraced the majority of the workers]." Vanguard workers began to decide by themselves, in the name of the workers, on the few things left to the unions. [47]

In May 1970, Castro acknowledged that the trade union movement had been abandoned and that it should be strengthened and democratized. Two months later, Minister of Labor Risquet, in one of the Revolution's most remarkable speeches of self-criticism, said:

> Theoretically, the administrator represents the interest of the worker and peasant state, the interest of all the people. Theory is one thing and practice another. . . . The worker may have a right established by the Revolution [that is not respected or a complaint against the administration] and there is no one to defend him. He does not know where to turn. He turns to the party and it does not know [about the worker's right] or it is busy mobilizing people for production . . . the party is so involved with the management that in many instances it has ceased to play its proper role, has become somewhat insensitive to the problems of the masses. . . . If the party and the administration are one, then there is nowhere the worker can take his problem. . . . The trade union either does not exist or it has become the vanguard workers' bureau. . . .[48]

To correct this situation, Risquet suggested two concrete measures: (1) Elections would be held for the directorate of all the trade union (local) sections in the country. He said that there should not be the slightest fear that conditions would be placed on the election of the representatives and that the elections should be free and open. (2) The unions should be given an opportunity to perform their natural role. Their *first duty* should be to see that labor legislation is applied and workers' rights protected. (Discussion of this point is left for the following section.)[49] In September Castro ratified the first point, announcing: "We are going to trust our workers and hold trade union elections in all locals. . . . They will be absolutely free, and the workers will choose the candidates [and] elect their leaders."[50]

This announcement was followed by meetings of both the National Council and the National Committee of the Confederation of Cuban Workers (CTC), which set the election dates (November 9 through December 9, 1970), enacted the electoral procedures, and defined the composition and functions of the local unions. The elections would be preceded by a general assembly held at the enterprise and attended by all its workers. At these assemblies, any worker could be openly and freely nominated as a candidate regardless of whether or not he was a trade union official. Next the assemblies would discuss the "merits" of the candidates for the job; this discussion would be intended for information only and all candidates would eventually appear on the ballot. There should be at least two or three candidates for each post in order to give voters a good option. The number of posts to be chosen would depend on the size of the enterprise: 3 to 5 in enterprises with 10 to 50 workers, 7 to 9 in those with 51 to 100 workers, and 11 in those with more than 100 workers. An electoral commission, composed of workers, would organize and conduct the election. Voting would be secret; the secretary general of the union would be selected directly by the workers, and the other posts would be distributed among those elected.[51]

The elections took place as announced and were widely publicized. The press reported partial electoral results in early December, but nothing else was said until May Day 1971, when Castro released one single figure on the elections (the number of unions established). Final results were given by Castro one year later. (See table 6.) The table shows that the ratio of candidates to posts was planned to be two or three to one, in the partial results the ratio was about two to one, and in the final results was one-and-a-half to one. It seems that in the small enterprises (which were probably reporting late) only one candidate appeared on the ballot. Only about half of the expected workers participated in the assemblies to select the candidates, and thousands of workers who attended the assemblies did not vote. The number of officials finally elected was 35 percent below the expected number. The average number of officials elected by each union section was four, a rather low figure when contrasted with the range of from three to eleven officials set by the electoral procedure. Nationwide, some 27 percent of those elected were old union officials, but in Havana about 40 percent of incumbent officials managed to keep their posts.[52]

Were the elections truly free and democratic? According to the official news media, they were. And yet there are some indica-

TABLE 6

Trade Union Elections in Cuba: 1970

	Planned Oct. 1970	Partial Results Dec. 1970	Final Results May 1972
Local sections established	———	26,427	37,047
Attendance at candidate-choosing assemblies	2,000,000	887,525	1,244,688
Number of voters		867,373	———
Number of candidates	500,000 to 750,000	224,875	262,967
Number of officials elected	250,000	117,625	164,367

Sources: Column 1: "Acuerdos del Comité Nacional de la CTC," *Granma,* October 30, 1972, p. 2, column 2: *Granma,* December 3, 1970, p. 1, column 3: F. Castro, "Speech at the May Day Parade and Worker's Rally," *Granma Weekly Review,* May 7, 1972, p. 2.

tions that the government used both pressure and manipulation throughout the electoral process. When the CTC was discussing the electoral procedure, strong criticism was voiced by some union members against the traditional methods. This embarrassed the old union leaders, one of whom candidly complained: "We turned the rabbit loose before the hunter had his rifle ready." The Minister of Labor had to intervene to stop the critics, calling them "counter-revolutionaries" and "demagogues" and warning that such "a nega-tive situation [had] to be changed radically."[53]

When breaking the news of the elections, Castro had said: "The [elected official] will have the moral authority of his election, and when the Revolution establishes a line, he will go all out to defend and fight for that line."[54] Thus he assumed that only those workers who would unconditionally follow government, management, and party orders would be elected. The election was important to legitimize a behavior typical of the 1960s.

The electoral procedure prohibited candidates from advertising their candidacy by any means, the electoral commission being the only one to publicize the candidates' "merits" on bulletin boards and in murals.[55] The CTC did not set the exact criteria for such merits, but Castro indirectly stressed revolutionary loyalty and militancy; hence, it is valid to assume that substantial weight was given by the commission to such merits. As table 6 shows, the participation of workers in the electoral process was below expectations (half of both the labor force and the government-announced figure), perhaps because they did not expect any real changes or they had one single candidate to vote for on the ballot.

Most of the new officials (almost three-fourths of those elected) fulfilled government aspirations (as obviously did the one-fourth of incumbents who stayed). Those few who did not meet the standard of loyalty soon came under fire as Minister of Labor Risquet revealed:

> In the great majority of work centers, the masses elected their best representatives. . . . There were some cases, however—very few of them we must say—where workers elected did not have sufficient merits or the merits which would entitle them to act as leaders. . . . [Every one of these cases] is a danger signal to the trade union movement and to the party, pointing out the location or the manifestation of the failures in our political work. . . . Each of these "warning lights" constitutes a challenge to our political strength, to the power of the ideas of the Revolution. . . .[56]

At the same time that the elections were taking place in the local unions, a reorganization of the national trade unions began which was not completed until late 1973. In October 1970, the CTC approved rules for the reorganization of the national trade unions. It was to be preceded by national assemblies on production, attended by government, administration, and union representatives, and in which problems of production and productivity would be discussed. Since most national trade unions had been organized prior to the revolutionary takeover (although there were some changes in 1961 and 1966), the trade union structure was not coordinated with the radical transformation of the administrative structure. Thus it was decided that instead of workers being partly organized by trade, all should be in vertical unions parallel to the central ministries and agencies; in other words, all workers employed by a central ministry or agency would be unionized together regardless of their trade. Each national union would be like a pyramid with the ministry or agency at the vertex, then the regional branches, then the consolidated enterprises and the plants (or farms or agencies) at the bottom thus facilitating control of production and productivity.[57]

From November 1970 to September 1973, a total of twenty-three national unions were established: Basic Industry; Mining and Metallurgy; Light Industry; Food; Sugar; Petroleum; Tobacco; Fishing; Agriculture and Cattle Raising; Forestry; News and Book Publishing; Construction; Transportation; Communications; Civil Aviation; Merchant Marine and Ports; Education and Sciences; Hotel and Restaurant; Commerce; Public Health; Public Administration; Civil Employees of the Armed Forces; and Arts and Entertainment. The first national unions established were all those in industry and transportation, plus the armed forces, next followed unions in other productive sectors, then services, and finally agriculture.[58] The unions first organized were those with a relatively small membership, high concentration, discipline, and skills which happened to be in the most strategic sectors (these were organized very fast: eleven in less than one year). Services and agriculture, with large numbers of workers, usually dispersed and less skilled, were slowly organized (it took two years to establish the remaining twelve unions).

The Role of the Unions: Defense of Workers' Rights and Participationism

In the fall of 1970 it was acknowledged that unions were transmission belts of the administration for the implementation of production plans. To correct this situation—it was promised—unions would be allowed to perform their natural role (the defense of workers' rights) and to participate in national decision making and enterprise management. One year later, however, there was no significant change in the official conception of the unions' role, as Raúl Castro stressed:

[Under capitalism] the trade unions are the instruments that organize and lead the working masses in the stuggle for their just demands. . . . However, when the working class is in power the role of the trade unions is changed. . . . There are no antagonisms between the working class and the revolutionary power [the government]. . . . One of the principal functions of the trade unions under socialism is to serve as a vehicle for the orientation, directives, and goals which the revolutionary power must convey to the working masses. . . . The trade unions are [also] the most powerful link between the party and the working masses. That is one of their principal missions. . . . Moreover, the work of the trade unions helps and supports that of the administration. . . . The principal tasks [in which the unions should be involved] are productivity and work discipline; more efficient utilization of the workday; norming and organization; quality, conservation, and most efficient and rational use of both material and human resources.[59]

Unions were also increasingly performing cultural and recreational functions for their membership, such as the organization of vacations (in 1972 a vacation plan for 250,000 workers was announced), education (a campaign is under way to recruit young workers into vocational schools), and recreation (such as the 1972 carnivals).[60]

To the promised "collective bodies" with worker representation to manage state enterprises, Jorge Risquet put stringent limitations:

The fact that Fidel and I have suggested that the workers should be consulted does not mean that we are going to negate the vanguard role that the Party must play. . . . [There should not be] expectations or hope for magic solutions. . . .[61] The decision and responsibility [in the enterprise] fall to the management, whose job is to take the daily, necessary measures required by the process of production. . . . One thing that is perfectly clear is that the management should have—and does have—all the authority to act. It is charged with a responsibility and it has the authority to make decisions.[62]

In mid-1971, Castro announced that the 13th National Congress of the CTC, to be held at the end of 1972, would debate the issues of union defense of workers' rights and participation in national and enterprise decision making.[63] (The 13th congress was the first to be held in six years, since 1966, when the 12th congress of the CTC endorsed the Sino-Guevarist line. The 11th congress of the CTC, held in 1962, endorsed the Soviet line prevalent at that time. The 10th congress of the CTC, the first under the Revolution, was held in 1959.) And yet the climate in 1971 was not propitious for such a debate. The brief discussion that preceded the elections in the local unions had been a warning of what could be expected by an uncontrolled membership at a national congress. The "safe" results of such elections provided minimum guarantees for avoiding embarrassing incidents, but the government probably wanted to complete the reorganization of the national unions and have enough time for the preparation of the debate. Thus the congress was postponed for one year, until November of 1973. In the meantime, the remaining reorganization of national unions was finished and the CTC made public nine "theses" for discussion prior to the congress.[64] Although about 88 percent of all workers in the state sector participated in the debate and this took considerable time and energy, the theses set a framework for and put limitations on the scope of the discussion. The following official quotation gives a good picture of the tone of the debate:

> During the discussion [of the theses] every worker who wanted to criticize the administration about concrete aspects of its work was given a chance to do so. . . . No political, moral, or any other pressures were applied to him. . . . The criticism voiced in the assemblies [however] cannot be viewed as the expression of any antiadministration trend, because, if such were to develop, the CTC would be the first to oppose it. . . . [The kind of criticism expressed was] in line with the role which the trade union movement can and should play.[65]

All the theses were approved by more than 99 percent of the votes, the highest opposing vote against a thesis being 0.2 percent. It has been officially reported that: (1) the voting was done by the public raising of hands; (2) figures for the number of opposition votes were exact because there were only a few of them and hence the accounting—and obviously the identification of the worker—was easy; and (3) there was no attempt to demand the inclusion of issues which were not within the framework of the theses.[66]

The 13th congress approved twenty-one resolutions which did not always coincide with the theses. Some of the latter were not subjects of resolutions, others were modified by them, and there were resolutions in areas not tackled by the theses. As secretary general of the CTC, the congress selected Lázaro Peña, an old member of the PSP. (Peña was one of the founders of the CTC back in 1939 and its first secretary general in 1939–47 mostly under the Popular Front of the PSP with Batista. He almost vanished from public life in the next fifteen years. Well trusted by the U.S.S.R., at the 11th congress of the CTC in 1962 he was elected by single ballot as Secretary General of the CTC and remained in the job until Cuban-Soviet relations deteriorated in 1966. A sexagenarian, Peña returned to public activities in 1970, became involved in the reorganization of the unions, and was elected by 99 percent of the vote in the 13th congress of the CTC as its Secretary General for 1973–77. He died in March 1974, after having served four months in office.) In the rest of this section, it is explained how the theses for and the resolutions of the 13th congress dealt with the issues of union defense of workers' rights, participation in national decision making, and in enterprise management; and the implementation of these theses is discussed.

The theses did not include any innovation on the subject of union defense of workers' rights. According to the theses, there are no conflicts but cooperation among the state administration, the party, and the unions because they share the same goal: "Always producing more and better." The congress approved new statutes and declarations of principles for the Cuban labor movement, in substitution of those enacted in the 1966 congress. The new principles state that unions are autonomous bodies which are neither part of the state apparatus nor of the party but that they are politically guided and directed by the party and must follow its policies. The objectives of the unions, as listed in the statutes, did not differ from those prevalent in 1966–70 or as summarized by Raúl

Castro in 1971. The general objectives are: support the revolutionary government, participate in national vigilance and defense activities, cooperate to improve managerial performance, strengthen labor discipline and fight any violations of it, and raise the political consciousness of their affiliates. More concrete objectives are to promote punctual daily attendance at work; maximum utilization of the workday; increases of output, productivity, and quality; saving raw materials and energy; adequate maintenance of the equipment; inventions to improve production; and development of cultural, recreational, and sports activities. The document also generally said that the unions should protect workers' rights, check the enforcement of labor legislation and safety measures, and assist affiliates who have complaints.[67]

Only one form of union participation in national decisions was endorsed by the theses: evaluation in public discussion of legal drafts on significant labor issues. This was a common practice in the 1960s and early 1970s, particularly when sensitive legislation had to be enacted (e.g., the law against loafing). In practice, the law eventually passed was a replica of the draft, suggesting that the laboc movement did not have real power to modify it. The theses recommended various innovations to correct that situation: (1) the draft should be distributed with enough anticipation and accompanied by explanatory materials in simple language; (2) all opinions voiced either for or against the draft, or suggesting its modification, should be heard; and (3) suitable suggestions arising from public discussion should be incorporated in the law and an official explanation given when such suggestions are rejected. In his main report to the congress, Secretary General Peña requested more direct participation of the unions in social security administration, setting price policies, and distribution of certain goods.[68] (By the end of 1977, no measures had been taken to implement either the theses or Peña's suggestions.) In his speech closing the congress, Castro suggested that a representation from the CTC should be invited to the meetings of the Executive Committee of the Council of Ministers where plans and other crucial administrative decisions are made.[69] (Three years later, Castro's suggestion was followed when the secretary general of the CTC was granted the right to attend sessions of the Council of Ministers and the Executive Council.)[70]

The theses prescribed that unions should participate in the administration of the enterprise through two institutions: "production assemblies" and "management councils." The assemblies are not new and have not changed their aims; they were common in the 1960s and, in 1971, the Minister of Labor described their functions as follows: "[Unions must] make every effort to get all the workers into the assemblies, [make them] approve and consider as their own the production plans or whatever activity is involved, [and turn the assemblies] into the tool that will make it possible for us to attain, day after day, [a high] degree of mobilization, interest, and enthusiasm behind the production goals."[71] The objectives of the new assemblies were listed by the theses: fulfilling and overfulfilling production plans, tightening labor discipline, increasing productivity, using resources more rationally, and improving the quality of the product or service. Prior to the congress, the assemblies could make recommendations to the manager concerning production problems and their potential solutions, but the follow-up procedure was not specified. The theses gave the manager the option to implement or reject the assembly's recommendation according to his judgment, but he had to explain the reasons for rejection in the next assembly or the results of the adoption of a recommendation. No sanctions were regulated for the manager who failed to fulfill his obligations with the assembly. The brief resolution on production assemblies passed by the congress did not enter into any of the details contained in the theses, but only set the overall goals of the assemblies and requested from the government the enactment of a law regulating their functions.[72] Concerning "management councils," the theses recommended that union representatives should participate in them but did not determine the number of such representatives, procedure for their selection, or concrete functions. According to the theses, the councils' function was to approve or make suggestions to modify production plans prepared by the manager following "directives issued by the state." The councils were also to be "informed" of any change in the production plan decided by the manager. There was no resolution passed by the congress on this matter.

In February 1975, a national council of the CTC was convened to discuss the implementation of the fourteen-month-old resolutions of the congress. The major report to the council delivered by Roberto Veiga, Peña's successor as secretary general of the CTC, took four full pages of *Granma*. The report discussed the role of the labor movement in a myriad of activities from the sugar harvest to the carnivals, but on the important subject of labor participation in decision making stated only that a law to institutionalize such participation was under study.[73] A resolution passed by the PCC congress at the end of 1975 stated that managers "are the highest authority" in state enterprises and "have maximum responsibility" for their functioning as well as for the results of their decisions. The resolution added that management would be advised by a board on which unions would be represented but that labor participation in management would be limited to the discussion of the plan, analyses of its fulfillment, use of the incentive fund, and organization of socialist emulation.[74] Finally in November 1976, the law that reorganized the state administration called for the introduction of two "new" types of councils in all central state agencies and enterprises, neither of which would truly include labor participation. "Leadership councils" are entrusted to study and make decisions on the most important administrative matters of the enterprise; membership of these councils is limited to "administrative leaders" of the enterprise while labor leaders of such enterprise are not eligible for membership. (However, the general secretary of the corresponding national union has the right to participate in the council when a measure affecting labor is discussed.) "Technical advisory councils" are entrusted with consultation on matters of science and technology related to the enterprise; these councils are composed of "outstanding specialists, highly qualified technicians and administrative heads," not of workers.[75]

A final comment is due on a series of measures taken since 1970—parallel with the reorganization of the unions—which seem to indicate a trend of governmental tightening of control over the workers. In September 1970, Minister of Labor Risquet referred to two steps that had already been taken to insure adequate control over the labor force: the elimination of the nonagricultural private sector (to expand state control over employment and avoid simulation of work); and the taking of a national population and housing census (to measure the size of the labor force and its distribution by occupation and location).[76] Measures to be discussed in this section are: the launching of a campaign to make managers more demanding of workers, the improvement of the system of worker's identity cards and labor records, the reestablishment of work quotas to measure output and productivity, the enactment of a law against loafing to curtail labor absenteeism and integrate loafers into the labor force, and the introduction of collective work commitments.

The campaign to make managers more demanding of their employees was a constant in the production assemblies held in 1971. In October, the Sixth Council of the CTC exhorted management "to strengthen itself [so] its standards of conduct should be one of demand rather than spiritlessness." At the council, Castro denounced managers who lacked "the character to make demands" as "one of the worst ills of the Revolution." The Minister of Labor, in turn, condemned "the demagogic manager, the politickers, and the characters who go around doing little favors" for the workers, and added: "We must reaffirm the role of the manager . . . in demanding that the workers come to work every day; that they make the most efficient use of the workday; that they comply with the established norms with regard to quantity and quality; that the equipment be kept in perfect working order; that no material is wasted; and that every possible measure which will contribute to consolidate work discipline be adopted."[77] By the end of 1971, an editorial of the party's newspaper *Granma* admonished the workers to be demanding of their own comrades, warning that those "who shut their eyes to sloppy work just because they don't want to look for trouble are committing acts of complicity and have an attitude unworthy of the working class." *Granma* exhorted the workers to "fight against this attitude and eliminate it from our industries and work centers."[78]

Each worker employed by the state (probably 90 percent of the labor force) has to have an identification card to get a job and a file with a complete record of his merits and "demerits" (faults). The merits include, among other things: voluntary (unpaid) labor in the sugar crop; overfulfillment of work quotas; overtime work without pay; postponement of retirement to continue working; defense of socialist (state) property; and a high level of political consciousness. Demerits (defined as "activities that negatively affect production, disturb labor discipline, and show a low level of consciousness") to be included in the file are, among others: absenteeism; negligence in handling equipment, raw materials, and fuel; nonfulfillment of work quotas; abandonment of the work in the enterprise without previous authorization; and deserting labor camps before completing the term to which the worker has committed himself. The "file" also registers any sanction applied to the worker by civil, military, revolutionary, and people's courts.[79]

As it has been explained in chapter 2, work quotas were first introduced and applied in Cuba in 1963–65, neglected in 1966–70 (when Sino-Guevarism was in vogue), and refixed and reinforced since mid-1970. Each worker is assigned a quota which determines how much should be produced by him at a given work schedule. Managerial control of fulfillment of the quotas (as well as exhortation for overfulfillment and sanctions for underfulfillment) is basic for enterprise productivity. As we have already seen, the labor file also registers the worker's performance in this matter.

In the spring of 1971, the government enacted a law against loafing which established the obligation of working upon all men from ages seventeen through sixty, who are physically and mentally capable. One of the main purposes of the law was to incorporate idle men into production, and more than 100,000 were indeed recruited even before the law went into force. Another objective was to curtail the increasing absenteeism of the labor force which reached some 20 percent by late 1970. Absentees for more than fifteen days are in a "precriminal stage of loafing" while recurrent absentees commit a "crime of loafing." Penalties fluctuate from house arrest to imprisonment in a rehabilitation center at forced labor for a period ranging from one to two years.[80] The CTC gave full endorsement to the law against loafing. Since the enactment of the law, four national meetings have taken place to check the work done by the courts. In a National Council of the CTC held in late 1971, Minister Risquet reported violations of the law, criticized managers who did not report absentee workers, and exhorted the strict enforcement of the law.[81] In a National Plenary Meeting on Labor Justice held at the beginning of 1972, some fifty recommendations were made (but not published) to improve management enforcement of the law, workers' cooperation in strengthening labor discipline, the courts' application of the law, and the behavior of those loafers incorporated into the labor force.[82]

The 13th congress of the CTC approved the introduction of "collective work commitments" between the enterprise management and the workers and their unions. Quantified commitments are made by the workers concerning the fulfillment and overfulfillment of daily, monthly, and annual work quotas; the savings of raw materials and energy; and the donation of unpaid labor. The workers also commit themselves to avoid absenteeism, tardiness, and any other violation of labor discipline. The union should use "persuasion in order that all workers make commitments in all the various aspects." The administration and the union join in keeping careful control of the commitments. Monthly and annual assemblies discuss the worker's fulfillment of his commitments in front of his job comrades and the results are put in a visible place in the work center.[83]

In early 1975 interviews were conducted in Cuba among local trade union leaders and rank-and-file workers employed in fifteen of the most important, prestigious, and efficient enterprises (in agriculture, industry, mining and services) to detect the labor response to the institutionalization process. According to the author of the survey, "those interviewed were more conscious, revolutionary, politically aware and militant than the average worker." When asked which was the most important role of the local trade union they answered: production-oriented (60 percent), educational (44 percent), both production and defense of workers' interest (14 percent), and defense of workers' interest (4 percent). As principal functions of work councils they gave: disciplinary (40 percent), educational (33 percent), both disciplinary and defense of workers' interest (14 percent), and defense of workers interest (5 percent). Almost 86 percent of those interviewed felt that workers must be consulted in enterprise affairs but only 52 percent of them thought that the manager had to respond to workers' inquiries, suggestions, or problems posed in production assemblies, and 58 percent were of the opinion that labor input in such assemblies was influential and significant.[84]

In summary, the main role of the unions in the 1970s does not seem to have changed much from their role in the 1960s: to cooperate with the state, the party, and the enterprise manager in the improvement of production and discipline of labor. A second function is to educate the workers and probably the least important function is to defend workers' interests. The "new" participatory powers of labor are small and essentially related to production; labor does not intervene in key decisions affecting the national economy (e.g., the distribution between investment and consumption), their own enterprise (e.g., hiring and firing managers), or their own welfare (e.g., fixing their salaries). The promised "management councils" with labor participation have not materialized; the councils introduced in 1976 are integrated by administrative and technical personnel, not by workers. The current trend seems to be for strengthening managerial powers in the enterprise and tightening of control over the workers.

Restructuration of Mass Organizations: The Small Farmers

Soon after Batista's ouster, the revolutionary leadership faced a crucial decision: whether to distribute the increasingly nationalized latifundia among the mass of landless rural wage workers that cultivated it or to keep it undivided.[85] The prevalent opinion (materialized in the 1959 agrarian reform) was to give away the ownership of land already divided into plots and held by sharecroppers, tenant farmers, and squatters, but against dividing the latifundia and converting the rural wage earners into private, independent farmers. The government's alleged reasons for this were of an ideological, political, and economic nature (that is, to impede a regression in the matter of ownership, to keep control over agriculture and the rural workers, and to avoid decline in productivity resulting from parcelization). The latifundia (mainly sugar plantations and cattle ranches) were briefly organized as pseudo-cooperatives which, by mid-1962, were transformed into state farms. One year later, the second agrarian reform eliminated the middle-sized independent farmer (the Cuban "kulak"). Although the resistance of private farmers in Cuba cannot be compared with that of the kulaks in the U.S.S.R., there were bloody clashes in the early 1960s between Escambray farmers who went to the mountains and state troops trained in guerrilla warfare.

At the end of 1966, there were some 234,000 small private farmers who controlled about 35 percent of the arable land. They were, however, incorporated into the National Association of Small Farmers (ANAP), which, in turn, was integrated into the national agricultural plans and supervised by INRA. Private farmers had to resort to government agencies for their supply of seed, fertilizer, tools, and credit, and to sell part of their crops to the state (*acopio*) at prices officially set below the market price. The size of the private sector was further reduced in 1967–71 (to 203,000 farmers and 32 percent of the arable land) through government purchases of farms and through the retirement and death of owners (ownership of land is not hereditary).[86] Furthermore, the size of the *acopio* was substantially expanded to embrace in some areas the total crop (e.g., the Havana "Green Belt"). In these cases the government paid "rent" to the farmer and allowed him to use a small plot of the farm for his own consumption. Until 1968, the small surplus of agricultural production (that part neither sold to the state nor consumed by the farmer and his family) was mostly sold at very high prices to urbanites who used it for their own consumption, transformation into other goods or services, or sale on the black market. During the "Revolutionary Offensive" of 1968 the government drastically curtailed these activities, hence reducing the marketability of the surplus. Small farmers still do some cash selling in very small quantities but mainly barter for other products that they need.

Most rural workers became state employees in 1962 when the cooperatives were transformed into state farms. Some of them, however, were hired by the private farms which began to flourish in spite of governmental restrictions. But gradually the government managed to reduce the number of these private wage earners from about 150,000 in 1962 to from 30,000 to 60,000 in 1966. This trend was accelerated in 1971 when, after passage of the law against loafing, the ANAP launched a campaign to detect and transfer to the state sector thousands of idle men partly employed on private farms, or working full time on them but at "low productivity."[87] The rural wage workers employed on state farms were allowed small family plots for their families' use and consumption. These plots were eliminated in 1967 under the allegation that the workers were giving more time to family plots than to the state land. A good number of rural workers (estimated at 6 to 10 percent of the total labor force) have been reluctant to become unionized and hold conservative views. In 1972, the CTC launched a campaign to incorporate some 150,000 of these rural workers into its membership.[88]

By the end of 1971, the Fourth Congress of the ANAP was held as part of the "new phase" of the Revolution and the reorganization of mass organizations. The complete record of the congress is not available (only Castro's closing speech was published in the press and the final resolutions transmitted on the radio). But it appears that there was a heated debate between the state administration and private farmers and between the latter and the workers employed on state farms. According to Castro, both the state administration and state-farm workers "made quite serious accusations" against the private farmers who "got the worst of it." The prime minister sided in favor of the state and against some of the "incredible" things requested by the private farmers: "Sometimes one must resort to rawness if one is to put a message across."[89] The four main resolutions approved by the congress reveal the main points of friction that arose and how the position of the private farmer was weakened by the congress.[90]

The first resolution exhorted the progressive incorporation of the private farms and their labor force into the state sector, with the objective of eradicating "every vestige left of class and private ownership of the means of production." (In spite of the government's efforts to accelerate such incorporation, by the end of 1971 only 50,556 farmers, equivalent to 25 percent of the total, had been incorporated.[91]) The resolution claimed that such incorporation would occur in a voluntary manner, without the use of force, violence, or coercion, but the ANAP is committed to the use of political education to convince the farmers of its advantages.

Another resolution dealt with the selling of agricultural surplus and the battle against the black market. Some small farmers requested that the congress annul Law No. 1035, which punishes the illegal traffic of agricultural products. The congress rejected the request, and Castro advised how to treat those farmers who would not accept the decision: "Those individuals who engage in black market operations should be made the object of political work. And the incorrigible ones should be deprived of all their rights [and] be treated as a class enemy."[92]

Two important resolutions dealt with the private farmers who are totally integrated into the *acopio* system. The congress decided that the "rent" paid to these farmers should not cover all their necessities in order that these farmers work part time on state land. Eventually the time devoted to the state should become the main source of the farmers' income "because in a nation of workers it would be illogical to develop a social class of rentists." The congress also showed concern about the small plots allowed to these farmers for family consumption. Although the plot was not abolished, the congress stated that in the future the plot should disappear and the farmer devote all his time to the state land.

As a result of the previous measures, by the end of 1975 the number of private farmowners had further declined to 162,126 and the arable land in their hands to 21 percent of the total.[93] Hence Castro could proclaim in 1977: "Of all the countries in the world today, ours with almost 80 percent of the land in the hands of state enterprises, has the highest percentage of [state] land."[94] Surprisingly the one-fifth of the land in private hands produced 80 percent of the total tobacco and coffee output, 60 percent of the vegetables, 50 percent of tubers and fruits, 33 percent of the cattle, and 18 percent of sugar cane.[95]

The Fifth Congress of ANAP, held in May 1977, acknowledged that the strategy approved in the previous congress would require thirty years to fully integrate private land into the state sector. In order to facilitate the transformation of private farms into "higher forms of agricultural production," the congress pushed for the voluntary aggregation of individual plots into cooperatives, probably following the model of the Soviet kolkhoz. Each new cooperative has to be approved by the Ministry of Agriculture and ANAP. Castro said about this: "Controls are necessary because tomorrow we might well have a strong and uncontrolled cooperative movement on our hands."[96] A resolution was also passed at the congress establishing taxes on cooperatives in order to contribute to the national economy and reduce income differences between the cooperative farmer and the worker.[97]

In summary, the private farmer who is not fully integrated into the *acopio* as yet is under political pressure to take that step or merge his farm into a cooperative. His incentive to generate a surplus for marketing is greatly reduced due to the stricter enforcement of sanctions against illegal traffic of agricultural products. On the other hand, the fully integrated private farmer should gradually yield his "rent" and reduce his work on the family plot in order to work more and more for the state land. The fate of the only private or quasi-private sector left in Cuba is clear: total absorption by the state sector.

Restructuration of Mass Organizations: The Youth

As part of the process of strengthening mass organizations, it was publicly acknowledged in 1970 that the work with the youth had been abandoned with grave negative consequences of a political, educational, and moral nature. Thus among the youth there was "a backward minority made up of those who neither study nor work, or do so only under pressure—those who, permeated by the old ideology which still remains at the bottom of certain strata of our society, maintain a conduct which is contrary to socialist morals."[98]

The secretary general of the Young Communist League (UJC), Jaime Crombet, said that this association, founded in 1962, had a "poor, rachitic membership" a decade later—120,000 members out of more than two million youngsters.[99] Due to the poor political work of the UJC, the objective of raising the consciousness and self-discipline of the youth could not be achieved and this failure affected, in turn, other areas such as education.

In spite of the remarkable progress by the Cuban Revolution in education (e.g., reduction of the illiteracy rate from 23 to 4 or 5 percent; doubling the number of elementary schools, student registration, personnel, and graduates; increasing the proportion of children of school age in school from 56 to 98 percent) serious deficiencies were reported. In April 1971, out of the total number of school-age youngsters (4 to 16) there were 300,000 who neither studied nor worked. Apparently the law against loafing reduced this figure to 215,513 one year after. This figure was equivalent to only 12 percent of the total student population, but the percentage dramatically increased with age (e.g., 23 percent among those 14 years old, 44 percent among those 15, and 60 percent among those 16). The dropout rate was very high: in elementary schools, 79 percent of those who entered the class of 1965 did not finish in 1971. The dropout rate was worse in rural areas (88 percent) than in urban schools (66 percent). The rate of dropout in junior high school was higher (86 percent) than in elementary school.

Some of the official reasons given to explain this phenomenon were of a material nature: poor school installations, difficult accessibility of schools, and deficient training of teachers (in elementary schools only 39 percent of the teachers had finished their studies, while in junior high only 27 percent had finished). But it was also reported that the students did not show enough enthusiasm, perhaps because they were spoiled: "Before it was papa who paid all the expenses for the student and, afterwards, it was the state. A lot of revolutionary talk, a lot of political indoctrination but, in the end, that man is not simply abstract ideas. The university will never educate a man more than a factory will."[100] The lack of systematic, constant, daily work and discipline among students was acknowledged by Castro: "Scholarship students and students in general are willing to do anything, except to study hard."[101]

The emphasis placed and the great efforts made by the Revolution to attract young farmers and workers into vocational and technological schools (especially agricultural ones) was crowned by success in the mid-1960s. But later the number of students registered at those schools declined dramatically and, in 1972, some were empty. In 1971, there were 24,033 students in language schools, but 16,203 in industrial schools and only 7,757 in agricultural schools. Castro explained that the idea of moral motivation had failed and there was a lack of material incentives: "Who wants to go to work in the countryside? [It] is rough, it is poor . . . it doesn't change from one year to the next [and will stay like it is] for years to come."[102]

Students also showed a lack of concern for and responsibility with socialist property. According to the Minister of Education, 50 percent of the books sent to schools were lost every year due to lack of care. Castro exploded in indignation: "There's something wrong when we have to educate our young people in the need to care for socialist property. . . . Loafers, people who don't work, criminals are the ones who destroy."[103]

Youngsters wore "extravagant foreign fashions" (too-short miniskirts in the case of girls; and the boys, too-tight pants and long hair), listened to American music, and liked "decadent" literature. In some cases these youngsters "were used by counterrevolutionaries in protests against the Revolution." It was also reported that "residual manifestations" of prostitution and homosexuality were found among the youth.[104] In 1967, minors had participated in 41 percent of crimes of all types committed in the nation; four years later the percentage had risen to 50 percent.[105]

There were also rumors about an incident that occurred in October 1970 at the University of Oriente in Santiago de Cuba. Apparently at a student assembly, four or five attendants criticized governmental policies and accused Castro of being an autocrat. Two days later the prime minister visited the campus, called a meeting, and engaged in a heated dialogue with one of his critics. After Castro left, another student assembly expelled all the students who had voiced criticism.[106]

To analyze the roots of the problems mentioned above and take measures to cope with them, two national meetings were held in Havana: the First National Congress on Education and Culture in April 1971, and the Second Congress of the UJC in April 1972. The

UJC Congress detected a "serious weakness" in the previous political work of this organization and launched a campaign to recruit the hundreds of thousands of youngsters outside of it or at least to exert political influence upon them. The UJC Congress also decided to raise the low political level of its cadres and militant members. Top priority was given by the UJC to children, recognizing that childhood is a crucial period for the future development of communist ideology. The political work of the UJC should be extended "to make every young person a self-sacrificing fighter" for increased production and productivity, reduction of production costs, careful use of material resources, and donation of overtime work when necessary. It was also agreed to work closely with the Minister of Education to reduce the dropout rate and direct the students to the fields in which they are most needed. The youth organization requested that "strict, revolutionary measures be taken in the shortest possible time" against youngsters who had antisocial behavior, especially those who neither worked nor studied, and those who were careless, negligent, and irresponsible in handling socialist property.[107]

Concrete measures were suggested by Castro in his speech closing the UJC congress. The dropout problem could be partially solved through the Compulsory Military Service (SMO) and the "Youth Centennial Column." The SMO recruits—in a three-year period—about one-third of all youngsters ages sixteen to seventeen, some 100,000 annually, for a regular force of 300,000 in 1972. Until 1973, most SMO recruits were integrated into the "Military Units to Aid Production" (UMAP). They worked in agriculture (mainly in the cane fields) and were trained in military discipline and some in a trade. The Column was formed in 1968 recruiting some 40,000 youngsters and in 1972 recruited about 55,000. It was integrated by militarized brigades which worked in construction, irrigation, and other projects. Originally the Column was intended as a one-year experiment, but later it was expected that it would continue until 1980. To cope with the remaining youngsters, compulsory education was to be extended after the sixth grade to cover the age bracket (thirteen to seventeen) with the highest dropout incidence. These youngsters would be subject to special internment combining work and study.[108] Three laws enacted in mid-1973 implemented some of Castro's suggestions through the following regulations: (1) the UMAP and the Column (together with other labor squads) were merged into the "Youth Army of Work" (EJT), a paramilitary body, dependent on the Ministry of Armed Forces, which is devoted to agricultural work (especially in the sugar harvest) and other "shock tasks"; (2) a new "Social Service" program (SS) was made mandatory for graduates who have not served in the SMO or the Column, these graduates having to serve three years working in rural areas; and (3) those who have neither been drafted into SMO nor served in the SS will be assigned for three years to the EJT.[109]

The Congress on Education recommended eradicating "extravagant foreign fashions, customs, and behavior" and impeding "rebellious groups from bourgeois societies" from becoming examples for Cuban youth. "Maladjusted minors" who commit offenses or have "antisocial behavior" should be interned in school workshops.[110] Two months later Castro alleged that the cause of the high rate of juvenile delinquency was that the youngsters were exempted from criminal sanctions (the prerevolutionary criminal code provided for special treatment of youngsters under eighteen) and suggested a reduction in the age of legal liability.[111] Following the prime minister's recommendation, in May 1973 the age of legal liability was reduced to sixteen years. In addition, tough sanctions (up to life) were introduced for crimes against the national economy, abnormal sexual behavior, and other offenses.[112]

Probably to avoid any repetition of rebellion among the students, the Secretary of Organization of the party announced at the University of Havana in mid-1971 the establishment of "standards for the political evaluation of both new and old students who lack the necessary and moral conditions" and stated that "the right to a university education is a right of revolutionaries only."[113]

In late 1972 an American journalist sympathetic to the Revolution asked a Cuban official why boys were not allowed to wear long hair. The official said that if one boy were allowed to be different in hair (or in dress or behavior) the rest might request the right to be different also. This in turn would create controversy, something that was considered incorrect.[114]

Some of the measures adopted in 1971–73 and described above were successful, others were not. Thus dramatic cuts in the dropout rates were reported in 1973–74 at all educational levels.[115] And in the Third Congress of the UJC, held in April 1974, an increase in membership to 400,000 (3.3 times the 1972 membership) was announced.[116] On the other hand, the Third Congress of the UJC acknowledged the persistence of old problems among the youth, such as "serious ideological weakness, undisciplined behavior, unthinking admiration of luxury items, search for foreign-made products, and existence of politically disruptive elements." The congress called again for ideological and political work "against all the imperialists' immoral attempts to pervert [the youth]" and "the poisoned bait of the cheapest sort of bourgeois propaganda," which shows that the scarcity of consumer goods was encouraging hoarding, discontent, and disruption.[117]

The Congress on Education and Culture and the Intellectuals

In the first decade of the Revolution, there was a remarkable improvement of material facilities for cultural expansion. The number of published books and journals increased four or five times; substantial state support was given to the national theater, cinema arts, and the national ballet; an excellent center for plastic arts and dancing was built; national and international literary contests were generously funded; and most writers and artists were well remunerated or subsidized. But the abolition of royalties; the nationalization of film companies, theaters, publishing houses, magazines, and newspapers; the centralization of cultural, publishing, and film activities under state agencies (respectively the National Council of Culture, the Book Institute, and ICAIC [Cuban Institute of Cinema Arts]); and the unionization of all writers and artists under the state-sponsored National Union of Writers and Artists of Cuba (UNEAC) made the writer and artist totally dependent on the state. The latter used this power to manipulate these intellectuals by hiring or dismissing them from jobs; facilitating, obstructing, or banning publication of their works, exhibition of their films, or staging of their plays; opening and closing publishing houses and journals; pressing the writers and artists to assume a revolutionary attitude in their works by appraisal and criticism through the news media; and rewarding them with national awards and travel abroad, or punishing them with internment in labor camps.

The government position vis-à-vis the intellectuals had been vaguely defined by Castro in 1961: "Inside the Revolution everything; against it nothing." Until 1968, all those who cautiously stayed within these limits were tolerated by the government, although the peace was interrupted by frequent controversies. However, during the Revolutionary Offensive both the government and the UNEAC bitterly criticized two Cuban writers who had been awarded prizes in a literary contest presided over by a jury which included foreign intellectuals. The writers were the poet Heberto Padilla and the playwright Antón Arrufat; both had proclaimed themselves revolutionaries but the government alleged that their works concealed criticism of the authoritarian nature of the regime. This incident was followed in 1969 by an attempt to select militant juries for international literary contests which would award prizes to revolutionary works, and by the expulsion from UNEAC of one writer accused of counterrevolutionary activities.[118] At the end of 1970, Castro expressed concern over "deviations in cultural activities" and announced that a Congress on Education and Culture—which he wanted to take place immediately but that had to be postponed until April 1971—would be the forum to discuss such problems.[119]

Before the congress began, a series of grave events occurred. In early February, a technician employed by the Cuban government, Raúl Alonso Olivé, who had been assigned as an assistant to Dumont while he was visiting Cuba in 1969, was accused of espionage and sent to prison. The charge against Olivé was that he had handed Dumont a list of black-market prices based on a survey that he had conducted.[120] On March 20, the poet Padilla was jailed. The news filtered abroad and on April 9, a large group of European and Latin American leftist intellectuals (among them Jean Paul Sartre, Gabriel García Márquez, Carlos Fuentes, Octavio Paz, and Mario Vargas

Llosa) addressed a letter to Castro expressing concern over Padilla's imprisonment and "the use of repressive methods against intellectuals and writers who exercise the right of criticism."[121] Ten days later Castro indirectly answered: "There are some gentlemen who aspire to intellectual tutelage and cultural colonialism . . . who want to teach our people from such places as New York, Paris, Rome, London, and West Berlin . . . our people must give a resounding call against . . . that inadmissible attempt to introduce and maintain [here] manifestations of a decadent culture, the fruit of societies that are rotten to the core."[122]

While the congress was in session, Castro attacked the "neocolonializing elements in the [Cuban] cultural movement" who had accepted "foreign cultural impositions" and developed a "snobbish, servile copy of decadent art."[123] Padilla was released on April 25 after handing a confession to the Ministry of Interior. Two days later, and three days before the closing session of the congress, Padilla read a letter of self-criticism to one hundred writers and artists gathered at the UNEAC headquarters. In this letter he admitted all his "errors against the Revolution," accused Dumont and Karol of being CIA agents, disclosed his links with several signers of the letter to Castro, and denounced the "errors" of four Cuban writers who were present at the meeting (one was his wife, the other three intimate friends of his). Three of the accused stood up, accepted their faults, and asked forgiveness; the only one who tried to defend himself from the accusation, alleging that it was false, was strongly criticized later by a UNEAC official.[124]

In this spiraling climate of tension, the congress on April 30 passed its final declaration which introduced a tougher line on cultural affairs. In the future it would not be enough for writers and artists to proclaim themselves revolutionaries and to abstain from criticizing the regime; they would also have to prove their militancy by producing political works: "Culture like education is not and cannot be apolitical or impartial. Apoliticism is nothing more than a reactionary and shamefaced attitude in the cultural field. Art is a weapon of the Revolution, a weapon against the penetration of the enemy." In the declaration it was stated that the mass media "are powerful instruments of ideological education whose utilization and development should not be left to spontaneity and improvisation." Control of the mass media should not be dispersed among various state agencies but centralized under "a single politico-cultural leadership." In staffing mass media, as well as universities and artistic institutions, "political and ideological conditions should be taken into account." The declaration also recommended a revision of the regulations of literary contests in order to check the revolutionary credentials of the juries and select the most revolutionary works. The declaration dealt with "foreign influences" in several passages: (1) condemning the Latin American writers who "took refuge in the capitals of the rotten and decadent societies of Western Europe and the United States to become agents of the metropolitan imperialist culture" (a clear reference to those Latin Americans who had signed the letter of protest to Castro); (2) warning that "many pseudorevolutionary writers, who in West Europe masquerade as leftists but in reality uphold positions against socialism, would be unmasked" (this was directed against Dumont and Karol); (3) combating the possible infiltration of "imperialist cinema, television, and art"; and (4) requesting the establishment of a "strict system" for inviting foreign writers and intellectuals to avoid the presence of persons whose work and ideology does not fit into those of the Revolution.[125]

All of these suggestions were immediately accepted by Castro in his closing speech to the congress. He said that criteria for and priorities on publications would be imposed upon the Book Institute: "There are privileged minorities writing things of no use, expressions of decadence. . . . Sometimes certain books have been printed [an obvious reference to Padilla's book of poems published in 1968] of which not a single copy, chapter, nor page should be published, not even a letter! . . . Our magazines will be only open to revolutionary writers." Then Castro set the rules for future literary contests: "In order for anybody to act as a member of a jury [or] to win an award, whether national or international, he must be a true revolutionary," that is, a revolutionary "without doubt, hesitation, or half-way measures." Finally Castro informed the "European pseudoleftists" and the "shameless Latin Americans" that they will never again be jury members or guests of the Cuban government: "Now you know it, bourgeois intellectuals, agents of the CIA, and espionage services of imperialism: you will not be allowed to come to Cuba! Our doors will remain closed indefinitely!"[126]

On May 20, sixty European and Latin American writers, filmmakers, and artists answered Castro in a second letter. They stated that Padilla's confession could have been obtained only through torture, and that this recalled "the most sordid moments of Stalinism," with its "dogmatic obscurantism," "cultural xenophobia," and "repressive system."[127] A week later Padilla released a statement saying that his confession was delivered completely voluntarily. (However, in his address to UNEAC he had shrewdly referred to the numerous sessions that he had held for more than a month with MININ [Ministry of Interior] officials whom he finally learned to "admire and love.") Almost at the same time, in a speech commemorating the tenth anniversary of the creation of MININ, Castro defended the integrity of the state security officials and indignantly repudiated "those miserable elements that in the international scene have said that the self-critical statement of a writer who held a counterrevolutionary position came as a result of physical torture." And then Castro acknowledged that the Revolution was under attack from "communist, socialist, Marxist, and leftist positions."[128]

That summer several American scholars, Marxists, or leftists, many of whom had visited Cuba before and were expected to return, found their visas cancelled or never received the expected visas from Cuba.[129] In the fall, a journalist who managed to enter Cuba reported the case of another writer who had been in trouble and lost his job, but transmitted the impression (received from interviews with state officials and writers) that the purge would not continue because the intellectuals had received the message and the government wanted to curb the bad publicity abroad.[130] Nevertheless, the American specialist of Caribbean affairs, Frank McDonald, who had spent two months in Cuba in 1970, returned in May 1971 as a guest lecturer at the University of Havana and published sympathetic reports on the Revolution, was arrested on Christmas eve of 1971. Accused of being a spy (a charge punishable by thirty years in prison or death), McDonald was held incommunicado for three months and frequently subjected to the interrogations of state-security officials. He was finally released because of "lack of evidence" but was deported and his notes confiscated under the allegation that he had gathered "sensitive socioeconomic information" for a book, thus violating a "freeze" imposed by the Cuban government in such studies.[131]

The tide of the ideological campaign did not recede in 1973. The Cuban press attacked "sociological research" conducted in Latin America by U.S. scholars sponsored by such institutions as the Ford Foundation, presenting such activities as espionage, and denouncing an increase of U.S. "cultural penetration" in this area.[132] An American political scientist who in the 1960s had visited Cuba several times and written sympathetic studies of the Revolution was refused a visa by the Cuban government because of his connections with the Ford Foundation. Two U.S. specialists on the Cuban patriot and writer, José Martí, both of whom had also been in Cuba several times, were attacked by the Cuban magazine *El Caimán Barbudo* ("The Bearded Crocodile") because in their works they presented a fragmented view of Martí which neglected his antiimperialist views, while both had received Ford support for a seminar and an institute on Martí.[133] The Cuban government also prohibited radio stations from transmitting U.S. and British pop and folk music (including protest songs) alleging that these caused alienation among the youth.[134]

In 1974–77, however, with the change in the U.S. presidency and the ensuing climate of relaxation of tensions, a few of the previous measures were softened or dropped: American pop and folk music was back on the Cuban radio, and a good number of U.S. scholars were allowed to visit the island (including top officials from the Ford Foundation, the Social Science Research Council, the Council on Foreign Relations, and the National Endowment for the Humanities). But there was no relaxation in the fundamental aspects of Cuba's intellectual and cultural policy. The resolution passed at the PCC congress on art and culture, as well as the new political constitution, both ratified the policy of the early 1970s. At the granting of the Casa de las Américas awards in 1977, Armando Hart, head of the newly created Ministry of Culture, said: "If a jury were to give an award to a work which went against the interest of Cuba or socialism, the *Casa de las Américas* would . . . denounce it as infamous before the Latin American literary movement."[135] Hart elaborated on the role of the writer in the Revolution at a meeting held in March 1977 with members of the literary section of UNEAC.[136] He began by stating that the ideological struggle between socialism and capitalism had become more acute and, since literature was one of the battlefields, Cuban writers were expected to: prepare for (instead of avoid) the ideological confrontation, pay greater attention to the party's line, and produce their "most artistic writings" basing their work on the life and needs of the workers and the accomplishments of the Revolution. Then Hart referred to "the small minority" that by setting itself up "as judge of the Revolution" and spreading "diversionary ideas" had damaged the literary family because it "awakened in the people a natural distrust for the work of writers." The diversionary writers, however, had "suffered the most": they "created a problem for themselves [and] have not been able to develop as writers." Claiming that he was not dogmatic, the Minister of Culture asserted that "writers must be true revolutionaries in order to develop a revolutionary literature" and that the writer who does not deeply understand the Revolution "suffers a serious intellectual deficiency." Finally Hart said that his ministry wanted UNEAC to "clear up [these problems] and forcefully put forward the line of principles proposed at the Party Congress." He also encouraged UNEAC to organize seminars to strengthen the writers and artists ideologically, gathering them together "in a body of common ideas."[137]

Institutionalization à la Soviet

The changes introduced in 1970–77 in the Cuban political structure suggest that a process of Soviet-style institutionalization is taking place highlighted by the following ten features:

1. Depersonalization of the government through delegation of power. There seems to be some substitution of the charismatic-per-

sonalistic regime prevalent in the 1960s by a technocratic-bureau-cratic administration closely resembling that of the Soviet Union.

2. Strengthening of socialist legality through the enactment of the new political constitution (heavily influenced by the Soviet constitution), the law of organization of central state administration, and other legislative measures.

3. Separation of functions on the central administration, the party, and the army. These three institutions were controlled in the 1960s by Castro and his inner circle, resulting in the absence of delimitation of their functions. Now there is a clear tendency to separate these institutions and assign specific functions to each of them. The center of power continues to be concentrated in the Castro brothers although it has been somewhat broadened.

4. Within the central administration, separation of legislative and executive functions (previously performed by the Council of Ministers) respectively assigning them to the newly created National Assembly and Council of State. The judiciary is now formally controlled by the central administration. Establishment of the OPP through national elections. Each of the new institutions has a counterpart in the Soviet system.

5. Building up the formerly stagnant Communist party (PCC) so that it will efficiently perform the political-guidance function. The membership of the PCC is being expanded and indoctrinated and the first party congress approved the PCC platform and elected all its officials.

6. Concentration of military functions in, and specialization and hierarchicalization of the armed forces. The latter have absorbed the militia and set a timetable for its demise. The armed forces have been reduced in size and centered on strictly military functions, while the productive activities they used to perform are now entrusted to a separate body. The military ranks have been reorganized twice, abandoning the modesty in ranks that was characteristic in the 1960s, and resembling now the complex hierarchy of the Soviety military.

7. Revival and strengthening of the trade unions but within the Soviet concept of transmission belts of the administration. The labor movement has been revitalized through elections in local units,

reorganization of national unions, and a national congress of the CTC. In spite of the 1970 rhetoric, however, the unions' primary objective continues to be cooperation with the administration in productive tasks instead of defense of the workers' interests. The promised participation of the unions in enterprise management has been limited to production issues and the really new participatory functions have still to be regulated and implemented. The current statutes of the CTC assert that the unions are not part of the state apparatus (although they have to follow the party's policy) but there are indications that they remain controlled by the administration, e.g., state manipulation in the local unions' elections, the reorganization of the national unions parallel to the central ministries and agencies (which suggests a better integration between the two), and the setting of a framework by the administration to the discussion preceding and during the CTC National Congress. Direct state control over the labor force has been reinforced with a better system of identification, record-keeping, measurement of output, and worker-absenteeism control.

8. Increasing political pressure to integrate private agriculture into the state sector as is common in Eastern Europe with the exception of Poland. There have not been major structural changes in the association of small farmers (ANAP). This organization, however, is expected to do political work on its members so that they will expand sales to the state (*"acopio"*), reduce production for their own consumption, and totally integrate their land into the state sector or cooperatives (*kolkhozy*). Those employed by private farmers are also under pressure to shift their services to the state farms.

9. Reorganization of the main youth organization (UJC) to expand its membership, improve the latter's political education, and cooperate with the administration in a series of measures to correct failures in the work with youth. These measures include reducing the number of school dropouts through drafting by militarily organized labor squads (e.g., UMAP, Centennial Column, EJT); attacking juvenile delinquency by reducing the age of criminal liability and introducing tougher sanctions for certain crimes; and fighting Western fashions, customs, and behavior to avoid differen-

tiation and rebellious attitudes and strengthen unity and compliance among the youth.

10. Politicalization of and tighter control over education and culture. A more rigid line has been introduced in ideological and cultural affairs to impede deviation from official thought, demand more militant works from writers and artists, control Western influences on art, centralize control over and politicize the communications media, and request unconditional support of the Revolution from Western advisors, magazine writers, jurors in cultural contests, and visitors.

The image projected in the second half of 1970 by Castro's promised reform was of a decentralized, democratic, independent, and mass-participation movement, in the mobilization style that was typical in Cuba during the 1960s. In real life there has been an institutionalization trend characterized by central controls, dogmatism, administrative-bureaucratic features, and limited mass participation resembling the pragmatism and institutionalization of the Soviet system.

In chapter 1, it was explained how the U.S.S.R. has increased its leverage over Cuba and induced Castro to revise the ideology that he so vehemently endorsed during the Sino-Guevarist stage so as to adapt it to conventional Soviet thought. Chapter 2 offered abundant evidence to support the viewpoint that Cuban economic organization in the 1970s has been dramatically transformed to comply with the Soviet system. The modification of Cuban foreign policy, to be discussed in chapter 4, also shows the Soviet imprint. The changes in government and society analyzed in this chapter uphold the hypothesis that the current process of institutionalization has been basically molded in the Soviet die.

4

Foreign Policy:
Multiple Roads to Socialism

Isolated from the rest of the Western Hemisphere for most of the 1960s, the Cuban leaders heartily embraced the principle that the guerrilla *foco* was the only road to socialism. An inter-American organization was established in Havana to promote continental revolution. The government launched armed expeditions to, supported subversion in, and trained guerrillas from Latin American countries. Cuba rejected any possibility of reestablishing relations with countries that did not meet its strict revolutionary criteria and launched a violent campaign against the United States.

Under the new policy of the 1970s, the pendulum has slowly swung to the other extreme: "non-guerrilla" roads to socialism have been accepted; the exportation of revolution to Latin America has been reduced to rhetorical proclamations of support; diplomatic and/or trade relations have been reestablished at one point or another with a dozen Latin American countries, most of which are not revolutionary; discrepancies in relations with several guerrilla leaders and insurrectional movements in Latin America have occurred; and negotiations with the United States have begun. At the same time, the Organization of American States (OAS) has liberalized its policy to accept diverse socio-politico-economic systems and freed its members to reestablish relations with Cuba, while the United States has ended its involvement in Vietnam, improved relations with China and the U.S.S.R., and exchanged diplomats with Cuba. At the end of 1977, the only remaining obstacle to a complete normalization of U.S.-Cuban relations seemed to be Cuba's military involvement in Africa.

Realpolitik with Latin America

In January 1962 the OAS agreed to expel Cuba from the OAS, alleging that Cuba's self-proclaimed socialism, Marxism-Leninism, and military links with the Soviet Union were incompatible with the inter-American system. In July 1964 the OAS, responding to evidence presented by Venezuela of a Cuban-armed expedition, agreed to cut diplomatic, economic, and transportation links with Cuba. At the time, only Mexico, Chile, and Uruguay opposed the sanctions, but eventually the last two countries accepted the OAS decision. Cuba resorted to increased aid to revolutionary groups in Latin America as the only way to break its hemispheric isolation. In addition, in 1966–67, Che Guevara, Regis Debray, and Fidel Castro proclaimed that the rural guerrilla *foco* "à la Cuba" was the only road for revolution in Latin America.

In the late 1960s, three events induced Cuba to stop sending armed expeditions abroad and to dramatically reduce its aid to Latin American guerrillas and revolutionary movements: the death of Che Guevara and the concomitant failure of his guerrillas in Bolivia (as well as previous failures in Argentina, Guatemala, Peru, and Venezuela); the deterioration of the Cuban economy which forced an inward concentration of all the nation's resources and efforts; and the rapprochement with the U.S.S.R., which allowed the latter to exert pressure on Cuba to normalize her relations with Latin America.[1] Early in 1970, Venezuelan guerrilla leader Douglas Bravo accused Castro of abandoning continental revolution for consolidating socialism in his own country, as Stalin had done in the U.S.S.R. in the 1930s. The premier answered defending his nation's "right and duty" to improve its economy and warned that, in the future, guerrilla fighters would have to meet Cuban criteria to receive aid.[2] Since 1970, almost nothing has been heard from the Organization of Latin American Solidarity (OLAS), founded in Havana in 1967 to promote continental revolution. In various speeches both Brezhnev and Castro have assured that Cuba will not attempt to export its revolution to Latin America.

In trying to break its hemispheric isolation and under pressure from the U.S.S.R., Cuba has become increasingly compromising with the socio-economic-political systems of other Latin American countries, first accepting the "progressive military," then "democratic socialism," and finally conventional military regimes and representative democracies. In mid-1969, Castro had set three preconditions in order for Latin American countries to restore relations with Cuba: (a) rejection of the OAS sanctions; (b) condemnation of the "crimes" committed against Cuba by "Yankee imperialism"; and (c) revolution. He then said that Cuba would never return to the OAS and would wait as long as necessary (ten, twenty, thirty years) until all Latin American countries would revolt and establish the Organization of Revolutionary States of Latin America.[3] Less than one year later, Castro replaced all these preconditions with a new one: that the country behave independently of the United States.[4]

Peru was the first country that offered Cuba an opportunity to practice the new realpolitik when, in 1968, General Juan Velasco Alvarado overthrew the democratic, but weak and inefficient, government of Fernando Belaúnde Terry, proclaimed a revolution, and nationalized the U.S. oil industry. Since then Cuban-Peruvian relations have warmed steadily. In 1969 Castro hailed the Peruvian leaders as a "new phenomenon," that of "a group of progressive military playing a revolutionary role"; in 1970, generous Cuban aid was given to help the victims of the devastating Peruvian earthquake; in the fall of 1971, Velasco invited a Cuban delegation to attend a meeting of the UNCTAD's Group of 77 held in Lima; and in late 1971, Castro made a stopover at the Lima airport (on his way back to Cuba from Chile) and met Velasco. Early in 1972, Peru presented a motion at the OAS requesting that its members be free to individually reestablish relations with Cuba if they wanted. The motion was defeated but, in July, Peru reestablished relations with Cuba.

For a brief period there was a chance that Bolivia, under the rule of leftist General Torres in 1970–71, would repeat the Peruvian example; but the military coup of conservative General Banzer in late 1971 erased that possibility.

Since 1971, Cuba has been courting Panama's military regime led by General Omar Torrijos. He has introduced a few minor socio-economic reforms and has challenged the United States over the Panama Canal. At the end of 1971, two vessels under Panamanian flag were captured by the Cuban navy, which alleged that the vessels had previously launched incursions against Cuba and that the captain of one of them (a Cuban by birth and a U.S. citizen) was a CIA agent. The U.S. government offered its aid to Panama and requested from Cuba the return of the vessels and the captain. Castro immediately denounced this as a U.S. plot to divert Panamanian attention from the canal and damage relations with Cuba. He invited Torrijos to send a plane to Havana to pick up all the crewmen who had not participated in acts of aggression. A Panamanian delegation soon arrived, heard the confession of those crewmen accused by Cuba, accepted the conditions, and hailed Castro for respecting Panama's sovereignty.[5] In 1972, Panama supported the Peruvian motion at the OAS and Panamanian Air Force planes made regular trips to Cuba carrying university professors and students as well as politicians. Later in the year, Torrijos followed the Cuban precedent at Guantánamo Base by refusing to collect the U.S. annual rent for the Canal Zone. In 1973 the conflict over the canal was taken by Panama to the UN Security Council with strong support from Cuba, Peru, the U.S.S.R., and China, and against U.S. objections. During council meetings held in March in Panama City, General Torrijos condemned the embargo of Cuba and Foreign Minister Juan Antonio Tack announced that Panama would soon recognize Cuba.[6] Relations between the two countries were finally reestablished in 1975, and General Torrijos visited Cuba in 1976.

In 1969, the Chilean Christian Democratic government of Eduardo Frei initiated trade exchanges with Cuba and in June 1970 signed a two-year trade agreement for $11 million. Later in the year, the Marxist candidate of the Popular Front *(Unidad Popular,* composed of Socialists, Communists, Radicals, and a leftist split of the Christian Democrats—MAPU), and Castro's friend, Salvador Allende, was elected president. Ten days after taking office, Allende reestablished diplomatic relations with Cuba, and early in 1971, a new trade agreement (increasing the trade volume by $6 million) was signed by both countries.[7] Castro and Allende exchanged visits in 1971 and 1972. Nevertheless, relations between the two nations were broken in September of 1973 by the Chilean military government immediately after the coup was implemented.

In 1971, Castro supported Uruguay's Popular Front *(Frente Amplio)* in that nation's elections. This front, more mixed a coalition than that of Chile, was composed of splits from the two traditional parties ("Blanco" and "Colorado") together with Communists, Socialists, and Christian Democrats and was led by retired General Liber Seregni. An illegal movement of urban guerrillas, the Tupamaros, could not participate in the elections and, although manifesting doubts that it could solve the problem, did not oppose the *Frente.* The latter lost the election to the conservative candidate of the incumbent party, Juan M. Bordaberry. In 1972–73, the military crushed the Tupamaros, closed down the congress, banned the Communist party, and shut the door to any potential resumption of relations with Cuba.

A surprising rapprochement took place in 1971–72 between Cuba and the conventional government of Ecuador led by the seventy-eight-year-old politician and quasi dictator, José María Velasco Ibarra. He had not introduced a single revolutionary measure in his term (nor in his previous two brief periods as president) but seized some fifty U.S. fishing ships that had entered the unilaterally established two-hundred-mile territorial waters of Ecuador. (The country is strategically important to Cuba because it is expected to become the second largest Latin American oil exporter by the end of the 1970s.) In the Soviet-Cuban communiqué released on the occasion of Premier Kosygin's visit to Havana, both parties hailed Ecuador's "independent posture" (as well as that of Panama). On his way back from Chile, Castro made a stop at Quito's airport and met Velasco Ibarra and part of his cabinet. The warming relationship was interrupted in early 1972 by a military coup that overthrew Velasco Ibarra (for the third time in his career!). The new military regime has been cautious in its statements and, although siding in 1972 with the Peruvians at the OAS meeting, did not follow them in immediately reestablishing relations with Cuba. In March 1973, during the ECLA (Economic Commission for Latin America) meetings held in Quito, the chief of the Cuban delegation, Rodríguez, met with Ecuadorian president General Guillermo Rodríguez Lara. When asked by journalists if the reestablishment of relations between the two countries was imminent, Rodríguez diplomatically replied "we are not in a hurry."[8]

Mexico never accepted the OAS decision to isolate Cuba. Diplomatic relations and small trade continued uninterrupted although several conflicts created tension and coolness between the two countries. Early in 1972, the situation apparently changed when, for the first time since Cuba's revolutionary takeover, an exchange of foreign trade missions took place. Cuba is interested in buying Mexican lubricants, manufactured products, and medicines (the latter suggests that the expected Soviet aid to develop a pharmaceutical industry in Cuba has not materialized) and receiving technical experience in the industrial processing of minerals and petroleum derivatives, in exchange for tobacco, rum, and minerals. Mexico's Foreign Trade Bank offered to finance the operation and an agreement was signed in March 1973. Two months later Mexico and Cuba signed an agreement on the treatment of hijackers.[9]

Jamaica and Trinidad and Tobago entered the OAS in the late 1960s. Instead of alleging that they were not bound by the 1964 OAS decision, the two countries abstained from establishing diplomatic and trade relations with Cuba. The two nations have rather conventional regimes, democratically elected, and at one point, Trinidad and Tobago accused Cuba of training some of its citizens in revolutionary warfare. The situation changed in 1971–72, however. An exchange of trade missions took place between Cuba and Trinidad and Tobago in late 1971, and a more liberal party gained power in Jamaica early in 1972. Both countries voted in favor of the Peruvian motion in the OAS in the spring of 1972, and Castro hailed them for doing so. In a conference of Commonwealth Caribbean leaders held in Port-of-Spain in October, Jamaica and Trinidad and Tobago (as well as Barbados and Guyana, the first of which entered the OAS in the early 1970s) decided to establish diplomatic relations with Cuba and the decision was implemented in December 1972. Castro paid short visits to Guyana and Trinidad-Tobago in September 1973 and met, in Port-of-Spain, the prime ministers of the four English-speaking Caribbean nations and thanked them for reestablishing relations with Cuba.[10]

The unexpected occurred in Argentina when in rapid succession President-General Alejandro Lanusse convoked presidential elections. These were freely held in March 1973 and won by the Peronist candidate, Dr. Héctor Cámpora, who was inaugurated as president in May. Cuban president Dorticós was invited to the inauguration and three days later Argentina and Cuba reestablished diplomatic relations. New elections, followed by the victory of General Juan Perón, consolidated the rapprochement between the two nations. In August, Argentina granted Cuba a credit of $1.2 billion to purchase agricultural, road-building, and railroad equipment. The Argentine Minister of Economy, José Gelbard, announced later that branches of U.S. corporations in his country would have to cooperate in view of the new Argentine trade policies with Cuba. At the end of the year, Chrysler-Fevre began negotiations with the Cuban trade mission in Buenos Aires, and General Motors-Argentina offered to sell 1,500 vehicles to the island. Ford rapidly joined the group. The three automobile corporations then requested the necessary authorization from the U.S. Treasury in order to sell vehicles to Cuba. In early 1974, Minister Gelbard headed a trade delegation to Havana which included representatives of the three U.S. corporations, and declared that the latter would sell to Cuba regardless of the U.S. Treasury's decision. The authorization was finally granted by Washington in April.[11] In spite of the death of Perón, the overthrow of his wife, Isabelita, by a military coup, and the increasingly repressive nature of the anti-communist military regime in Argentina, diplomatic and commercial relations with Cuba have continued.

In Central America surprising changes began to take place. At the end of 1972, Cuba sent two "medical brigades" to help the victims of the earthquake that destroyed Managua (interestingly, the same gesture that opened the door to the Peruvians), and they were received by the Minister of Public Health.[12] Cuba stated that this was an act of solidarity to the suffering people of Nicaragua and did not necessarily mean support of Nicaraguan dictator Anastasio Somoza, Jr. But even this gesture would have been difficult to imagine three years before. On the other hand, then Costa Rican president José Figueres (another former archenemy of Castro), addressing a meeting of Cuban exiles in Puerto Rico in 1973, advised them to be realistic (in view of the U.S. rapprochement with China) and to be open-minded of the possibility of rapprochement between Cuba and the United States.[13] In late 1973, Honduras renewed trade relations with Cuba signing a $2.3 million agreement to buy sugar from the island.[14] In 1977, Costa Rica and Cuba agreed to exchange consuls.

Finally, relations with Venezuela, the nation which in 1963 had requested the OAS to impose sanctions against Cuba, improved considerably since 1969 as a result of a change in attitude by the Christian Democrat government. The first step was taken by President Rafael Caldera's "pacification program" which included legalization of the Venezuelan Communist party, amnesty to revolutionary activists who agreed to respect the democratic process, and relaxation of tensions with Cuba. In 1972 top Venezuelan officials from the Ministries of Education and Agriculture visited Cuba; there were professional, scholastic, and sports exchanges; the Cuban press agency *Prensa Latina* was allowed to establish a branch in Caracas; and one of the two Cuban guerrillas arrested in the 1963 landing was freed. (Another Cuban guerrilla captured in 1967 was freed in early 1974.) Early in 1973 Caldera stated that the guerrillas in Venezuela had disappeared, that Cuba's conflicts with other Latin American countries had been considerably reduced, that the normalization process between

Venezuela and Cuba was evolving positively, that his government was endorsing Cuba's entrance into international agencies (e.g., the Group of 77), and that although Venezuela would not formally present the Cuban case in the next OAS General Assembly, the theme would be discussed informally. The assembly held in April was headed by Venezuelan foreign minister Arístides Calvani who played a crucial role in obtaining approval for the new doctrine of "ideological pluralism"—which meant the acceptance by the OAS of nations with divergent socio-politico-economic systems, including Marxist ones.[15] At the same time the OAS assembly was taking place, the Christian Democrat presidential candidate Lorenzo Fernández was in Moscow discussing with Soviet leaders the possibility of shipping oil from Venezuela to Cuba.[16] In his 1973 May Day speech, Castro for the first time openly courted Venezuela by welcoming its recent step to annul the commercial treaty with the United States and announcing that Cuba would support the Venezuelan government "regardless of its economic system" in case of a serious conflict with international oil corporations.[17] In June Venezuela presented a motion to the OAS (eventually defeated) by which a majority of votes (and not two-thirds as before) would be enough to lift the sanctions against Cuba. Less than one month later an anti-hijacking agreement was signed between Venezuela and Cuba. In September Castro praised as "progressive" the Venezuelan action in the OAS and said that Cuba would welcome a visit of President Caldera to Havana. The following month a Venezuelan official delegation led by a minister and close friend of Caldera went to Cuba, spurring the rumor that relations would be reestablished immediately.[18] This warming trend was temporarily halted in December 1973 when the opposition's candidate, Carlos Andrés Pérez (from Acción Democrática), was chosen as president in national elections. In his platform Pérez had sustained a more conservative policy vis-à-vis Cuba but, by the end of 1974 he had reestablished relations with Cuba.

The previous pages show that, in spite of several setbacks, Cuba has assumed an increasingly compromising attitude vis-à-vis Latin American countries[19] with divergent revolutionary stands: the former Chilean Marxist government of Allende; a group of nations that have proclaimed themselves revolutionaries but are mostly reformist or have not changed their status quo at all (e.g., Jamaica, Mexico, Panama, and Peru); a group of conventional regimes that do not pretend to be revolutionary (e.g., Barbados, Colombia, Guyana, Trinidad and Tobago, and Venezuela); and military regimes of a conservative and even repressive nature (e.g., Argentina and Ecuador). A Hungarian journalist posed the problem to Castro while he was in Chile, asking him: "You have said a number of times in your speeches that there are many ways to achieve socialism; could you give us a general picture of the Latin American scene in this respect?" Castro answered employing the "Cantinflas style" (the deliberately confusing and contradictory manner which the famous Mexican comedian, Mario Moreno, uses to get away from difficult situations):

> I don't think I ever said that there were many ways, I might have said there was more than one way, which remains to be proven and, to a certain extent, is being proved. Also, that new variants might come up. . . . Here's a new way: the Chilean process. A variant which may very well set the beginning of a process whose future we cannot predict, as in the case of Peru.

A Chilean journalist tried to get a more concrete definition from the Cuban premier by asking: "In view of the experience of the last ten years of revolutionary struggle in Latin America, do you think that the theory of the revolutionary nucleus [the guerrilla *foco*] is now subordinate to other forms of struggle or is that theoretical stand still valid?" Castro diplomatically chose to remain silent.[20]

Conflicts with Old Allies and Friends

The new realpolitik of the Cuban Revolution has generated a series of conflicts due to the abandonment of Castroite revolutionaries who oppose in their countries the governments with whom Cuba has reached a detente. There are also contradictions between Cuba's manifested principles or ideology and those of the new allies. As Karol has pointed out, in 1968 Castro's criterion for sorting friend from foe was their prevailing attitude toward the U.S.S.R. Three years later, having come to terms with the Soviets, Castro's criterion changed to weigh on his allies' prevailing attitude toward the United States. In both cases, the Cuban leader was willing to accept as an ally a country which shared his antagonism toward his main enemy at that time, neglecting the internal system of such an ally. This inconsistency was masterfully presented to Castro while in Chile by a journalist from Iceland:

> You have self-determined yourself as a revolutionary but at the same time you said that you wanted to have relations with any country that had an independent policy [from the United States]. It seems to me that there is a contradiction between the two positions. One would be nationalistic and the other would be revolutionary. If tomorrow you discover that Ecuador or Argentina offers you good relations [and you decide to accept], you can fall in the same contradictions as the Soviet Union has with its aid to Iran and Bolivia, or as Communist China has with its aid to Pakistan.

Castro answered:

> If you want to be an accurate observer of reality and not a theoretician passing judgment on the problems of this world from an ivory tower . . . you have to understand politics as a principle, one bound by conditions or reality. . . . The thing that would be most displeasing to U.S. imperialism today would be if—in defiance of the accords that imperialism imposed through its colonial administration, which is what the OAS is—various governments should establish relations with Cuba. . . . There would be no contradiction if the government of Ecuador wants to establish diplomatic relations with Cuba. Because we subordinate whatever other differences or whatever other problem exists to the fundamental one: defiance of the dictates of the United States.[21]

The question that could have been asked then was: what about the revolutionaries in Ecuador and the contradictions between that system and Cuba's? This conflict is not a theoretical one but has actually occurred in Peru, Chile, Mexico, Argentina, and other countries. (It could have happened in Bolivia if the 1971 coup had not impeded the rapprochement between Cuba and the military regime led by a man who belonged to the same armed forces which killed Guevara in 1967.)

In 1969, Castro began praising the Peruvian military junta which had kept imprisoned two guerrilla fighters who had been pro-Castroites: Hugo Blanco (condemned to twenty-five years) and Héctor Béjar. Both were released at the end of 1970 and took different positions, one against the junta and the other working within it, but both critical of Castro. Blanco's militant antagonism earned him political exile in September 1971; he did not, however, go to Cuba but went to Mexico instead. (His destination could have been the decision of either Blanco or the Cuban government.) He later moved in succession to Argentina, Chile, and back to Mexico. Blanco has stated that when he was leading his guerrillas he did not receive the human and material aid that Cuba claimed it had sent but only the support of Radio Havana. Now "Castro, the guerrilla par excellence, believes it possible that in Peru socialism will come about without destroying the present government by force of arms." Blanco added that he is "disheartened" when he listens to the Cuban radio supporting the military government "which represents the exploiters" instead of the true revolution.[22] Béjar explained almost at the same time the opposition between the Peruvian and Cuban approaches to continuity and change. He said that he supported the military government of his country, because it had assumed a pragmatic and flexible position vis-à-vis sources of financing for development and degree of state control. Thus Peru accepted economic aid from the United States, Japan, the U.S.S.R., and international agencies in order to guarantee the country's independence, as well as domestic private financing to avoid grave economic sacrifices to its people and to facilitate increasing political freedom in the nation. Conversely, Béjar suggested, Cuba had substituted dependence on the Soviets for its former dependence on the United States and had collectivized everything, subjecting its people to tremendous hardships and establishing absolute state control in politics.[23]

In Chile, the conflict between the Movement of the Revolutionary Left (MIR), a Castroite type of movement, and Allende's
Front put Castro in a difficult position. The MIR encouraged the illegal occupation of land, thus disobeying Allende's warnings; it also
wanted the abolition of institutions that Allende had promised to
preserve; finally the MIR (together with some socialists) demanded
faster and deeper revolutionary change, while Allende tried to consolidate the process itself. This conflict came to the fore in the last
days of Castro's visit to Chile. Upon his arrival at Santiago airport,
Castro cautiously said: "We aren't holding our Revolution up as a
model. . . . We don't claim that we are free of defects, that we ha-
ven't made any mistakes. . . . It would be ridiculous for us to tell
you: 'Do as we have done.' "[24] In his farewell speech, he stated, certainly pleasing Allende: "We didn't come to teach [but] to learn, to
see something extraordinary . . . taking place in Chile. Something
more than unique: unusual! It is a revolutionary process [he had
pointed out before that "a revolutionary process is not a revolution"]
practically the first in humanity's history . . . in which revolutionaries are trying to carry out changes peacefully." But then
(taking the MIR's stand), he bluntly rejected that he had gone to
Chile to learn about elections, parliament, and freedom of the press
and suggested that these were "anachronisms" which would eventually be eradicated by the people. According to him, these institutions were used to confuse, deceive, and divide the peasants, the
workers, and the middle class, trying to win them over to the "counterrevolutionary cause," thus weakening the revolutionary forces.
"In this ideological struggle, the odds are against the revolutionaries; [because they] are not equal to the reactionaries." Castro then
explained the sophisticated techniques that the opposition used in
Chile (and that had bothered him, such as indiscreet questions
posed by journalists and criticism from students) and claimed that
the revolutionaries had shown little ability in mobilizing the masses
(which also upset him when his farewell speech in Santiago's stadium had a poor attendance). Cuba, Castro assured, had a greater
power for mobilization than Chile because the former had mechanisms and instruments for mobilization that the latter lacked. Castro
concluded by saying that what he had learned in Chile made him

identify more with the Cuban model.[25] Thus, in the last minute, he broke his promise to avoid interference in Chilean affairs, advising Allende to get rid of all those institutions that made possible the "unique" Chilean revolutionary process and to adopt instead the state mobilization techniques.

The military coup of September 11, 1973, broke a forty-year tradition of constitutionalism in Chile, overthrew a democratically elected government, and took Allende's life. It was also a dramatic blow to the attempt of reaching socialism through democratic, peaceful means and, in some way, a confirmation of the Castroite position. Concerning the latter, it could be conversely argued that Allende's position was the only one possible and that the radicalization of the revolution would have only precipitated the military intervention. Castro strongly condemned the coup, blamed the U.S. government as its instigator and organizer, declared that Allende had won a place of honor among the great martyrs, invited Mrs. Allende and her daughter to visit Cuba, and launched a campaign against the military junta. And yet, when asked if Cuba would try to reestablish socialism in Chile by exporting the revolution to that nation, Castro rejected that action as impossible. Even more significant was the moderation with which Cuban officials and the press handled the Christian Democrat support of the coup, presenting it as a decision of personalities and rightist factions of the party but not of the movement as a whole.[26] This cautious attitude was probably intended to avoid further embarrassment and loss of support to the Venezuelan Christian Democrats with whom Cuba was reaching an understanding at the time.

The Cuban leadership paid a high price for trying to save its link with Mexico, the only Latin American country with which the island had diplomatic relations, airline connections, and some trade in the second half of the 1960s. Friction between the two countries was common. Mexico derived an immediate gain from the Cuban-U.S. split: an enlarged U.S. sugar quota. The Mexicans steadily improved their relations with the Americans as the presidential meetings of Díaz Ordaz/Johnson and Echeverría/Nixon exemplified, and the Mexican police collaborated with U.S. intelligence in checking travelers to Cuba (stamping their passports and taking photos of them). Cuban trade with Mexico was small and systematically at a deficit. In 1969 a few Mexican airplanes were hijacked to Cuba, and a member of the Mexican Embassy in Havana was accused of being a CIA agent by Castro and was expelled from the country.[27] In 1968, hundreds of Mexican students who were protesting against the government in the Plaza de Tlatelolco were killed, wounded, or imprisoned; several university professors and intellectual figures were also sent to jail. Press reports were published suggesting that Cuba was behind the student revolt, an alleged leftist plot to disrupt the Olympic games to be held in Mexico City. To the dismay of the Mexican left, not only did Cuba fail to condemn the massacre and massive imprisonment, it also sent its athletes to the Olympics. In 1971, the Mexican government captured a small guerrilla *foco* and reported that its members had been trained in North Korea with the U.S.S.R. serving as an intermediary. In the news media campaign that followed, some newspapers suggested that Cuba was also involved in the affair. But the Cubans again remained silent, probably because they did not want to jeopardize the exchange of trade missions that took place a few months later.

The establishment of relations between Cuba and Guyana was a serious blow to the opposition, the People's Progressive Party of Cheddi Jagan, a close friend of Castro in the 1960s. Almost at the same time that relations were established, a progovernment Guyanan magazine reported that the friendship between Castro and Jagan had been dissolved because of the embezzlement of $20 million sent previously to Jagan from Castro.[28] In his visit to Guyana in September 1973, Castro was asked about Cuba's position on reactionary regimes and the kind of struggle that should be fought against them. He answered: "It's for the people and not for us to decide which form of struggle is necessary."[29]

Most revealing was Cuba's cautious attitude vis-à-vis the ill-fated expedition of Colonel Francisco Caamaño Deñó to the Dominican Republic in February of 1973. Caamaño was the leader of the 1965 Dominican uprising crushed by the U.S. intervention; since 1967 he had disappeared, although it was generally assumed that he was in Cuba. He landed in the Dominican Republic with a tiny guerrilla group and a week later had been killed and his guerrillas disbanded. The Cuban press reported the tragic events factually by using international news agencies' wires (e.g., UPI, AFP, EFE,) and did not endorse the action. One surviving guerrilla and a nephew of Caamaño, who escaped to Mexico, reported that the expedition was not launched from Cuba but from the island of Guadeloupe in the Caribbean.[30]

The following two statements from Castro summarize the current position of the Cuban government concerning the exportation of revolution to and support of revolutionary movements in Latin America:

> No country in Latin America, regardless of its social system, has to fear from Cuba's Armed Forces. . . . The Cuban government has never thought of carrying the revolution with the weapons of Cuba's military units, to any nation in this hemisphere. This would be an absurd and ridiculous idea.[31]

> We sympathize with revolutionary movements. However, if a revolutionary movement emerges in a nation that has relations with Cuba and respects our sovereignty, in spite of our sympathy for that revolutionary movement, we will abstain from supporting it.[32]

Changes within the OAS

For a decade Castro systematically rejected the possibility of Cuba's return to the OAS, abhorring it as a "putrid, revolting den of corruption," a "disgusting, discredited cesspool" and a "ministry of colonies of the United States." At one point Castro said that Cuba would return to the OAS only if the "imperialists and their puppets were kicked out first"; afterward he spoke of the substitution of the OAS first by the Organization of Revolutionary States of Latin America and later by the Union of Peoples of Latin America. (It should be noted that the second title, suggested in 1971, conveniently excluded the word "Revolutionary.")[33]

The position of OAS officials in the matter was an embarrassing one: violently rejected by Castro, strongly criticized by several Latin American countries, and confronting strong opposition to change from the most authoritarian-conservative countries in the area in an awkward marriage with the powerful United States. In November 1971, trying to avoid a repetition of the Chilean example (Allende individually reestablished relations with Cuba), the Secretary General of the OAS, Galo Plaza, began consultations in Mexico on the "normalization" of relations with Cuba. Besides the support of the openly favorable countries, he apparently received an endorsement from both Bolivia (then under leftist Torres) and the open-minded democratic countries. But the strong opposition of conservative military regimes and that of the United States put an end to the move. [34]

In the spring of 1971, Nixon's overtures to China raised the possibility that Cuba would be next. The majority of the OAS members became fearful of losing their scapegoat and bait for juicy U.S. aid as Taiwan had done. The open-minded minority showed concern over an embarrassing Cuban-U.S. agreement behind their backs. Galo Plaza hurried to ask the White House and the State Department to keep him, and the OAS members, informed of any changes in policy toward Cuba and resumed his efforts to find a satisfactory compromise within the OAS framework. The Cuban Ministry of Foreign Relations quickly rejected any move to restore Cuba to OAS membership but welcomed the restoration of relations with Latin American countries on an individual basis. Toward the end of the year, Peru presented a motion at the OAS freeing its members to make individual decisions on the matter but later withdrew the motion. In May 1972, Peru reintroduced the motion which was defended at an extraordinary meeting of the OAS by Chancellor General Mercado Jorrín. [35] The final vote (thirteen against, seven in favor, and three abstentions) showed some surprises: Colombia and Costa Rica (reportedly favorable) voted no, and Argentina and Venezuela (the first reportedly against, the second in favor) abstained. [36] Castro's strong statement from Sofia, at the same time that the meeting was taking place, rejecting any "neutralization" of Cuba and endorsing the Latin American revolution (see below) could have affected the voting adversely.

The changes that occurred in Latin America in the second half of 1972 and the first half of 1973 significantly altered the OAS voting pattern in the Cuban case. In April 1973 the majority of the OAS members accepted the new doctrine of "ideological pluralism" and Galo Plaza stated that possibly the next General Assembly would lift the sanctions against Cuba. [37] At the time, there were in the OAS eleven countries solidly in favor of lifting the sanctions, six strongly against, and seven weren't clearly decided. This was a remarkable shift in one year, but still only eight votes (one-third of the membership) were needed to maintain the sanctions. On May Day 1973, Castro said that the new doctrine of "ideological pluralism" made the 1962 OAS resolution (declaring the Cuban Marxist system incompatible with the "inter-American system") null and void. And yet he did not help break the deadlock by stating that it was the OAS that was incompatible with Marxism-Leninism and by rejecting a return to the OAS unless the United States was excluded from the organization. (He also added a new condition: that the OAS headquarters be moved to a Latin American country.)[38]

In June 1973 an OAS commission rejected a Venezuelan motion substituting a simple majority of twelve votes instead of the previously required two-thirds majority of fifteen votes to lift the sanctions against Cuba and allowing each country to individually decide about diplomatic and trade relations. Two countries previously reported as not clearly decided (Colombia and Costa Rica) voted in favor of the amendment raising to thirteen the number of those favorable to rapprochement. On the other hand, the military coup in Chile dramatically turned a militant positive vote into an equally vehement negative one. In early 1974 the United States took two significant steps to ease tensions in Latin America: it reached an agreement over expropriation of U.S. property with Peru and established a basis for negotiation over the canal issue with Panama. The results of these events were clear in the Inter-American Conference of Chancellors held in Mexico City in February. Although the issue of U.S. economic sanctions had been included in the agenda and five Latin American countries had informally requested a discussion of relations with Cuba, the conference did not reach any conclusion on the subject. However, in another hemisphere foreign ministers' meeting held in Washington in April 1974, Argentina proposed (supported by Mexico, Peru, and Venezuela) that Cuba be invited to the next of such meetings to be held in Buenos Aires in March 1975. The proposal was adopted almost unanimously.[39]

In November 1974, the OAS met in Quito to discuss again the change in policy vis-à-vis Cuba, but the necessary two-thirds majority of votes was not reached. Among the countries in favor of the policy shift were the Dominican Republic, El Salvador, and Honduras; five countries abstained (Bolivia, Brazil, Guatemala, Haiti, Nicaragua, and the United States), and only three voted against (Chile, Paraguay, and Uruguay).[40] Tired of playing the OAS game, Colombia and Venezuela decided almost immediately to reestablish relations with Cuba. The change in the U.S. presidency and the increasing threat that the necessary majority would be reached by Latin American countries independently from the United States finally resulted in a compromise: on July 29, 1975, the OAS met in Costa Rica and agreed to free its members so that they could individually decide their policy toward Cuba. (The sanctions were not officially lifted because such action would have required ratification by the legislative bodies of all approving Latin American countries.) The majority was reached due to a shift of four countries that had previously abstained in Quito: Bolivia, Guatemala, Haiti, and the United States.[41] (For changes in the stand of OAS members on the Cuban issue, see table 7.)

The change in attitude of the United States vis-à-vis Cuba obviously permitted the OAS to "defuse" the Cuban issue. Although no additional countries in the hemisphere have fully reestablished relations with Cuba since the Costa Rican meeting, the United States has begun the long process of rapprochement with the island.

The Conditions for U.S.-Cuban Rapprochement

In the late 1960s, a U.S.-Cuban rapprochement was mainly the subject of intellectual discussion with a few practical overtures which did not produce the expected results.[42] In the first half of the

TABLE 7

OAS Members' Stand on the Cuban Issue: 1970–75

Stand	1970	May 1972	June 1973	Nov. 1974	July 1975
In favor of rapprochement	4	7	13	15	19
With diplomatic relations	1	2	8	11	11
Without diplomatic relations	3	5	5	4	8
Dubious	5	3	5	6	2
Against	14	13	6	3	3
Total	23	23	24	24	24

Sources: See explanation in the text.

1970s, however, an era of realpolitik began which has created better opportunities for negotiation: on the U.S. side, the understanding with China, agreements with the U.S.S.R., and the end of the war in Vietnam; on the Cuban side, the decline in the exportation of revolution to Latin America and a more compromising attitude toward divergent systems in the area. These and other events reduced the importance of or made irrelevant some of the conditions set for negotiations by both countries, but a rapprochement between them was blocked largely by personal antagonism between their chief leaders. [43]

In October 1969—with an eye on the increasing number of military and authoritarian regimes in Latin America—President Nixon pragmatically stated that, in the future, the United States would deal with these countries realistically as they are. This justified the close U.S. economic and military cooperation with Brazil and its compromising policy vis-à-vis Peru. U.S. officials have not mentioned again the incompatibility of the Cuban regime with the inter-American system as a deterrent for normalizing relations between the two countries. (The "inter-American system" was never clearly defined but loosely meant representative democracy plus market economy, a formula which is now absent in most of Latin America and has been substituted within the OAS by the new

doctrine of "ideological pluralism.") The U.S. government, however, maintained the two other preconditions established for the
restoration of relations with Cuba: (1) cutting its military ties with
the U.S.S.R., and (2) stopping its subversion in Latin America.
Throughout 1970–73, the president of the United States, the Secretary of State, and the assistant secretaries for Inter-American Affairs
reiterated (in reports to the U.S. Congress, the OAS, the Latin
American countries, and the news media) that Cuba had not
changed its position on these two points.[44] In 1971, the State
Department accepted that "Cuba's active assistance to subversive
elements was apparently at reduced levels" but pointed to her
intransigent rejection of a return to the OAS as proof that the
situation was not ripe for a revision.

This deadlock was slightly altered by events which aggravated the
existing tension: the hijacking of U.S. planes to Cuba; the capture of
or attacks on Cuban fishing vessels by groups of Cuban exiles; the
establishment, late in 1970, of a Soviet servicing facility for
submarines in the Cuban port of Cienfuegos; and the seizure, at the
end of 1971, of two vessels under Panamanian flag by the Cuban
Navy. The latter was probably the gravest incident of all: the State
Department qualified it as "an intolerable threat" to free trade and
navigation in the Caribbean; Pentagon sources indicated that air and
naval units were being placed on alert and that they would go to the
aid of any attacked ship under a foreign registry, if the corresponding government requested it; and the navy reported that warships
stationed in Guantánamo (that is, in Cuban territory) would be sent
to the Caribbean to engage in potential confrontation with Cuban
war vessels.[45]

Only in a few cases were there positive exchanges between the
two nations, the only significant one being the anti-hijacking
agreement signed in 1973. It was precipitated when in November
1972 a hijacked airplane almost caused a disaster in both the United
States and Cuba. (The hijackers threatened to crash the plane into
the Oak Ridge Atomic Center and the landing in Havana presented
serious problems because the airplane had been damaged by FBI
agents' bullets.) Discussions began immediately through the Swiss
Embassy in Havana and the agreement was simultaneously signed

in that capital city and Washington on February 15, 1973. The document granted to each nation the right to deport the hijacker of an aircraft or vessel or to try him in its own territory and according to its own law. In the latter case hijacking for "strict political reasons" may be considered as a mitigating or extenuating circumstance providing that the hijacker: (a) was in "real and imminent danger of death"; (b) did not have a "viable alternative for leaving the country"; (c) did not use financial extortion (any funds obtained through this means are to be returned without delay); and (d) did not cause physical injury to members of the crew, passengers, or other persons. These conditions, together with careful checking of passengers at U.S. airports, have considerably reduced airplane hijackings. Another important clause in the agreement stipulates penalties for those who conspire, prepare, or take part in an expedition to carry out acts of violence against the territory, aircraft, or vessles of the other party.[46] This was obviously intended to protect Cuba against attacks from exiles and may explain why the agreement has received no publicity in the United States.

In 1971–72, Castro spoke several times on his own preconditions for a rapprochement with the United States. When visiting Chile, he remarked that to reach an understanding it would not be necessary for a revolutionary or socialist government to be in office in the United States but just a realistic government ("a president of wide vision and broad understanding") aware of the U.S., Latin American, and world situation and aspirations and, hence, assuming a policy of peace. According to Castro, Nixon did not represent those trends and had been aggressive and reactionary in the past: "Nixon will never visit Havana!" Cuba would wait until the proper man is installed in the White House. Two conditions would also have to be met by the ideal government for normalization of relations with Cuba: (1) an end to the war in Vietnam, and (2) an end to the U.S. role of gendarme in Latin America, that is, its abstaining from any intervention as in the past.[47]

In a press conference in Sofia, Bulgaria, in May 1972, Castro dismissed as false a newspaper report stating that he was planning to meet Nixon in Warsaw: "We are not at all interested in such a meeting [and] would refuse [it]." He then stated that Cuba would never yield to the two U.S. conditions: "We will not give in one iota in this respect." Since Cuba had been able to overcome the most difficult tests posed by the United States, Castro argued that "it would be absolutely senseless for us to make any concessions to the U.S.A. [now]." Then he said: "Nixon is the one who's got to do something." He would have to meet, "with no strings attached," the two conditions set by Castro in Chile: (1) an end to the Vietnam war, and (2) an end to U.S. intervention in Latin America; plus two additional ones: (3) lifting the economic embargo of Cuba, and (4) getting the naval base out of Guantánamo. Castro added that Cuba would wait two, four, ten years until such conditions were met and further stated that "Kissinger and all those advisors and 'big brains' will never come to Havana or hold any kind of meeting with us."[48]

In his speech of July 26, 1972, Castro reiterated that Cuba's doors would be closed to "Nixon's cheap politicking and dirty deals." At the same time, he expressed satisfaction at seeing "the advances and new formulations in the policies of the U.S." made at the Democratic Convention and that "one of the presidential candidates [McGovern] was in favor of lifting the blockade against Cuba." However, he violently attacked another point of the Democratic platform which stated that Cuba could not become a Soviet military base. "In our territory we do as we damn please! And no [U.S.] party platform has any right to establish prerequisites of any kind with regard to Cuba." Finally he reiterated the four conditions, enumerated in Bulgaria, necessary to begin negotiating the restoration of relations with the United States.[49]

Let us now discuss the changing relevance of the conditions for negotiations set by both parties. It is clear that the socialist system of Cuba is no longer at issue and that the United States has concentrated all its emphasis on external matters. As shown in chapter 1, Cuba's military and economic links with the U.S.S.R. have increased in the last decade, especially in the 1970s; hence, the U.S. demand that Cuba close the door to its Soviet friends has induced the opposite result. Without having some guarantees from the United States first, Cuba could not cut its links with the U.S.S.R. To do so would have left Cuba vulnerable to the United States. The Soviet-Cuban military relationship presented a serious threat to the internal security of the United States in October 1962, but during the Missile Crisis the leaders of the two superpowers reached an agreement. This apparently has been honored by the U.S.S.R., which gave explanations to the United States at the time of the installation of its submarine base in Cienfuegos. (In early 1974, Dr. Kissinger apparently accepted these realities and indicated that the United States had dropped its demand that Cuba cut military ties with the U.S.S.R.[50]) The second U.S. condition was directed mainly at protecting the security of the American allies in Latin America. In many cases, however, those allies exaggerated the real threat in order to increase U.S. aid; in others, they managed (with or without U.S. aid) to capture the expeditions or defeat the guerrillas coming from Cuba. Since 1968, the island has dramatically cut its efforts to export revolution to Latin America. With its increasingly compromising attitude toward divergent systems in Latin America—as shown in this study—Cuba has proven that she can be a peaceful neighbor. (The Soviet interest in normalizing the Cuban situation in the Western Hemisphere has been an important factor in this change;[51] thus, the increasing Soviet leverage on Cuba has paradoxically helped in closing the gap to meet one of the two U.S. conditions for negotiation while widening the gap in the other.) When U.S.-Cuban relations are fully reestablished, the two U.S. security objectives will probably be achieved anyway; peaceful relations with the United States and Latin America could result in the increased independence of Cuba vis-à-vis the U.S.S.R. and in an even more conventional foreign policy of the island toward its neighbors. Two conditions, which were not initially set by the United States, have been added in the second half of the 1970s: compensation to U.S. citizens for property confiscated by Cuba, and respect for human rights on the island (more on this below).

The first condition set by the Cubans was met with the end of the war in Vietnam. (In his speeches of December 1972 and May 1973 Castro dropped this condition.) Concerning the second condition, the last open U.S. intervention in Latin America occurred more than a decade ago in the Dominican Republic; in view of the U.S. experience there and in Vietnam, it is doubtful that such an action would be repeated. There is a probability, however, of U.S. covert intervention in the region as in the case of Chile under Allende. In the hemispheric conference of foreign ministers held in Mexico in 1974, Kissinger declared that, in the future, inter-American relationships will be based on nonintervention, renunciation of the use of force and coercion, and on the "respect for the right of countries to choose their own political, economic, and social system."[52] The United States could promise to abstain from intervention provided that the Cubans do the same. The third condition set by the Cubans (raised to the first condition May 1973 by Castro, who added that it should precede any discussion and be unconditional) could be accepted without any significant disadvantages to the United States and probably with some gain. The economic embargo caused serious problems to Cuba at the time of its inception, but most of them have since been overcome. In early 1974, the U.S. government eased the embargo by allowing American subsidiaries of motor vehicles in Argentina to export cars and trucks to Cuba, and in August 1975, extended this measure to all American subsidiaries abroad and for most products. Still some difficulties remain: the increased cost of freight (Cuba's main markets moved from 90 to 6,000 miles away); the higher costs paid on U.S. spare parts bought by Cuba through intermediaries (according to the Cubans the overprice ranges from 20 to 30 percent); the difficulties with shipping (Cuba's merchant marine carries only 7 to 8 percent of the island's trade); the relatively poor assortment and low quality of goods in Eastern Europe (as compared with the United States); and the higher price the Cubans pay for their imports from the Soviet bloc.[53] But Cuba is capable of selling all that it produces (actually the problem is that it does not produce enough) and of buying practically everything that the island needs either from socialist or market-economy countries. The embargo, instead, has provided the Cubans with an excuse for their poor economic performance and a propaganda tool for despising the United States as a superpower strangling a small nation. Dropping an economically unoperative embargo would probably result in an improved political image of the United States abroad. The fourth condition is for the United States to get out of Guantánamo. This naval base, according to the opinion of military experts, does not have strategic significance today and is not really necessary to the United States. Its doubtful psychological value ("in spite of Castro we are still there") is offset by the risks of a grave incident that it constantly poses. (Castro seems to have placed a low priority on this condition; he attributed less importance to it in December 1972, although reconfirming it on May 1, 1973. Hence this condition may be negotiable.) Since mid-1974, Castro has maintained in several speeches and interviews that there is one precondition to negotiations with the United States: the unilateral, total, and unconditional lifting of the embargo. The other conditions (e.g., Guantánamo) have not been entirely dropped but now have a lower priority both in importance and in time.

Personal animosity between Castro and Nixon was often pointed out as the main obstacle to rapprochement. The former commonly deprecated the latter as a "war criminal" and a "fascist," and the Cuban press exacerbated the issue by systematically spelling Nixon's name with a swastika (instead of an x) and ridiculing the American president in political cartoons. Nixon, in turn, showed his personal dislike of Castro as early as 1959, when he was vice-president, and this feeling—reportedly—was kept afloat by his intimate friend Charles ("Bebe") Rebozo, the son of Cuban immigrants, and Nixon's Cuban-born valet. In August 1974, Nixon's resignation from the presidency removed the major obstacle to U.S.-Cuban rapprochement. President Ford soon took the initiative and, after a temporary setback, President Carter pushed further for the normalization of U.S.-Cuban relations.

The Beginning of the Dialogue

In November 1974, scarcely three months after Ford became president, secret U.S.-Cuban talks began in New York and Washington. Apparently it was Kissinger who took the initiative and Castro promptly sent two special envoys. At the talks, which lasted one year, position papers were presented by both sides and discussions held on several crucial issues: compensation for property confiscated from U.S. citizens or corporations, release of $30 million of Cuban frozen assets in the United States, trade and the embargo, freedom of political prisoners, reunion of Cuban families, mutual visitation rights, and the status of the Guantánamo naval base. As bona fide gestures toward Cuba, in the summer of 1975, the United States shifted its vote at the OAS meeting in Costa Rica—from abstention to favorable—and partially lifted the embargo by allowing U.S. subsidiaries abroad to trade with Cuba. In the meantime, Cuba became heavily involved in the Angolan civil war by sending troops and military advisors (reaching a height of twenty-two thousand personnel by the end of the year) which were supplied with Soviet weapons.[54] In addition, Cuba sponsored in the fall of 1975 a Latin American conference in support of the independence movement of Puerto Rico. In November, the Assistant Secretary of State for Inter-American Affairs, William D. Rogers, warned the Cuban envoys to the secret talks in Washington that continuation of Cuba's military intervention in Angola would put a stop to the talks. The Cubans did not answer Rogers and there were no further meetings.[55] These events and the forthcoming presidential elections, in which Ford was under attack from the right wing of the Republican party, reversed the trend. In December, President Ford declared that the Cuban actions vis-à-vis Angola and Puerto Rico "precluded any improvement in relations with Cuba . . . ended any efforts at all to have friendlier relations with Cuba."[56] Fidel Castro angrily answered Ford saying that Cuba would not comprise its principles and foreign policy in order to establish relations with the United States. To compound the situation, in 1976 a Cuban fishing vessel was attacked by Cuban exiles and several fishermen died, and on October 6, a Cubana de Aviación airplane in which Cuban exile terrorists had planted a bomb, exploded in the air, killing all its occupants. Castro accused the CIA of involvement in the airplane bombing and other sabotages perpetrated against Cuba and, in retaliation, denounced the U.S.-Cuban anti-hijacking agreement announcing that it would expire in six months.

The impasse in the dialogue was broken by the election of Jimmy Carter to the presidency.[57] Immediately after taking office in

January 1977, Carter suspended reconnaissance flights over Cuba and informed the Cuban government that withdrawal from Angola would not be a precondition for negotiations. Later, Secretary of State Cyrus Vance publicly stated that the United States was no longer holding any preconditions for negotiations with Cuba. Castro replied to the American friendly gestures saying in a CBS interview with Bill Moyers that he considered Carter a man with a sense of morals who would abide by international principles and might bring an end to sixteen years of hostility between the United States and Cuba. In February and March, however, President Carter made a series of statements setting the following old and new conditions for "full normalization of relations" with Cuba: (1) noninterference of Cuba in internal affairs of countries in the Western Hemisphere; (2) decrease of military involvement in Africa; and (3) respect for human rights and release of political prisoners. The U.S. president explained that these were conditions for "full normalization" (i.e., establishment of embassies in both countries and complete freedom of trade), not conditions for "negotiations." From the Cuban side, Castro reiterated that the U.S. should lift the embargo as a precondition for "negotiations" but not for "contacts." While the two chiefs of state were publicly performing this minuet of political rhetoric, representatives from both parties were busily negotiating two important agreements: one on maritime boundaries and fishing rights and another on exchange of "interest sections." The talks, now open, began in New York in March and continued in Havana in April; besides the two main issues listed above, the two parties discussed Cuban involvement in Africa, compensation of U.S. property, and respect for human rights. On April 29, the U.S.-Cuban fishing agreement was signed; it set a midpoint boundary in the maritime overlapping zone between U.S. and Cuban shores, allowed Cuban fishing vessels (licensed by the United States) to have access to the U.S. zone and ports, and established the bases for U.S.-Cuban cooperation in scientific research on fishing.[58] On June 3, the U.S.-Cuban agreement on interest sections was signed: each side would have a small delegation of eight to ten members, headed by a counselor, the United States in Havana under Swiss flag, and Cuba in Washington, D.C. under Czech flag.[59]

Maintaining the momentum, both countries took a series of positive steps. In the United States: (1) the State Department let the regulations prohibiting travel of U.S. citizens to Cuba expire; (2) the Treasury Department legalized the expenditure of money in Cuba by U.S. visitors; and (3) the policy of granting visas to Cuban scholars, technicians, and artists was considerably relaxed. In Cuba: (1) although the anti-hijacking agreement expired on April 15, Castro promised to continue its enforcement; (2) several U.S. prisoners held in Cuba on drug charges were released; (3) Castro promised to allow the Cuban families of some one hundred U.S. citizens to leave the island and reunite with their relatives; (4) Castro and Rodríguez told important U.S. visitors that Cuba had reduced by half its military force in Angola, that Cuba was not involved at all in Zaire's conflict with Katanga, and that Cuba would not send new combat forces abroad except in response to foreign military intervention and under very unique circumstances; and (5) Cuba extended invitations to visit the island to a basketball team from South Dakota, a group of businessmen from Minnesota, and a good number of American politicians and scholars. In April 1977, Raúl Castro stated in a conversation with U.S. reporters: "The war [between the United States and Cuba] has ended. . . . We are reconstructing the bridge, brick by brick. . . . When both sides reconstruct that bridge, we can at the end shake hands without having winners or losers."[60] Culminating these events, on September 1, 1977, the "interest sections" were opened in Washington and Havana.

What should we expect in the future? Both Castro and Carter have publicly expressed cautious views on a rapid reestablishment of full relations. Castro even said in an ABC interview with Barbara Walters that he did not expect U.S.-Cuban relations to be reestablished during Carter's present term in office, maybe in the second term or perhaps even later. Some American observers have taken these statements, and the absence of dramatic new developments, as indications of cooling off or freezing of the trend. Conversely, they could be interpreted as healthy signs that both countries understand the complexity of the process and of the long and complicated period of negotiations that lies ahead. Both parties need time to study the situation and their bargaining strategies and implications before deciding on further steps.[61] But the bases seem to have been established—through the interest sections—to continue the dialogue.

The U.S. policy of isolation of Cuba and wait-and-see, practiced in 1961–74, allowed increasing Sovietization and totalitarianism of the Cuban Revolution with the consequent curtailment of political and individual freedoms and the disappearance of the autochthonous characteristics of the Cuban process. The initial American-manifested concern over the negative domestic features of the Cuban regime (be it rhetorical or real) has been displaced by U.S. interests in external affairs. The normalization of American-Cuban relations could help to gain some independence for the island and perhaps more freedom and less economic hardships for its people. These results are by no means assured beforehand but would largely depend on the attitude and concerns of the United States. If it decides to take the initiative and does not neglect the interests of the Cuban people at the bargaining table, it may induce the slow transformation of the current centralist-dogmatic and Soviet-dependent Cuban regime into a more democratic and independent socialist system. In an era of realpolitik, this may be considered a rather naïve and romantic suggestion with which to close this chapter, but not for those who dream of a better world for tomorrow.

5

An Analysis of the Past
and a Forecast of the Future

The previous four chapters of this book have described the transformation that took place in Cuba in the 1970s and suggested some of the factors behind it. The first section of this chapter analytically illustrates the interrelation among those changes and better identifies their causes. For that purpose, a model that coherently integrates the most significant features of socialist systems is applied to Cuba at different points of its socialist history. Comparisons are also made between the Cuban and Soviet systems both in 1968 and 1973. The causes of the Cuban transformation of the 1970s and the alternatives that the country may have had are discussed here too. The second section of the chapter attempts to forecast how various features of the Cuban system will behave in the late 1970s and early 1980s. This is done by contrasting the features of the Cuban and Soviet systems in 1973 and by assuming that the current trend reducing differences between the two will continue. Finally internal and external factors that may either support or impede such an approximation are evaluated.

An Attempt at Integration and Analysis

It is my contention that the changes that have taken place in several facets of the Cuban system (i.e., the economy, the government, the society, foreign relations) are not independent from each other and have not been generated by separate and disconnected causes but that those changes are interrelated and have been induced by a set of connected forces. To discuss these hypotheses and test them, we will use a model that I previously designed to compare and interrelate the most significant socio-politico-economic features of socialist systems.[1] (See table 8.)

This model is a continuum divided into two fields by a "center" with two opposite "poles": X (positive) and Y (negative). Each of the poles represents an ideal system abstracted from reality and its features are described by sixteen pairs of opposing variables (e.g., variable 1 in pole X is concentration of government functions in a clique, while in pole Y it is separation of government functions). Pole X is mainly (but not exclusively) characterized by emphasis on ideological development (the goals of a "New Man," world revolution, and so on.), a mobilization regime, and antimarket tendencies. It is represented in reality by a few countries (e.g., China, Cuba) that at certain periods of their history have attempted to skip the socialist, transitional stage of evolution (or at least pass rapidly through it) and enter directly into a communist society. Pole Y is predominantly characterized by emphasis on material development (pragmatic goal as opposed to idealistic goal), institutionalization of politico-administrative processes, and market-oriented tendencies. It is represented in reality by countries (e.g., Yugoslavia) which have accepted the need for a transitional stage and temporarily postponed the ultimate goal of a communist society.

The comparison is static in time (mid-1968) because each of the countries selected has gone through important changes since socialism was introduced in them. Some of these countries have moved in a linear direction (e.g., Yugoslavia) while others in a cyclical manner (e.g., China). Therefore it is inappropriate to refer to "a system" in one country regardless of the time period. The Soviet system of War Communism (1918–20), for instance, is

TABLE 8

A Static Comparison of Socialist Systems in Mid-1968

Predominance of:	Pole X	China	Cuba	Center	U.S.S.R.	Czech.	Yugos.	Pole Y
1. Concentration of a clique over separation of gov't functions	2	2	2	0	-1	-2	-1	2
2. Mobilization over institutionalization	2	2	2	0	-2	-1	-1	-2
3. Military over party power	2	2	2	0	-1	-2	-2	-2
4. Rigidity over flexibility in cultural expression	2	2	0	0	1	-2	-2	-2
5. Centralized over decentralized planning	2	1	0	0	1	-1	-2	-2
6. State administrator over self-management	2	0	2	0	1	0	-2	-2
7. Loyalty over expertise in selection of managers	2	2	2	0	0	-1	-1	-2
8. Communes and state farms over collective and private farms	2	2	1	0	0	0	-2	-2
9. Utopian over realistic output targets	2	2	2	0	0	-1	-1	-2
10. Capital accumulation over consumption	2	2	2	0	1	0	-1	-2
11. Budgetary finance over self finance	2	0	2	0	0	-1	-2	-2
12. Moral over material incentives	2	2	2	0	-1	-2	-2	-2
13. Equality over stratification	2	2	2	0	-1	-1	-2	-2
14. Full employment over high labor productivity	2	2	2	0	1	-1	-2	-2
15. Isolation over integration with outside world	2	2	2	0	-1	-1	-2	-2
16. Commitment to world revolution over coexistence	2	2	2	0	0	-2	-2	-2
TOTALS	32	27	27	0	-2	-18	-27	-32

Sources: Based on Carmelo Mesa-Lago, "A Continuum Model to Compare Socialist Systems Globally," *Economic Development and Cultural Change* 21 (July 1973): 573–90.

different from Lenin's New Economic Policy (1921–28), from the Stalinist era (1929–53), and from the Economic-Reform system (1965 on). On the other hand the Chinese, Cuban, Czech, and Yugoslav systems during the early years of the first long-range plans had many features in common with the Stalinist system. The Cuban Sino-Guevarist system (1966–70) at its peak in the 1968 "Revolutionary Offensive" showed strong similarity to the Chinese system of the "Great Leap Forward" (GLF) (1958–60) and the "Great Proletarian Cultural Revolution" (GPCR) (1966–68). The year 1968 was chosen for the comparison since by the middle of that year most of the countries in the model had reached a peak in the evolution of a stage, thereafter changing the direction or velocity of the movement.

The sixteen variables selected in the model embrace the most distinctive features among systems, hence similar features for all systems (e.g., collectivization of industry) are excluded. Variables have been qualitatively evaluated (based on published information on the five countries and a ranking made by some twenty specialists) rather than quantitatively measured. The set of variables evaluate the polarization of each system in relation to pole X with a five-point scale: 2 = very strong; 1 = strong; 0 = medium; -1 = weak; and -2 = very weak. The total score of a system places it in an appropriate position in the continuum. (The five countries in the model were selected for the comparison because, in 1968, they stood up as the best representatives of the poles and the center.) The ranking of sixteen "very strong" (a total of 32 points) is only achieved in the ideal system represented by pole X which is approximated in reality by the Chinese and Cuban systems. Conversely a ranking of sixteen "very weak" (a sum of -32) is only achieved in the ideal system represented by pole Y and approximated by Yugoslavia and, to a lesser extent, by Czechoslovakia. A ranking of sixteen "medium" (a total of zero) would describe the perfect center position, with the Soviet Union close to it but leaning toward pole Y. Each set of variables in the ideal systems at the poles of the continuum has internal cohesiveness. Variables in a real system have relative cohesiveness; that is, they tend to reinforce each other and to move in the same direction.[2]

The model shows how far apart Cuba and the U.S.S.R. were in mid-1968. The former had a ranking of 27, was in the same position as China, and was rapidly approximating pole X. The U.S.S.R. had a ranking of -2 and was slowly departing from the center toward pole

Y. Cuba had fourteen variables ranked as very strong, one as strong, two as medium, and none as weak or very weak. Conversely the U.S.S.R has six variables ranked as very weak or weak, five as medium, five as strong, and none as very strong. There were 29 points between the two systems.

In table 9, the same continuum model is used but to simplify it the poles and the center have been deleted. In addition, the comparison in table 8 is static while in table 9 it is dynamic. The latter traces the evolution of the Cuban system since socialism was introduced in 1961, at the peak of four stages: 1962 for the introduction of features of the Stalinist Soviet system; 1965 for the experimentation with opposing systems (Chinese of the GLF versus Soviet of the Economic-Reform system); 1968 for the adoption of Sino-Guevarism (an adaptation by Guevara and Castro to Cuba of the Chinese system of the GLF and the GPCR); and 1973 for the movement toward the Soviet Economic-Reform system. The Cuban variables evaluated in table 9 roughly correspond with those features summarized in chapter 1, table 1, although in the latter they were ordered differently.

Table 9 clearly indicates that in 1962–65 Cuba was moving toward the center thus approximating the Soviet position. As a result of the 1961–63 attempt to apply the Stalinist system to Cuba, central planning was introduced, there was a reversion in the previous consumptionist policy (1959–60) to increase capital accumulation, the budgetary system of finance was organized in the recently collectivized state sector, and full employment was achieved. But autochthonous features of the Cuban Revolution were still salient: charismatic leadership, mobilization, predominance of the army (the ORI organized in 1961 was controlled by the Castroites in 1962), and the guerrilla mentality shown in utopian output targets, distaste for technicians, egalitarianism, and strong commitment to continental revolution. In 1964–65 Cuba moved closer to the U.S.S.R. by the partial introduction in the former of some of the economic reforms that had been tested in the latter, such as self-financing and decentralization techniques which also resulted in more realistic output targets in certain sectors of the economy. In addition, the PCC was established and there was a temporary

TABLE 9

A Dynamic Comparison of the Cuban System at the Peak of Each Stage and with the Soviet System in 1973

Predominance of:	Cuba				U.S.S.R.
	1962	1965	1968	1973	1973
1. Concentration on a clique over separation of gov't functions	2	1	2	0	-1
2. Mobilization over institutionalization	2	1	2	0	-2
3. Military over party power	2	2	2	1	-1
4. Rigidity over flexibility in cultural expression	-1	-1	0	1	1
5. Centralized over decentralized planning	1	0	0	1	1
6. State administrator over self-management	2	2	2	1	1
7. Loyalty over expertise in selection of managers	1	1	2	0	0
8. Communes and state farms over collective and private farms	1	1	1	1	0
9. Utopian over realistic output targets	1	0	2	0	0
10. Capital accumulation over consumption	1	1	2	1	1
11. Budgetary finance over self finance	2	1	2	1	0
12. Moral over material incentives	-1	-1	2	-1	-1
13. Equality over stratification	1	1	2	0	-1
14. Full employment over high labor productivity	2	1	2	1	1
15. Isolation over integration with outside world	1	2	2	-1	-2
16. Commitment to world revolution over coexistence	2	1	2	0	-1
TOTALS	19	13	27	6	-4

Sources: Based on chapter 1, table 1, and other data scattered in this book.

compromise with pro-Soviet Communist parties in selected Latin American countries to play down guerrilla warfare in them.

But in 1966 the adoption of Sino-Guevarism generated a dramatic shift in the opposite direction: Castro became the undisputed ideologist of the Revolution (after Rodríguez's dismissal and Guevara's departure), mobilization was accentuated while several institutions declined (e.g., the party, the unions, JUCEPLAN), the army expanded its influence enormously, several journals that had participated in the controversy over alternative systems were closed down (steps against deviant intellectuals were taken), planning remained centralized but became politicized in decision making (mini or sectorial plans were substituted for macro-national plans also), grandiose sugar output targets were set up, capital accumulation grew to be an obsession, self-financing was eradicated, moral incentives and egalitarianism were vigorously expanded in the pursuit of the "New Man," work quotas declined and labor productivity was completely disregarded, and the exportation of the Revolution took momentum.

The climax of the Cuban movement away from the U.S.S.R. and toward pole X occurred in the first half of 1968. Nevertheless, the death of Che Guevara a few months before had sealed the fate of the exportation of the Revolution, and Castro's endorsement of the Soviet invasion of Czechoslovakia in August put in motion the shift in Cuban foreign policy (variables 15 and 16): accommodation with the U.S.S.R. and a more moderate attitude toward Latin America in order to break the island's isolation. In spite of these external changes, the domestic policy of Cuba (represented by variables 1 through 14) remained unchanged until 1970. The economic dislocation created by the sugar harvest failure proved the unfeasibility of the development strategy and the necessary foundation for building the "New Man" collapsed. The Cuban debt with the U.S.S.R. was astronomical and to get the nation out of the abyss in which it had fallen massive aid and viable economic strategy and organization were desperately needed. The U.S.S.R. was willing to postpone the debt payments, to grant more credit and technical help, and to increase the price paid for Cuban exports on the condition that such aid would be used rationally and that Cuba would honor its export commitments. That meant that the Cuban system had to be transformed into the Soviet image. Castro accepted the deal as evidenced by Cuba's dramatic shift to the center of the continuum shown for 1973 in table 9: delegation of Castro's power and separation of government functions (rise of old members of PSP to top positions); decline in mobilization and move to institutionalization; development of the party; tightening of controls in ideology, culture and education; reintroduction of macro-, long-run technical planning; revitalization of the unions with potential to make suggestions in production issues; stress on managerial skills; setting up of rational output targets, especially in sugar; reduction of the investment rate with a parallel increase in capital efficiency; reintroduction of self-financing; return to material incentives; the justification of wage differentials; concern over labor productivity and acknowledgment of the appearance of unemployment pockets; proclamation of total unity of ideas between Cuba and the U.S.S.R. with the former becoming the unconditional defender of the latter in the Third World; breaking of Cuba's isolation by reestablishment of diplomatic and/or trade relations with a dozen Latin American countries and the halt in the exportation of revolution; setting up of conditions for negotiation with the United States and the beginning of an acceptance—even if reluctantly—of peaceful coexistence. While in 1968 Cuba was close to pole X and separated by 29 points from the U.S.S.R. in the continuum, in 1973 Cuba was close to the center and only 10 points apart from the U.S.S.R. Between 1968 and 1973 Cuba moved 21 points to the right in the continuum. (See the last two columns of table 9 which compare the Cuban and Soviet systems in 1973.)

The question could be raised if Cuba, facing defeat in both the external and internal fronts (death of Guevara in 1967 and economic dislocation in 1970), had no other alternative but to yield to Soviet pressure. In trying to answer that question a brief review of the peculiarities of Cuba is necessary.[3] It is an island lacking many vital resources, with a low degree of development, and it has traditionally been economically dependent on a foreign power. The main source of Cuban foreign exchange is still sugar (about 80 percent of its exports) and, to a lesser extent, tobacco and nickel. The country lacks basic energy sources (oil, coal, or rivers with strong currents) and has to import about 98 percent of the oil that it needs. The industrial base is very small (basically U.S. or Soviet made) and heavily dependent on imported inputs and spare parts, as well as foreign technical aid. Most manufactured products have to be imported. In spite of good physical conditions and the expansion of the agricultural infrastructure, planning errors, incorrect incentives, climatological factors (hurricanes and drought), and the excessive concentration on sugar have impeded self sufficiency in food and maintained a high proportion of imports of foodstuffs.

At the beginning of the 1960s the U.S.S.R. replaced the United States as the supplier of capital, intermediate and manufactured goods, as well as oil and foodstuffs in exchange for Cuban sugar and other raw materials. The inability of Cuba to expand its exports and the small degree of import substitution resulted in a growing deficit in the balance of payments with the U.S.S.R. Such deficits were mostly covered with Soviet credit; the Cuban foreign debt with the U.S.S.R. in 1970 had risen above $3 billion (equivalent to the Cuban average annual GNP during the 1960s). The possibility of shifting the direction of trade and external financing to the Western Hemisphere was nil in the 1960s due to the breaking of trade and diplomatic relations with all countries except Canada and Mexico. China's aid in the first half of the 1960s was small and the confrontation of this country with Cuba in 1965 resulted in a subsequent sharp decline in trade between the two. In spite of the similarities of the Cuban and Chinese systems in 1966–68 there was no significant interaction between the two countries. China was seriously handicapped at the end of that period by the internal turmoil caused by the Cultural Revolution. Western Europe and Japan did not open large lines of credit to Cuba at the time because they knew of the island's poor capacity for repayment and did not want to alienate the United States. Third World countries were either not independent, not interested, and/or not powerful enough to come to Cuba's aid; the Arab world in particular was in disarray after their calamitous defeat in the 1967 war against Israel.

The development strategy based on steady gigantic sugar crops in the 1970s could, in theory, have generated a large surplus to gradually repay the debt to the U.S.S.R., expand trade with capitalist countries, and allow Cuba to increase its independence. The feasibility of such a strategy, however, was not a subject of a serious prior analysis but largely the personal decision of Castro. He became totally and directly involved in the sugar plan, played his last card in 1970, and lost the battle. The difference between final output (8.5 million tons) and the target (10 million) was precisely the surplus that Cuba needed (after satisfying internal consumption and export commitments) to begin reducing the foreign debt. Furthermore the chances of repeating a harvest above 8 million tons in the 1970s were zero. During the second half of the 1960s the Cuban masses had been promised again and again that the sugar target would be fulfilled and that their sacrifices would be rewarded with a better life in the 1970s. Thus the failure to reach the goal was a psychological blow aggravated by the decline in production in the non-sugar sector. Discontent, skepticism, and withdrawal of the labor force were the visible results. Castro's prestige was severely damaged and his charisma—as a unifying force in the Revolution—was eroded.

The United States could have played a crucial role in that juncture by associating with Mexico, Chile, and Peru in lifting economic sanctions against Cuba, facilitating her reintegration into the Western Hemisphere, and offering an alternative to Cuba vis-à-vis the U.S.S.R. There is evidence that some consideration was given to this strategy in influential circles of the U.S. government. (For example, a sophisticated study conducted at Rand Corporation in early 1971 made a computerized analysis of several Cuban leaders ranking them according to their stand in numerous issues and their proclivity to a potential rapprochement.[4]) And yet at that time Nixon was working out the preliminary details for the detente with the U.S.S.R. and any movement to "neutralize" Cuba would have seriously hampered his strategy. For the United States, detente with the Soviet Union had a much higher priority than neutralization of Cuba. Finally the Americans could easily foresee that increased Soviet control over Cuba would retain the economic burden upon Soviet shoulders (instead of upon the United States) and reduce the exportation of the Revolution to Latin America.

The continuation of the Sino-Guevarist system was not feasible.

Economically it would have deteriorated the situation even more without any serious hope of eventual improvement. Politically it would have dangerously exacerbated the discontent among the masses, created the preconditions for a grave conflict or upsurge (such as the ones which occurred in Germany, Hungary, and Poland in the 1950s) and eventually destroyed the remnants of support behind Castro. The possibility of a compromise, making some economic changes to immediately alleviate the situation of the masses (e.g., increase in consumption, decline in voluntary labor) but retaining other features of the Cuban system, had to be ruled out because it would have required substantial economic aid from outside Eastern Europe (e.g., the United States) which was not available. It seems, therefore, that the only real alternative open to Castro was to yield to the Soviets. He would have to relinquish part of his power and Cuba its independence but he and the Revolution would continue.

A Forecast for the Remainder of the 1970s and Early 1980s

Let us start with the assumptions that, for the remainder of the 1970s, the current Soviet influence over Cuba will continue and that the Economic-Reform Soviet system will remain basically unchanged. Based on these two premises, it can be predicted that Cuba will proceed in its movement toward the center of the continuum and close the gap with the U.S.S.R. Using the knowledge accumulated in the previous four chapters and the two columns of table 9, a cautious forecast can be made of the behavior of the sixteen features of the Cuban system in the rest of the 1970s.*

There will be a continuation in the separation of government functions and the delegation of Castro's power. The prime minister will probably devote more time to foreign trips and less to domestic

---

*With very few exceptions, the predictions made in mid-1974 (in the first edition of this book) using this model materialized in 1975–77 and hence have been deleted in this section. The few predictions that proved incorrect have also been deleted. Finally, some new predictions have been added and a few of the old ones refined.

technical issues such as economic decision making. The trends of declining mobilization and increasing institutionalization will proceed. The trend toward socialist legality will continue. The PCC will expand its membership and possibly augment the proportion of workers in its ranks. The second PCC congress will be held and the party program and bylaws promulgated. The party prestige and influence will rise approximating that of the army. The latter will be basically limited to military functions. There will be an expansion in the membership of most mass organizations except the ANAP. Unions will remain active but their main role will abide as transmission belts of the administration. Rigidity in cultural expression will endure, although increasing communication with the outside world (especially Latin America and probably the United States) may generate an opposite tendency in favor of flexibility.

The strengthening of central planning with computers, more accurate statistics and technicians will gain momentum with the implementation of the first five-year plan in 1976–80. Administrators in state enterprises will retain decision-making authority although unions' and workers' suggestions in production matters receive some attention. The OPP will provide some feedback from the masses and allow them to participate in the administration of municipal and provincial services, but will be basically controlled from above. Emphasis in skills will be maintained, with a growing number of graduates in accounting, economics, and technological careers (many of them studying in the U.S.S.R.) and gradual substitution of technocrats for political cadres (or the latter raising their skills). Private agriculture will shrink even more due to deaths of private farmers, state purchases, expansion of *acopio*, merging into cooperatives, and reduction of wage earners employed in this sector.

Caution and realism in fixing output targets will be entrenched. GNP will probably grow at a modest but steady rate of from 5 to 6 percent annually or from 3 to 4 percent per capita. The modern industrial sector, nickel, fishing, and mechanized agriculture will steadily increase their output. Sugar harvests will yield from 5 to 6 million tons. If the KTP-1 harvest combines are produced on schedule (and fulfill expectations in efficiency), sugar crops will gradually rise, perhaps reaching 7 million tons. Results in the rest of agriculture will be ambiguous. The reduction in private agriculture and the lack of adequate incentives to the farmers will be negative factors in terms of output and efficiency. Investment rates will likely be set at about 20 to 22 percent of GNP. Consumption of manufactured products will increase and, if mechanization of sugar materializes and sugar prices recuperate, there should be some reduction in rationing of foodstuffs (through an increase in imports). The Economic Management System will be applied in most if not all of the economic sectors, and economic calculation, self-financing, credit, interest, profit, mercantile relations among enterprises, and the national budget will be reintroduced. The price system will be the subject of study and, perhaps, of reform to make prices better allocators.

Material incentives will keep up and tie closer to labor skills and productivity. The equilibrium between population income and consumer goods will be improved further by reducing the monetary surplus to a manageable amount. Inequality will probably increase through expansion of wage differentials, substitution of prices for rationing, and freezing (or reduction) of available free social services. Work quotas will become more technically fixed in industry thereby helping to improve labor productivity but still facing serious difficulties in non-mechanized agriculture. Production bonuses will hold on while the use of voluntary labor and overtime will decline if the labor surplus grows. Also if unemployment pockets become more frequent, there may be an attempt to introduce family planning and/or to export the labor surplus, possibly to the United States.

A majority of Latin American countries will reestablish diplomatic and/or trade relations with Cuba, among them probably Costa Rica, the Dominican Republic, and Ecuador. Exchange of visits of chiefs of state between Cuba and other Latin American and socialist countries will be frequent. Although it is not likely that Cuba will return to the OAS (unless it is dramatically reformed), the former will become integrated with several hemispheric institutions, some of them linked to the OAS. The trend toward normalization of

U.S.-Cuban relations will proceed unless Cuban involvement in Africa is increased. If the American-Soviet detente continues, such normalization will not result in the "neutralization" of Cuba but will give greater flexibility to the latter in trade, credit, oil, and spare-part supplies, and reduce its freight costs. The degree of resumption of economic relations with the United States will largely determine the degree of dependence of Cuba upon the U.S.S.R. and Comecon. The exportation of revolution to Latin America will come to a halt and peaceful coexistence will be gradually accepted by Cuba, although the latter will probably maintain military advisors and similar personnel in Africa and Asia and perhaps send troops to selected countries on these continents.[5]

Let me now discuss some external and internal factors that may affect Soviet influence over Cuba and indirectly the accuracy of the previous forecast. In order to reduce dependency on the Soviets, Cuba would have to find alternative sources for credit, oil, and military aid as well as trade partners capable of substituting for the U.S.S.R. We have already seen that this possibility is a poor one. Due to the American-Soviet detente and the Cubans' distrust of the United States, it is not likely that the latter will substitute for the U.S.S.R. significantly. And yet without promoting Cuban total independence from the U.S.S.R., the United States can help to reduce the island's current degree of dependency on the Soviets. An American-Cuban relationship, however, will tend to move Cuba toward pole Y, which is to say in the same direction in which it is being pushed by the U.S.S.R. And yet, there could be important differences in some variables, for instance, in the matter of flexibility in cultural expression. We have ruled out the possibility of China taking the place of the U.S.S.R. and hence of reversing the current movement of Cuba. The Arab countries could substitute for the Soviets in oil but not in capital equipment, military aid, and other vital supplies. Western Europe has the potential but not the interest to take up the Soviet role. Chile's military coup, reformism in Peru, and conservatism in Argentina have practically eliminated the possibility of a grouping of socialist countries in Latin America which could integrate an anti-U.S. axis and act as a bargaining agent with the U.S.S.R. In the present situation, Latin America does not have the resources and willingness to substitute for the U.S.S.R. and is busy trying to make agreements with the United States, taking advantage of the high prices of raw materials.[6]

Internally, even if the economic recuperation of Cuba continues, it will not be significant enough to reduce dependency on the Soviets to any noticeable degree. Castro no longer enjoys the capacity for maneuver that he had in the 1960s. Both the pro-Soviet group and the young generation of technocrats have a vested interest in the current process of institutionalization, professionalization, and pragmatism. These are increasingly powerful forces that, in alliance with the U.S.S.R., may stop Castro in any attempt to turn back to mobilization, radicalization, and idealism. Castro himself, being a consummate politician, has probably learned by now that the only way that he can keep his power is to hold the Revolution on its current path. Even if he is uncomfortable with his somewhat reduced role in the process, he is being induced to compromise due to the absence of a viable substitute for the Soviets. Unless something totally unexpected occurs, and this cannot be ruled out in politics, we should see Cuba moving in the direction forecast above for the rest of the decade and into the early 1980s.

Notes

Chapter 1

1. For details on the politico-economic-social aspects of the 1959–70 stages, see Carmelo Mesa-Lago, ed., *Revolutionary Change in Cuba* (Pittsburgh: The University of Pittsburgh Press, 1971).

2. On the 1963–66 debate see Bertram Silverman, *Man and Socialism in Cuba: The Great Debate* (New York: Atheneum, 1971); Robert M. Bernardo, *The Theory of Moral Incentives in Cuba* (University, Alabama: The University of Alabama Press, 1971); and my articles "Ideological, Political and Economic Factors in the Cuban Controversy on Material Versus Moral Incentives," *Journal of Interamerican Studies and World Affairs* 14 (1972): 49–111, and "Revolutionary Morality?," *Society* 9 (1972): 70–76.

3. On this new stage of the Revolution, see: Charles Vanhecke, "Cuba: de l'utopie aux réalités," *Le Monde*, March 17–20, 1971; Charles Bettelheim, "La révolution cubaine sur la voie soviétique," *Le Monde*, 12 May 1971; Jacques Valier, "Cuba 1968–1971: le développement des déformations bureaucratiques et des difficultés économiques," *Critiques et L'Economie Politique*, no. 6 (1972); "Cuba: From Dogma to Pragmatism?" *Bolsa Review* (London), April 1972; and "Cuba: The New Realism," *Latin America* (London), 19 May 1972; Edward Gonzalez, *Cuba Under Castro: The Limits of Charisma* (Boston: Houghton Mifflin Co., 1974), pp. 217–36; Andrés Suarez, "The Politics of Cuba Under Castro: How Socialist is Cuba?" (Paper delivered at the Meeting of the American Political Science Association, New Orleans, September 1973); "Cuba: La Revolución en marcha," *Latin American Perspectives* 2 (Supplement 1975); and Nelson Valdés, "Revolution and Institutionalization in Cuba," *Cuban Studies/Estudios Cubanos* 6 (1976): 1–37 and other articles published in the same volume under the title "Cuba: The Institutionalization of the Revolution."

4. See K. S. Karol, *Guerrillas in Power: The Course of the Cuban Revolution* (New York: Hill & Wang, 1970); Edward Gonzalez, "Relationship with the Soviet Union," in Mesa-Lago, ed., *Revolutionary Change in Cuba*, pp. 81–104; Charles Bettelheim, "La révolution cubaine sur la voie soviétique"; and Leon Gouré and Julian Weinkle, "Cuba's New Dependency," *Problems of Communism* 21 (1972): 68–79.

5. Radio Moscow, transmissions of 9 December 1970, and 22 February 1971. The extension of the trade agreement was not reported by the Cuban press.

6. *Granma Weekly Review*, 2 and 16 May 1971, p. 12 and 20 and 27 June, p. 1.

7. "Cuban-Soviet Commission for Economic, Scientific and Technical Collaboration Holds First Session," *Granma Weekly Review*, 12 September 1971, p. 7.

8. "Novikov and Carlos Rafael Rodríguez Sign Protocol of Collaboration between

161

Cuba and the USSR" (and in smaller print: "Prime Minister Castro Attends Signing"), *Granma Weekly Review*, 19 September 1971, p. 3.

9. Radio Moscow, transmission of 25 September 1971.

10. "Palabras en el Reparto Alamar," Instituto Cubano de Radiodifusión, transmission of 27 October 1971. See also the daily edition of *Granma*, 25–30 October 1971, p. 1 (except for 27 October edition which is pp. 1–3).

11. "Joint Soviet-Cuban Communique," *Granma Weekly Review*, 7 November 1971, p. 1.

12. *Granma Weekly Review*, 9 January 1972, p. 10.

13. See Marcel Niedergang, "La récent voyage de M. Fidel Castro a confirmé son alignement sur Moscou," *Le Monde Diplomatique*, August 1972; "Brazil, Sugar Challenge to Cuba," *Latin America* 2 (1972): 9–10; and "Inestabilidad del mercado azucarero," *Progreso* (August 1972): 35–76.

14. "Cordial Nixon-Mao Interview; Chou-Nixon Friendly Meeting; Paper Tiger Gives Syrupy Speech in Peking," *Granma Weekly Review*, 27 February 1972, pp. 1, 7, 12. See also ibid., 5 March 1972, pp. 1, 12. Chinese-Cuban relations reached a low ebb in January 1974 when the New China News Agency excluded Cuba from the Latin American countries worthy of receiving socialist support. (Argentina, Ecuador, Mexico, Peru, and Venezuela were the countries mentioned.)

15. "Sale Nixon en viaje a la URSS," *Granma*, 17 May 1972, p. 5; "Llegó Nixon a Moscú," ibid., 23 May, p. 6; "Actividades de Nixon en Moscú," ibid., 24 May, p. 5; "Llegó Nixon a Varsovia," *Granma*, 1 June, p. 6; "Terminó Nixon su visita a Polonia," ibid., 2 June, p. 7. The weekly editions of *Granma* did not publish news on the visit.

16. "Firman Cuba y la URSS protocolo de la segunda sesión de la Comisión Intergubernamental de Colaboración Económica y Científico-Técnica," *Granma*, 17 April 1972, p. 6. See also A. Voronov, "Soviet-Cuban Cooperation Enters New Stage," *International Affairs* (Moscow) (September 1972): 81.

17. Raúl Castro, "Speech at the Naval Parade on Revolutionary Navy Day," *Granma Weekly Review*, 13 August 1972, p. 5.

18. Radio Rebelde, transmission of 18 April 1972. See also *Granma Weekly Review*, 23 April 1972, p. 2.

19. F. Castro, "Speech at the May Day Parade and Workers' Rally," *Granma Weekly Review*, 7 May 1972, p. 5. Information on the trip comes from ibid., May–July editions and the Cuban radio. See also "Fidel por 10 países," *Cuba Internacional* 4 (1972): 4–71.

20. Until Cuba's entrance Comecon was composed of the seven Eastern European countries visited by Castro, plus Mongolia. Observers were Cuba, North Korea, North Vietnam, and Yugoslavia. In 1962, Albania was excluded. China neither entered Comecon nor sent observers.

21. C. R. Rodríguez, "Speech at the 26th Session of the Council for Mutual Economic Assistance," *Granma Weekly Review*, 23 July 1972, p. 10.

22. See for instance the opinion of Leon Gouré and Julian Weinkle, "Cuba's New Dependency," *Problems of Communism* 21 (1972): 77, published three months before Cuba entered Comecon.

23. See Theodore Shabad, "Cuba Becomes Full Member of Soviet Economic Bloc," *The New York Times*, 12 July 1972, p. 2.

24. Boris Gorbachov, "Cuba: Algunas cuestiones de su integración económica con los países del socialismo," *Panorama Latinoamericano* (Moscow), no. 171 (1 August 1973): 10–12.

25. Rodríguez has argued that statistical similarity could not hold in economic and political terms. See "Diálogo con Carlos Rafael Rodríguez," *Cuba Internacional* 3 (1971): 86–91.

26. See my chapter, "Economic Policies and Growth," in Mesa-Lago, ed., *Revolutionary Change in Cuba*, pp. 301–3.

27. Soviet sources are: *Vneshniaia torgovlia SSSR: statisticheskii sbornik 1918-1966* and *Vneshniaia torgovlia SSSR za 1968 god* (Moscow: Mezhdunarodnie Otnosheniia, 1967 and 1969), pp. 69 and 15; *Foreign Trade* (Moscow), no. 6 (1970): 55, and no. 5, (1971): 48. Cuban sources are Junta Central de Planificación, *BE Boletín Estadístico 1970* (Havana: JUCEPLAN, 1971), pp. 188–91. See also Eric N. Baklanoff, "International Economic Relations," in Mesa-Lago, ed., *Revolutionary Change in Cuba*, pp. 258–76.

28. The trade deficit was close to five billion pesos in 1977. See Carmelo Mesa-Lago, "Present and Future of the Cuban Economy and International Economic Relations," in Cole Blasier and Carmelo Mesa-Lago, eds., *Cuba in the World* (Pittsburgh: University of Pittsburgh Press, 1978).

29. By Gouré and Weinkle, "Cuba's New Dependency," p. 75, without giving a clear source.

30. F. Castro, "Speech at the Main Event in Commemoration of the Victory of Playa Girón," *Granma Weekly Review*, 2 May 1971, p. 6.

31. Martin Schram, "Cuba Today: The Party Seeks Economic Revival," *Newsday*, 13 September 1971; and Gouré and Weinkle, "Cuba's New Dependency," p. 78. The Soviet official figure of its technicians in Cuba is of 1,000 only. See Gorbachov, "Cuba: Algunas cuestiones," p. 3.

32. *Granma Weekly Review*, 17 February 1974, p. 11.

33. See Gonzales, "Relationship with the Soviet Union," pp. 82–86.

34. F. Castro, "Speech on the 19th Anniversary of the Attack on the Moncada Garrison," *Granma Weekly Review*, 6 August 1972, pp. 3–6.

35. "Executive Committee of Council of Ministries Established," *Granma Weekly Review*, 3 December 1972, p. 2.

36. F. Castro, "Speech at the Solemn Session in Honor of the 50th Anniversary of the USSR," *Granma Weekly Review*, 31 December 1972, p. 9. Castro also said (p. 16) that he felt at home in Moscow and that a man could have two homelands.

37. F. Castro, "Report to the People on the Economic Agreements Signed with the Soviet Union," *Granma Weekly Review*, 14 January 1973, pp. 2–3.

38. "3rd Session of the Cuban-Soviet Intergovernmental Commission for Economic, Scientific and Technical Collaboration Opened," *Granma Weekly Review*, 4 March 1973, p. 3.

39. See *Granma Weekly Review*, 25 March 1973, pp. 4–5.

40. See Janette Habel, *Proceso al sectarismo* (Buenos Aires: Jorge Alvarez Editor, 1965).

41. *Granma Weekly Review*, 15 April 1973, p. 4.

42. F. Castro, "Speech Analyzing Events in Czechoslovakia," *Granma Weekly Review*, 25 August 1968, pp. 2–3.

43. TANJUG (Yugoslav News Agency), Belgrade, 27 June 1973.

44. F. Castro, "Speech Analyzing Events in Czechoslovakia," p. 3; and "Discurso en el séptimo aniversario de la derrota del imperialismo yanqui en Playa Girón," *Granma Resumen Semanal*, 28 April 1968, p. 6. Castro and Tito had a meeting during the Conference of Nonaligned Countries in Algiers which opened a "new stage of relations" between Cuba and Yugoslavia. In February 1974, a Cuban delegation led by Raúl Castro visited Yugoslavia, hailed Tito and the League of Communists, acknowledged Yugoslav achievements in the "construction of socialism," agreed to expand cooperation between the two countries, and invited Tito to visit Cuba. See *Granma Weekly Review*, 3 March 1974, pp. 10–11 and March 10, 1974, p. 11. In February 1976, Fidel Castro visited Yugoslavia.

45. For a coverage of the trip see *Granma Weekly Review*, 15, 23, and 30 September 1973.

46. F. Castro, "Speech at the Fourth Conference of Nonaligned Nations," *Granma Weekly Review*, 16 September 1973, p. 12.

47. As quoted by George Volsky, "Cuba Fifteen Years Later," *Current History* 66 (1974): 13.

48. "Cuba: Sentimental Journey," *Latin America* (4 January 1974): 4–5.

49. As reported by TASS and transmitted by the Associated Press, 29 January 1974. For Western coverage of the visit see "Cuba: Brezhnev Visit" and "Cuba: The Russian Perspective," *Latin America* (1 and 8 February 1974): 34–36, 46–47; and "Bienvenido Brezhnev," *Time*, 11 February 1974, pp. 37–38.

50. Information on the visit discussed in this chapter comes from *Granma* and Cuban radio transmissions, 26 January through 4 February 1974. The 29 January issue of *Granma* was totally devoted to the visit.

51. Work on a two-way station satellite between Cuba and the U.S.S.R. began in December 1970 by a Soviet team of thirty engineers. Three years later Cuba was incorporated into the Intersputnik System of Communications. The first direct television transmission, from Moscow to Havana, was the military parade held on 7 November 1973, in Red Square on the 56th anniversary of the Bolshevik Revolution. On 2 January 1974, the Cuban military parade commemorating the fifteenth anniversary of the Revolution was transmitted to Moscow. The transmission of Brezhnev's visit was the third. A final stage in the project will permit direct telephone and telegraph communication between the two countries. Cuba became thus linked with the U.S.S.R. before Eastern Europe. (Czechoslovakia and the GDR would be the first to be connected in 1974–75.) "The Satellite Station in Cuba," *Granma Weekly Review*, 20 January 1974, p. 6.

52. F. Castro, "Discurso en la concentración popular en honor del compañero Brezhnev," *Granma*, 30 January 1974, pp. 2–3.

53. L. Brezhnev, "Discurso en la concentración popular," *Granma*, 30 January 1974, pp. 4–5.

54. "Declaración cubano-soviética," *Granma*, 5 February 1974. Cuban support for the Soviets' moves toward detente with the United States and international peace revised its former stand as expressed in 1968 by Castro's criticism of the socialist countries' "constant, foolish, and inexplicable campaign in favor of peace." Castro, "Speech Analyzing Events in Czechoslovakia," p. 2.

55. F. Castro, "Discurso en el X aniversario de la constitución de la FMC," *Granma Revista Semanal*, 30 August 1970, pp. 4–5.

56. F. Castro, "Speech at the Closing Session of the National Plenary Meeting of Basic Industry," *Granma Weekly Review*, 20 December 1970, pp. 2–3.

57. F. Castro, "Franco debate obrero sobre ausentismo y trabajo voluntario," *Granma*, 8 September 1970, p. 5.

58. F. Castro, "Speech at the Closing Session," p. 4.

59. F. Castro, "Speech in the Rally to Celebrate May Day," *Granma Weekly Review*, 16 May 1971, pp. 7–8.

60. F. Castro, "Speech to the Workers in Chuquicamata," *Granma Weekly Review*, 28 November 1971, p. 6; and press interview, *Granma Weekly Review*, 19 December 1971, pp. 12–13. In his interview with Barbara Walters in 1977, Castro was even more apologetic: "At times we have had public disagreements with the U.S.S.R. But . . . I think they were due to our lack of political maturity. . . . [Our Soviet comrades] were extremely patient with us at the time of our differences." "An Interview with Fidel, by Barbara Walters," *Granma Weekly Review*, 24 July 1977, pp. 4–5.

61. At the concluding session of the Cuban-Soviet Commission's first meeting, Rodríguez had stated that Cuba was "constructing socialism." Later, in the communiqué released on the occasion of Kosygin's visit, the Soviet side said that Cuba was "constructing the foundations of socialism." The importance of the Dorticós-Brezhnev statements is that they were made at Moscow, using the correct Russian terminology and, then, were reproduced in the Cuban press. See *Granma Weekly Review*, 2 January 1972, p. 12. On 28 January 1974, in an interview for Soviet television, Castro said in Havana: "In the U.S.S.R. a *new man* has been forged corresponding to a society that has built socialism and is constructing communism." (Emphasis is mine.)

62. See *Granma*, 19 November 1972, pp. 8–9. For a cautious review of the incentives controversy see interview with Carlos Rafael Rodríguez in *Economía y Desarrollo*, no. 14 (1972): 149–53.

63. See as an example, Felipe Carneado, "Social Being and Social Consciousness," *Granma Weekly Review*, 1 April 1973, p. 2.

64. F. Castro, "Speech at the Main Ceremony Marking the 20th Anniversary of the Attack on the Moncada Garrison," *Granma Weekly Review*, 5 August 1973, p. 5. Contrary to his custom of improvising his speeches, Castro read this one from a written text.

65. F. Castro, "Discurso en el Acto de Clausura del XIII Congreso de la CTC," *Juventud Rebelde* (16 November 1973): 2–11.

Chapter 2

1. For details on planning in the 1960s, see Carmelo Mesa-Lago and Luc Zephirin, "Central Planning," in Mesa-Lago, ed., *Revolutionary Change in Cuba*, pp. 145–84.

2. W. Leontief, "Notes on a Visit to Cuba," *New York Review of Books*, 21 August 1969, p. 16.

3. By the end of 1977 Cuba had published three biannual statistical yearbooks and four yearbooks. See República de Cuba, Dirección Central de Estadística, *BE Boletín Estadístico 1966, 1968, 1970* and *1971* (Havana, 1968, 1970, 1971, and 1973), and *Anuario Estadístico de Cuba 1972, 1973* and *1974* (Havana, 1974, 1975, and 1976). For details on Cuban statistical sources and accuracy see my article, "Availability and Reliability of Statistics in Socialist Cuba," *Latin American Research Review* 4 (1969): 53–91 and 47–81.

4. O. Dorticós, "Control económico y perspectivas del desarrollo de la economía cubana," *Economía y Dessarrollo*, no. 11 (May–June 1972): 10, 27–28.

5. "First Congress of the Party Resolution on Economic Management and Planning System," *Granma Weekly Review*, 11 January 1976, pp. 10–11.

6. Based on a statement by A. Kosygin quoted by *Granma Weekly Review*, 23 July 1972, p. 10.

7. "Franco debate obrero," *Granma*, 8 September 1970, p. 5.

8. See chapter 1.

9. Orlando Carnota, "La aplicación de las computadoras en el campo económico y social en un país en vías de desarrollo: Cuba," *Economía y Desarrollo*, no. 9 (1972): 84–129; "Cuba and the Computer," *Granma Weekly Review*, 2 April 1972, p. 5; Luis Gutiérrez, "El desarrollo de la computación electrónica en Cuba," *Economía y Desarrollo*, no. 12 (1972): 144–49; Osvaldo Dorticós, "Desarrollar cultural, científica y técnicamente los cuadros administrativos," *Economía y Desarrollo*, no. 20 (1973), pp. 27–57; and Ramon C. Barquín, "Cuba: The Cybernetic Era," *Cuban Studies* 5 (1975): 1–23.

10. Dorticós, "Control económico," pp. 30–31.

11. F. Castro, "Speech at Rio Verde Sheep Farm, Magallanes," *Granma Weekly Review*, 5 December 1971, p. 8.

12. F. Castro, "Discurso en la inauguración del primer edificio del Plan de Participación Masiva en las Construcciones," transmitted by Radio Havana, 26 April 1971. (Only a few excerpts of this speech were published in the newspapers.)

13. O. Dorticós, "Análisis y perspectivas del desarrollo de la economía cubana," *Economía y Desarrollo*, no. 12 (1972): 49–53 and "El combustible: factor esencial para el mantenimiento de la actividad económica," ibid., p. 80.

14. F. Castro, "Primera Plenaria Nacional de Producción y Productividad de la Industria de Materiales," transmitted by Radio Havana, 21 December 1971.

15. Orlando Carnota, "El Analista de Sistemas y el Licenciado en Control Económico: profesionales básicos en la informática de gestión," *Economía y Desarrollo*, no. 10 (1972): 121–34.

16. See interview with Carlos Rafael Rodríguez for the Chilean magazine, *Chile Hoy*, 9 August 1972, reproduced in *Economía y Desarrollo*, no. 14 (1972): 154–55.

17. O. Dorticós as quoted by *Latin America* (2 November 1973): 252.

18. "Proyecto de Resolución acerca de la capacitación cultural y técnica y la formación profesional de los trabajadores," XIII Congreso de la CTC, 11–15 November 1973.

19. R. Castro, "Speech at the Inauguration of Three Courses at the National School for Management," *Granma Weekly Review*, 14 March 1976, p. 2.

20. Ibid. and "First Congress of the Party Resolution on Economic Management and Planning System," pp. 10–11.

21. Mario Nuti, "Contra la ganancia," answered by Ricardo A. Hernández, "Contra la ganancia: un comentario," *Economía y Desarrollo*, no. 8 (1971): 3–17. See also Zoila González Maicas, "Algunas consideraciones acerca de la evaluación de inversiones," *Economía y Desarrollo*, no. 12 (1972): 150–71. See also Manuel Castro Tato, "Análisis general de las etapas fundamentales de decisión en los proyectos de inversión," ibid., no. 15 (1973), pp. 30–47; and Eduard Sheinin, "Rumbo del Partido comunista de Cuba hacia el perfeccionamiento de la gestión económica," *America Latina* (Moscow), no. 4 (1976): 41.

22. Boris Gorbachov and Olga Darusenkov, "Cuba en la nueva etapa de la construcción socialista," *Ciencias Sociales* (Moscow), no. 3 (1973): 91.

23. "Podemos aumentar la producción," *Bohemia*, May 1970, pp. 32–37.

24. For details see my book, *The Labor Sector and Socialist Distribution in Cuba* (New York: Praeger Publishers, 1968).

25. Jorge Risquet, "Comparecencia sobre problemas de fuerza de trabajo y productividad," *Granma*, 1 August 1970, p. 4.

26. O. Dorticós, "Discurso en la inauguración de la Escuela de Cuadros del Ministerio de la Industria Ligera" quoted in "Organización y normación del trabajo en 500 grandes centros industriales," *Granma*, 16 September 1970, p. 5.

27. Information from F. Castro, "Speech at the Closing Session of the National Plenary Meeting of Basic Industry," *Granma Weekly Review*, 20 December 1970, p. 5; "Speech in the Rally to Celebrate May Day," ibid., 16 May 1971, p. 6; and F. Castro, "Speech at the May Day Parade," p. 2; "Primer Encuentro Nacional de Organización y Normación," transmitted by Radio Havana, 24 January 1972; information released in the 13th Congress of the CTC, 11–15 November 1973; and *Granma*, 1 March 1976.

28. Minerva Salado, "El puerto por dentro," *Cuba Internacional* 5 (1973): 36–45.

29. See note 27.

30. R. Castro, "Palabras en la clausura del acto de constitución del Sindicato Nacional de Trabajadores Agropecuarios," *Granma*, 10 September 1973, pp. 2–3.

31. See note 27.

32. Dorticós, "Análisis y perspectivas," p. 52.

33. F. Castro, "Discurso en el acto de clausura del XIII Congreso de la CTC," *Juventud Rebelde* (16 November 1973): 7.

34. "Resolución sobre trabajo de la mujer," XIII Congreso CTC, 11–15 November 1973.

35. Dorticós, "Análisis y perspectivas," p. 38.

36. Recent visitors to Cuba have given contradicting versions on the importance of

the black market. In 1969 Gil Green (*Revolution Cuban Style* [New York: International Publishers, 1970], p. 22) could not find evidence of it but René Dumont (*Cuba: est-il socialiste?* [Paris: Editions du Seuil, 1970], p. 242) did find it in Havana. In mid-1971 Castro reported that the black market was still operating ("Speech in the Rally to Celebrate May Day," *Granma Weekly Review*, 16 May 1971, p. 6) but a U.S. journalist visiting the island at the time reported that it had virtually disappeared in food but it was still operating in clothing although declining (Joe Nicholson, Jr., "Inside Cuba: A Reporter's Notebook; After Fourteen Years of Revolution," *Harper's*, April 1973, p. 56).

37. F. Castro, "Speech at the Closing Session," p. 6.

38. Ibid.; "Speech in the Rally," p. 6; and information gathered in Cuba by Lourdes Casal, August 1973.

39. Nevertheless, families with a per capita income of $25 or less per month were exempted from house rent. *Granma Weekly Review*, 17 January 1971, p. 8.

40. *Latin America* (19 February 1971): 60; (19 May 1972): 154–56; and (8 September 1972): 283; "Incentive Program for Cubans Offers More Goods and Food," *The New York Times*, 15 May 1972, p. 12; information gathered in Cuba by Lourdes Casal, August 1973; Joanne Omang, "Cuba Has Problem: Too Much Money," *Washington Post*, 4 January 1976; and Jerry Flynt, "Cubans Admit their Economy is in Serious Trouble," *New York Times*, 25 April 1977.

41. "Theses of the 13th Congress of the CTC," *Granma Weekly Review*, 2 September 1973, p. 9; and Lázaro Peña, "Main Report to the 13th Congress of Central Organization of Cuban Trade Unions," *Granma Weekly Review*, 18 November 1973, p. 4.

42. *New York Times*, 25 November 1976.

43. According to the American journalist, James Higgins, Cuban officials told him in early 1971 that the investment ratio had increased from 31 percent in 1968 to 33 percent in 1970 but declined to 28 percent in 1971. Conversation at Harvard University, 14 May 1971. Information on 1974 from *Economía y Desarrollo*, no. 32 (November–December): 196.

44. See note 40; "Cuba: Shadows over Carnival," *Latin America* (July 23, 1971): 239; *Granma Weekly Review*, December 24, 1972, p. 3; *Anuario Estadístico de Cuba 1974*, pp. 128–29; and Comité Central del PCC, *Directivas para el desarrollo económico y social del país en el quinquenio 1976–1980* (Havana, 1976).

45. "El cambio de libretas," *Bohemia*, 31 August 1973, pp. 26–31.

46. F. Castro, "Speech at the May Day Parade," p. 3.

47. F. Castro, "Discurso en el acto de clausura," p. 6.

48. Ibid.

49. F. Castro, "Speech in the Rally," p. 7.

50. F. Castro, "Discurso en el acto de clausura," pp. 2, 7, 9.

51. "Theses of the 13th Congress," pp. 8–9. (Subsequent references to the congress proceed from this source unless a specific source is provided.) See also *Granma*, 1 March 1976.

52. "Proyecto de Resolución sobre Organización del Trabajo y Salarios," XIII Congreso CTC, 11–15 November 1973; and Peña, "Main Report," p. 4.

53. Peña, "Main Report," p. 4.

54. "Proyecto de Resolución sobre la Emulación Socialista," XIII Congreso CTC, 11–15 November 1973.

55. See Nicholson, "Inside Cuba," p. 56; and "Proyecto de Resolución sobre la Distribución de Artículos Electro-domésticos," XIII Congreso CTC, 11–15 November 1973.

56. F. Castro, "Speech at the Closing Session," p. 3; "Prime Minister Meets with Representatives from 487 Havana Work Centers," *Granma Weekly Review*, 25 April 1971, pp. 2–3; "Speech at the Rally to Celebrate the 11th Anniversary of the Committees for the Defense of the Revolution," *Granma Weekly Review*, 10 October 1971, p. 3.

57. "Speech at the Rally," p. 3; Radio Havana, several transmissions in late 1971 and early 1972; F. Castro, "Speech in the Rally," p. 4, "Speech at the May Day Parade," p. 2, and "Speech at the International Workers' Day Parade," *Granma Weekly Review*, 13 May 1973, p. 2; *Granma Weekly Review*, 19 August 1973; and "La construcción veinte años despues," *Bohemia*, 31 August 1973, p. 23.

58. "First Congress of the Party Resolution on Economic Management and Planning," pp. 10–11.

59. Information on sugar in this section comes from Mesa-Lago, ed., *Revolutionary Change in Cuba*, pp. 301–11, several issues of *Granma Weekly Review*, and transmissions from Radio Havana.

60. F. Castro, "Speech in the Graduation of 2,095 Students of the University of Havana," *Granma Weekly Review*, 17 December 1972, p. 9.

61. For a detailed study of voluntary labor in the 1960s see my article, "Economic Significance of Unpaid Labor in Socialist Cuba," *Industrial and Labor Relations Review* 22 (1969): 339–54.

62. "Theses of the 13th Congress," pp. 8–9; and "Proyecto de Resolución sobre Trabajo Voluntario," XIII Congreso CTC, 11–15 November 1973.

63. F. Castro, "Speech at the Closing Session," pp. 3–5.

64. *Granma Weekly Review*, 10 December 1972, p. 9 and 14 January 1973, pp. 2–3; José Vásquez, "Cinco preguntas sobre la zafra," *Cuba Internacional* 5 (1973): 16–17; Marcelo Fernández Font, "The United Nations Conference on Sugar 1973," *Granma Weekly Review*, 24 June 1973, p. 10; "Cuba: Cane Mechanization," *Direct from Cuba*, no. 173, 5 July 1977, pp. 5–6; and "The KTP-1 Cane Harvester Plant in Holguín," *Granma Weekly Review*, 24 July 1977, p. 10.

65. Centro de Investigaciones de la Caña, "Efecto de la quema de los campos en la producción de azúcar," *Economía y Desarrollo*, no. 10 (1972): 92–118.

66. Centro de Investigaciones de la Caña, Centro de Información Científica y Técnica, Universidad de La Habana, *Sistema australiano de corte, zafra 1971* serie 8, no. 8 (Havana: Investigaciones Agrícolas Agroindustriales, December 1971) and "Introducción en Cuba del sistema australiano de corte," *Economía y Desarrollo*, no. 15 (1973): 48–71.

67. F. Castro, "Speech at the Rally to Celebrate the 18th Anniversary of the Attack on Moncada," *Granma Weekly Review*, 1 August 1971, p. 4; idem, "Speech at the May Day Parade," p. 3.

68. O. Dorticós, Radio Havana transmission of 1 July 1972. Two months later the president confirmed his previous statement and said that targets for 1973–75 had been "more or less quantitatively defined" and that work had begun on the 1976–80 targets; but he did not release any data on those targets. "Closing Speech at the 40th Conference of Sugarcane Technicians," *Granma Weekly Review*, 10 September 1972, p. 2.

69. *Granma Weekly Review*, 20 May 1973, p. 11.

70. Antonio Núñez Jiménez. "Ceremony Honoring the 10th Anniversary of the Academy of Sciences of Cuba," *Granma Weekly Review*, 5 March 1972, pp. 4–5.

71. F. Castro, "Main Report Presented to the 1st Congress of the Communist Party of Cuba," *Granma Weekly Review*, 4 January 1976, p. 2.

72. Ibid.

73. See Mesa-Lago, ed., *Revolutionary Change in Cuba*, p. 331.

74. For a comprehensive analysis of Cuba's economic performance in 1971–77 see Carmelo Mesa-Lago, "Present and Future of Cuba's Economy and International Economic Relations," in Cole Blasier and Carmelo Mesa-Lago, eds., *Cuba in the World* (Pittsburgh: University of Pittsburgh Press, 1978).

75. Ibid.

76. F. Castro, "Speech at the Closing Session of the 4th Congress of the ANAP," *Granma Weekly Review*, 9 January 1972.

77. F. Castro, "Speech at the Main Ceremony Commemorating the 20th Anniversary of the Attack of the Moncada Garrison," *Granma Weekly Review*, 5 August 1973, p. 5.

Chapter 3

1. For a picture of the Cuban situation in these years, see my essay "Ideological Radicalization and Economic Policy in Cuba," in Irving Louis Horowitz, ed., *Cuban Communism* (New Brunswick, N.J.: Transaction Books, 1972), pp. 93–122.

2. L. Huberman and P. Sweezy, *Socialism in Cuba* (New York: Monthly Review Press, 1969), pp. 201–18.

3. The controversy was published in *Monthly Review* in 1968–69 and compiled as *On the Transition to Socialism* (New York: Monthly Review Press, 1971).

4. M. Zeitlin, "Inside Cuba: Workers and Revolution," *Ramparts*, March 1970, pp. 20, 70–78.

5. R. Dumont, *Cuba: est-il socialiste?* (Paris: Editions du Seuil, 1970), pp. 134–223.

6. K. S. Karol, *Guerrillas in Power: The Course of the Cuban Revolution* (New York: Hill & Wang, 1970), pp. 329–30, 410, 457–58.

7. F. Castro, "Comparecencia . . . sobre la zafra azucarera de 1970," *Granma Resumen Semanal*, 31 May 1970, p. 12.

8. F. Castro, "Discurso en conmemoración del XVII aniversario del asalto al Cuartel Moncada," *Granma Resumen Semanal*, 2 August 1970, pp. 2–6.

9. J. Risquet, "Comparecencia sobre problemas de fuerza de trabajo y productividad," *Granma*, 1 August 1970, pp. 5–6.

10. F. Castro, "Discurso en el X aniversario de la constitución de la FMC," *Granma Resumen Semanal*, 30 August 1970, pp. 4–5.

11. F. Castro, "Discurso en la plenaria provincial de la CTC," *Granma Resumen Semanal*, 20 September 1970, pp. 4–5.

12. F. Castro, "Discurso en la concentración para celebrar el décimo aniversario de los CDR," *Granma Resumen Semanal*, 4 October 1970, pp. 4–5.

13. F. Castro, "Speech at the Closing Session of the National Plenary Meeting of Basic Industry," *Granma Weekly Review*, 20 December 1970, pp. 2–3.

14. See, for a detailed discussion of this subject, Andrés Suárez, *Cuba: Castroism and Communism, 1959–1966* (Cambridge, Mass.: MIT Press, 1967) and "Leadership, Ideology and Political Party," in Mesa-Lago, ed., *Revolutionary Change in Cuba*, pp. 3–21.

15. "Executive Committee of Council of Ministries Established," *Granma Weekly Review*, 3 December 1972, p. 3.

16. B. Roca, "Nuevo sistema judicial," *Cuba Internacional* 3 (1971): 72–75.

17. José Gabriel Gumá, "Unification of the Judicial System," *Granma Weekly Review*, 5 September 1971, p. 8. See also Osvaldo Dorticós, "Speech at the Inauguration of the Council of Government of the People's Supreme Court," *Granma Weekly Review*, 15 July 1973, pp. 4–5.

18. *Prensa Latina* (Havana), 1 July 1971.

19. Gumá, "Unification of the Judicial System," p. 8.

20. Author's estimates based on list published as "Comité Central del Partido," *Verde Olivo* 6 (10 October 1965).

21. Raúl Castro, "At the 15th Anniversary of the Triumph of the Revolution," *Granma Weekly Review*, 13 January 1974, p. 3.

22. *Partiynaya Zhizn* (Moscow), 10 April 1973, quoted by George Volsky, "Cuba Fifteen Years Later," *Current History* 66 (1974): 11.

23. Ibid.; O. Dorticós, *Primer Activo Nacional de Educación Interna del Partido* (Havana: Ediciones COR, no. 16, 1971); and F. Castro, "Main Report Presented to the 1st Congress of the Communist Party of Cuba," *Granma Weekly Review*, 4 January 1976, p. 2.

24. Information gathered in Cuba by Lourdes Casal, August 1973.

25. Materials used in these courses were published in numerous issues of *Granma* throughout 1973.

26. Suárez, "Leadership, Ideology and Political Party," pp. 10, 18; F. Castro, "Discurso en el acto de clausura del XIII Congreso de la CTC" *Juventud Rebelde* (16 November 1973): 10.

27. Secundino Guerra Hidalgo, "The Congress: The Party's and the Nation's Most Important and Decisive Meeting" and "The Party Program: Analysis and Objectives for Changing an Objective Reality," *Granma Weekly Review*, 23 December 1973, pp. 8–9.

28. Edward Gonzalez, "The Party Congress and Poder Popular: Orthodoxy, Democratization and Leader's Dominance," *Cuban Studies/Estudios Cubanos* 6 (1976): 1–14.

29. Ibid.; *First Congress of the Communist Party of Cuba, Havana, December*

17–22, 1975: Collection of Documents (Moscow: Progress Publishers, 1976); and "The First Party Congress: Institutionalization of the Revolution," *Center for Cuban Studies Newsletter* 3 (1976). The list of membership in the three PCC bodies was published in *Granma Weekly Review*, 4 January 1976, p. 12.

30. Leonel-Antonio de la Cuesta, "The Cuban Constitution: Its Originality and Role in Institutionalization," *Cuban Studies/Estudios Cubanos* 6 (1976): 15–30. The full text of the constitution was published in a special supplement of *Granma Weekly Review*, 7 March 1976.

31. Gonzales, "The Party Congress," p. 6.

32. De la Cuesta, "The Cuban Constitution," p. 29.

33. R. Castro, "At the 15th Anniversary," pp. 2–3.

34. Law 1,269 of 9 May 1974, *Granma Weekly Review*, 19 May 1974, p. 1. See also N. Kishin, E. Smirnov and A. Bezvenezhnig, "URSS: Los Organos de Poder del Pueblo; estructura y función de los Soviets," *Bohemia*, 11 January 1974, pp. 30–35; and Blas Roca, "Matanzas: Organos de Poder Popular," ibid., 3 May 1974.

35. The functions of the OPP are specified in the Constitution and in "First Congress of the Party Resolution on the Organs of People's Power," *Granma Weekly Review*, 11 January 1976, pp. 8–9. The law regulating the OPP national elections was published in ibid., 25 July 1976, p. 1; the election results in ibid., 24 October 1976, p. 11; and the list of deputies to the National Assembly in ibid., 14 November 1976, p. 7.

36. "Law on the Organization of Central State Administration," *Granma Weekly Review*, 19 December 1976, p. 12.

37. Ibid. The list of members of the Council of State and the Council of Ministries was published in ibid., 12 December 1976, p. 5.

38. For detailed studies of Cuba's armed forces in the 1960s and 1970s, see Jorge I. Domínguez, "The Civic Soldier in Cuba," in Catherine Kelleher, ed., *Political-Military Systems: A Comparative Analysis* (Beverly Hills: Sage Publications, 1974) and "Institutionalization and Civic-Military Relations in Cuba," *Cuban Studies/Estudios Cubanos* 6 (1976): 39–65.

39. "Cuba: Discipline and Incentives," *Latin America* (21 September 1973): 302–3.

40. "Militia Day," *Granma Weekly Review*, 22 April 1973, pp. 1–2, 6–7.

41. Law 1,257 of 1 December 1973. See "Law of Council of Ministers on New System of Rank in Revolutionary Armed Forces," *Granma Weekly Review*, 16 December 1973, p. 2.

42. See F. Castro comments on the law, ibid., p. 3.

43. "Law on the System of Military Rank in the Revolutionary Armed Forces of the Republic of Cuba," *Granma Weekly Review*, 5 December 1976, p. 12.

44. F. Castro, "Speech at the Solemn Session to Set Up the National Assembly of People's Power," ibid., 12 December 1976, p. 3.

45. Ibid., pp. 2–3.

46. Ibid. and F. Castro, "Speech at the Closing Session of the First Congress of the Communist Party of Cuba," ibid., 11 January 1976, p. 3.

47. Lionel Martín, "Reestructuración sindical en Cuba," *Cuba Internacional* (April 1971): 28–30.

48. J. Risquet, "Comparecencia sobre problemas de fuerza de trabajo," pp. 5–6.

49. Ibid.

50. F. Castro, "Discurso en la concentración," pp. 4–5.

51. "Acuerdos del Comité Nacional de la CTC" and "Orientaciones para el proceso eleccionario," *Granma*, 30 October 1970, p. 2.

52. Radio Rebelde, transmissions of 2 and 3 December 1970.

53. J. Risquet, "Palabras en la Plenaria Provincial de la CTC," *Granma*, 9 September 1970, pp. 4–5.

54. F. Castro, "Discurso en la concentración," pp. 4–5.

55. *Granma*, 30 October 1972, p. 2.

56. J. Risquet, "Speech at the Closing Session of the 6th National Council of the Central Organization of Trade Unions," *Granma Weekly Review*, 24 October 1971, p. 4.

57. See F. Castro's explanation at the establishment of the National Trade Union of Basic Industry, "Speech at the Closing Session," p. 2.

58. Information from Radio Havana, *Granma* and Castro's speeches especially "Speech at the International Workers' Day Parade," *Granma Weekly Review*, 13 May 1973, p. 5.

59. R. Castro, "Speech at the Closing of the National Conference of Civilian Workers of the FAR," *Granma Weekly Review*, 26 September 1972, p. 5.

60. Martín, "Reestructuración sindical en Cuba," p. 30; and "Cuba: Trade Unions," *Latin America* (28 July 1972): 234, 236.

61. J. Risquet, "Palabras en la Plenaria," pp. 4–5.

62. J. Risquet, "Speech at the Closing Session of the 6th," p. 4.

63. F. Castro, "Speech in the Rally to Celebrate May Day," *Granma Weekly Review*, 16 May 1971, p. 2; "Speech at the Rally to Celebrate the 18th Anniversary of the Attack on the Moncada," *Granma Weekly Review*, 1 August 1971, p. 1.

64. "Theses of the 13th Congress of the CTC," *Granma Weekly Review*, 2 September 1973, pp. 11–12. Following quotations from and references to the "theses" come from this source.

65. Lázaro Peña, "Main Report to 13th Congress of Central Organization of Cuban Trade Unions," *Granma Weekly Review*, 18 November 1973, p. 4.

66. "Over 1½ Million Workers Participate in Discussion of 9 Theses of 13th Workers' Congress," *Granma Weekly Review*, 4 November 1973, pp. 4–5.

67. "Estatutos de la Central de Trabajadores de Cuba y Declaración de Principios o Fundamentos," XIII Congreso CTC, Havana, 11–15 November 1973, pp. 1–10.

68. Peña, "Main Report to 13th Congress," p. 5.

69. Castro, "Discurso en el acto de clausura del XIII," p. 8.

70. "Law on the Organization of Central State Administration," p. 9.

71. J. Risquet, "Speech at the Closing Session of the 6th," p. 4.

72. "Proyecto de Resolución sobre las Asambleas Regulares de Producción y Servicios," XIII Congreso CTC, Havana, 11–15 November 1973.

73. Roberto Veiga, "Informe Central del XXXIV Consejo Nacional de la CTC," *Granma*, 6 February 1975, pp. 3–6.

74. "First Congress of the Party Resolution on Economic Management and Planning System," *Granma Weekly Review*, 11 January 1976, pp. 10–11.

75. "Law on the Organization of Central State Administration," p. 9. It should be recalled that in 1960–62 "technical advisory councils" were temporarily set up in state enterprises but these were made up of delegates from the workers chosen by them. See Cuban Economic Research Project, *Labor Conditions in Communist Cuba* (Coral Gables: University of Miami Press, 1963), p. 8. In addition to the councils discussed in the text, there have been "labor councils" operating in Cuba for more than a decade. These do not perform managerial functions, however, but act in a conciliatory capacity. They attempt to solve labor conflicts at the enterprise level, and their decisions may be appealed to the courts. A law modifying the "labor councils" is now under study by the National Assembly. See "Texto del Dictamen de la Comisión de Trabajo, Seguridad Social, Prevención y Asistencia Social sobre el Proyecto de Ley de Organización y Funcionamiento de los Consejos de Trabajo," *Granma*, 15 July 1977, p. 2.

76. J. Risquet, "Palabras en la Plenaria," pp. 4–5 and "En la clausura . . . ," *Granma Revista Semanal*, 17 August 1969, p. 2. See also "Franco debate obrero," *Granma*, 8 September 1970, p. 5.

77. Quotation and information come from J. Risquet, "Speech at the Closing Session of the 6th," p. 4.

78. "A Battle Already under Way," *Granma Weekly Review*, 5 December 1971, p. 1.

79. Law No. 1,225 of 29 August 1969; "Proyecto de evaluación laboral," *Granma*, 8 July 1970, p. 1; "Proyecto sobre méritos y deméritos laborales," ibid., 12 September 1970, p. 3; and Resolution No. 425, 15 October 1970, ibid., 16 October 1970, p. 1.

80. The draft of the law was published in all newspapers in early January 1971 ("Draft Law against Loafing," *Granma Weekly Review*, 17 January 1971, p. 7). The draft was to be discussed in meetings by hundreds of thousands of workers, which would "enrich it with numerous, astute observations" ("A Legislative Forum of the Working Class," ibid., 30 January 1971, p. 3). But when the final law was enacted in March there were practically no changes made in the draft (Law No. 1,231, of 16 March 1971, ibid., 28 March 1971, p. 2).

81. "Statement by the CTC . . . ," *Granma Weekly Review*, 28 March 1971, p. 2; and J. Risquet, "Speech at the Closing Session of the 6th," pp. 4–5.

82. Jesús Montané, "Speech at the National Plenary Meeting of Labor Justice," *Granma Weekly Review*, 23 January 1972, pp. 10–11.

83. "Theses of the 13th Congress," p. 9; and "Proyecto de Resolución sobre la Emulación Socialista," XIII Congreso CTC, Havana, 11–15 November 1973, pp. 3–4.

84. Marifeli Pérez-Stable, "Institutionalization and Workers' Response," *Cuban Studies* 6 (1976): 31–54.

85. For a detailed discussion of the status of small farmers and rural workers under the Revolution see Mesa-Lago, ed., *Revolutionary Change in Cuba*, chapters 11 and 12.

86. Data on the reduction of the private agricultural sector come from José Acosta, "La revolución agraria en Cuba y el desarrollo económico," *Economía y Desarrollo*, no. 17 (1973): 155–59.

87. Radio Havana, transmission of 4 March 1971.

88. "Cuba: Trade Unions," pp. 234, 236.

89. F. Castro, "Speech at the Closing Session of the 4th Congress of ANAP," *Granma Weekly Review*, 9 January 1972, pp. 2–4.

90. Radio Havana, transmission of 13 January 1972.

91. Acosta, "La revolución agraria," pp. 158–59.

92. Castro, "Speech at the Closing Session of the 4th," pp. 2–4.

93. F. Castro, "Main Report Presented to the 1st Congress of the Communist Party of Cuba," p. 6.

94. F. Castro, "Speech at the Closing of the 5th Congress of ANAP," *Granma Weekly Review*, 29 May 1977, p. 3.

95. *Direct from Cuba*, no. 169, 15 May 1977.

96. F. Castro, "Speech at the Closing of the 5th Congress of ANAP," pp. 2–4.

97. Ibid.

98. Jaime Crombet, "Summary of the Report of the National Committee of the Young Communist League," *Granma Weekly Review*, 9 April 1972, pp. 2–3.

99. Ibid.; and Radio Havana, transmission of 1 March 1972.

100. *Granma Weekly Review*, 21 November 1971, p. 8.

101. F. Castro, "Speech at the Final Session of the 2nd Congress of the Young Communist League," ibid., 16 April 1972, pp. 2–4.

102. Ibid.

103. F. Castro, "Speech at the Final Session of the 2nd," pp. 2–4; and Belarmino Castilla, "Speech at the Opening of the National Congress on Education and Culture," *Granma Weekly Review*, 9 May 1971, pp. 4–5.

104. "Declaration by the First National Congress of Education and Culture," *Granma Weekly Review*, 9 May 1971, pp. 4–5.

105. "El Fórum logró acercarnos aún más a nuestro pueblo," *Granma Revista Semanal*, 11 May 1969, pp. 7–10; and F. Castro, "Speech at the Tenth Anniversary of the Creation of the Ministry of Interior," *Granma Weekly Review*, 13 June 1971, pp. 4, 6.

106. Martin Schram, "Cuba Today: Universities 'Open to All,' But . . . ," *Newsday*, 10 September 1971. Mr. Schram visited the university and spoke with students and professors about the incident.

107. "Final Declaration of the 2nd Congress of the Young Communist League," *Granma Weekly Review*, 23 April 1972, pp. 7–8.

108. F. Castro, "Speech at the Final Session of the 2nd," pp. 5–7.

109. Raúl Castro, "Important Battles are Being Waged in the Field of Production," *Granma Weekly Review*, 12 August 1973, pp. 2–3.

110. "Declaration by the First National Congress of Education and Culture," pp. 4–5.

111. F. Castro, "Speech at the Tenth Anniversary," pp. 4, 6.

112. *Granma*, 26 May 1973.

113. Jesús Montané, "Speech at the Second Party Assembly at the University of Havana," *Granma Weekly Review*, 11 July 1971, p. 4.

114. Joe Nicholson, Jr., "Inside Cuba: A Reporter's Notebook; After Fourteen Years of Revolution," *Harper's*, April 1973, p. 57.

115. Raúl Castro, "Speech at the Ceremony Marking the Anniversary of the Founding of the UJC," *Granma Weekly Review*, 14 April 1974, pp. 2–3; and F. Castro, "Speech at the Main Rally in Celebration of Construction Workers Day," ibid., 15 December 1974, p. 2.

116. Raúl Castro, "Speech at the Closing of the 3rd Congress of UJC," ibid., 17 April 1977, p. 6.

117. Antonio Pérez Herrero, "Speech at the 3rd Congress of the UJC," ibid., 17 April 1977, p.5.

118. For details on the events of 1959–70 see the chapters by Lourdes Casal on literature and Julio Matas on cinema and theater in Mesa-Lago, ed., *Revolutionary Change in Cuba*.

119. F. Castro, "Speech at the Closing Session," p. 4.

120. "The Olivé Case," *Granma Weekly Review*, 21 February 1971, p. 7.

121. *Le Monde*, 9 April 1971, p. 32.

122. F. Castro, "Speech at the Main Event in Commemoration of the Victory of Playa Girón," *Granma Weekly Review*, 2 May 1971, p. 5.

123. F. Castro, "Speech in the Inauguration of a Junior High School in Jagüey," ibid., 2 May 1971, p. 9.

124. Padilla's statement of self-criticism was released by the Cuban press agency *Prensa Latina* in Paris. Excerpts were published in *Le Monde*, 29 April 1971, and *The New York Times*, 26 May 1971. The complete text in Spanish was published by *Casa de las Américas* 11 (1971): 191–203.

125. "Declaration by the First National Congress of Education and Culture," pp. 5–6.

126. F. Castro, "Speech at the Closing of the First National Congress of Education and Culture," *Granma Weekly Review*, 9 May 1971, pp. 7–9.

127. *Le Monde*, 20 May 1971, and *The New York Times*, 22 May 1971. These and other documents are in a compilation by Lourdes Casal, *El caso Padilla: Literatura y Revolución en Cuba* (New York: Ediciones Nueva Atlántida, 1972). For a good analysis see José Yglesias, "A Cuban Poet in Trouble: The Case of Heberto Padilla," *New York Review of Books*, 3 June 1971, pp. 3–8. See also the compilation and debate in *Libre* (Paris) 1 (1971) and (1971–72).

128. F. Castro, "Speech at the Tenth Anniversary," p. 3.

129. Personal information made available to the author in June–December 1971. Among those rejected were two well-known political scientists and one economist. On the other hand, American experts on education and public health entered Cuba with relative facility.

130. Schram, "Cuba Today: Universities 'Open to All', But . . . .".

131. "U.S. Writer Describes Months in Cuban Prison," *Los Angeles Times*, 13 June 1972, p. 4; and Frank McDonald, "Report from a Cuban Prison," Institute of Current World Affairs, several issues from September 1972 to August 1973 (see especially the latter, no. 18, pp. 6–7).

132. Augusto E. Benítez, "Marginality: A Case of Sociological Espionage," *Granma Weekly Review*, 4 March 1973, p. 10.

133. See Virgilio Perera and Leonardo Acosta, "La campaña anti Martí," *El*

Caimán Barbudo, no. 65 (1973): 19–24, and no. 66 (1973):12–15. In July 1974, however, the Cuban government invited a top Ford official to visit Cuba.

134. "All Cuban Stations Ban U.S. Music," *The New York Times,* 22 April 1973.

135. *Granma Weekly Review,* 30 January 1977, p. 5.

136. Armando Hart, "Abridged Transcript of the Address at a Meeting Held with the Literature Section of UNEAC," ibid., 24 April 1977, pp. 4–6. The press release did not record the writers' positions but only Hart's reply.

137. Ibid.

Chapter 4

1. See Ernesto F. Betancourt, "Exporting the Revolution to Latin America," and Irving Louis Horowitz, "The Political Sociology of Cuban Communism," in Mesa-Lago, ed., *Revolutionary Change in Cuba,* pp. 105–41.

2. F. Castro, "Speech in the Ceremony to Commemorate the Centennial of the Birth of V. I. Lenin," *Granma Weekly Review,* 3 May 1970, pp. 2–5.

3. F. Castro, "Speech at the Close of the Main Rally Marking the Beginning of the Ten-million-ton Sugar Harvest," ibid., July 20, 1969, p. 5.

4. F. Castro, "Discurso en conmemoración del Centenario del Natalicio de Lenín," *Granma,* 23 April 1970, pp. 2–4.

5. *Granma Weekly Review,* 26 December 1971, and 2 January 1972. In March 1973, Cuba freed one of the two remaining Cuban-born prisoners as a friendly gesture toward Panama.

6. Ibid., 25 March 1973, pp. 8–11.

7. CORFO, *Chile Economic News* (27 February 1971): 3.

8. *Granma Weekly Review,* 1 April 1973, p. 8.

9. *Comercio Exterior* (Mexico), March 1972; *Latin America* (16 March 1973): 83; and *Granma Weekly Review,* 13 June 1973, p. 3.

10. "Caribbean: Cuba Back in the Fold?" *Latin America* (20 October 1972): 229; *Granma Weekly Review,* 24 December 1972, p. 13, and 16 September 1973, p. 1.

11. *Granma Weekly Review,* 20 May and 3 June 1973, p. 1, and 10 March 1974, p. 2; *Latin America* (31 August 1973): 280, (7 December 1973): 387, (1 March 1974): 66; *Time,* 11 February 1974, 38; and *The New York Times,* 19 April 1974, p. 1.

12. *Granma Weekly Review,* 7 January 1973, p. 8.

13. Cuban exiles reacted negatively to Figueres's suggestions with a few remarkable exceptions, e.g., Castro's former minister of finance, Rufo López Fresquet.

14. *Latin America* (7 September 1973): 28.

15. Marvine Howe, "Venezuela Opens Cuban Contacts," *The New York Times,* 22 April 1973, p. 17.

16. *Time,* 16 April 1973, p. 38.

17. F. Castro, "Speech at the International Workers' Day Parade," *Granma Weekly Review,* 13 May 1973, p. 3.

18. Ibid., 15 July, 16 September, and 21 October 1973.

19. Cuban relations have not only improved with Latin America but with other nonsocialist countries as well. Trade with Japan, France, Italy, Canada, Great Britain, Spain, and Sweden increased notably in 1970–73, reaching the half-billion peso mark. Cuba imported equipment (for transportation, agriculture, industry, and construction) and received technical assistance and credits from these countries in exchange for sugar, nickel, tobacco, and rum. See *Svea Örnstedt SIDA* (Stockholm), 15 July 1971; "Cuba," *Barclay's Economic Intelligence Department* (London), 17 December 1971; "Cuba: From Dogma to Pragmatism," *Bolsa Review* (London), April 1972; and "Cuba's Links with Nonsocialist World Expanding," *Business Latinamerica*, 20 April 1972. At the end of 1971, Castro stated that Cuba was in the process of overcoming the economic embargo and that the island had a growing foreign market and could sell all that it was capable of producing. *Granma Weekly Review*, 21 November 1971, p. 8, and 28 November 1971, p. 4.

20. "Press Conference with Newsmen from Different Countries," *Granma Weekly Review*, 19 December 1971, pp. 8–9.

21. Ibid., p. 15. Castro also justified (ibid., pp. 13–14) his increasingly good relations with Franco's Spain (with which Cuba signed, at the end of 1971, a new four-year trade and payments' agreement including a most-favored-nation clause) on the basis of Spanish resistance to U.S. pressure to isolate Cuba in the 1960s. For a detailed account of Castro's 1971 trip to Chile and stops to Lima and Quito, see George W. Grayson, "The Significance of Castro's Trip to South America," *World Affairs* 135 (1972): 220–39.

22. Hugo Blanco, *Land or Death: The Peasant Struggle in Peru* (New York: Pathfinder Press, 1972), pp. 63, 74. See also "Hugo Blanco Leaves Mexico," *Intercontinental Press*, 10 July 1972.

23. Heinz Rudolf Sonntag, "Discusión con Héctor Béjar," *Libre* 1 (Paris), (1972): 44–52.

24. *Granma Weekly Review*, 21 November 1971, pp. 9, 12.

25. F. Castro, "Speech at the Farewell Meeting Arranged for Him by the People of Chile at the National Stadium," ibid., 19 December 1971, pp. 2–4. See also press conference on pp. 9–11.

26. See ibid., 23 and 30 September and 7 October 1973. Castro's detailed version of the coup is given in the latter.

27. The only reaction of the Cuban press to some of these problems was "Respuesta a cierta prensa mexicana," *Granma*, 18 August 1969. See also Patricia Nelson, "Mexican-Cuban Relations," *The Christian Science Monitor*, 11 November 1969, p. 4.

28. *New Nation* (Georgetown), 14 October 1972.

29. *Granma Weekly Review*, 16 September 1973.

30. Cuban reports were published in ibid., 11, 18, and 25 February 1973; see also *Latin America* (23 February 1973): 57–58, (1 June 1973): 176.

31. F. Castro, "Discurso en el Acto Central con Motivo del XV Aniversario de la Victoria de Playa Girón," *Granma*, 16 April 1976.

32. F. Castro interview with Fernando Morais: "Quatro horas de entrevista com Fidel Castro," *Veja* (Brazil), 13 July 1977, p. 43.

33. F. Castro, "Speech at the Close of the Main Rally," p. 5; "Discurso en conmemoración del Centenario," pp. 2–4; and "Speech at the Main Event in Commemoration of the Victory of Playa Girón," *Granma Weekly Review*, 2 May 1971, p. 6.

34. Benjamin Welles, "More Latin Lands Seem Willing to End Ban on Cuba," *The New York Times*, 14 August 1971, p. 3.

35. Ibid.; and "Peru: End of Story," *Latin America* (2 June 1972): 169–70.

36. "Cuba: From Dogma to Pragmatism"; and "Cuba and the Recent Vote in the OAS," *Granma Weekly Review*, 18 June 1972, p. 12.

37. Galo Plaza's statement was made on 26 April 1973 at the Conference "The OAS Today and Tomorrow" at the University of Pennsylvania, Philadelphia.

38. F. Castro, "Speech at the International Workers' Day Parade," pp. 2–3.

39. See *The New York Times*, 19 April 1974, pp. 1, 12 and 6 May 1974, p. 8. *Granma* reported the event in a responsive manner. See *Granma Weekly Review*, 28 April 1974, p. 12.

40. For details and analysis of the Quito meeting see "A Round Table on U.S.-Cuban Rapprochement," *Pitt Magazine* 30 (May 1975): 31–38.

41. See *The New York Times*, 30 July 1975.

42. For example, the 1968 conversations between Antonio Núñez Jiménez, president of the Cuban Academy of Sciences, and American intellectuals who tried to facilitate the interchange of scholars and publications; the 1968–69 agreements of the Hispanic Foundation, Library of Congress, and of the Latin American Studies Association in order to promote intellectual interchange; the seminars held in 1968–69 by the Center for Inter-American Relations (CIAR) of New York with the purpose of recommending to the U.S. government a new policy with respect to Cuba; and the 1969 Ford Foundation grants made available for field research in Cuba. See also the articles by John N. Plank, "We Should Start Talking with Castro," *The New York Times Magazine*, 30 March 1969, p. 29; Irving Louis Horowitz, "United States-Cuba Relations: Beyond the Quarantine," *Trans-action* (April 1969): 43–47; Richard Fagen, "United States-Cuban Relations," in Yale H. Ferguson, ed., *Contemporary Inter-American Relations: A Reader in Theory and Issues* (New York: Prentice-Hall, 1972), pp. 192–203 (this is Fagen's report to the CIAR meetings of 1968–69); and Jorge I. Domínguez, "Taming the Cuban Shrew," *Foreign Policy*, no. 10 (1973): 94–116.

43. For background on U.S.-Cuban relations see Cole Blasier, "The Elimination of U.S. Influence," in Mesa-Lago, ed., *Revolutionary Change in Cuba*, pp. 43–80; and Edward Gonzalez, "The United States and Castro: Breaking the Deadlock," *Foreign Affairs* 50 (1972): 722–37.

44. For instance Robert A. Hurtwitch in February 1970 in the television program "The Advocates," in July 1970 before the House Foreign Affairs Committee, in September 1971 before the Senate Foreign Relations Committee, and in February 1973 before the Congress; a State Department report to the OAS in March 1970; Secretary Rogers to the Congress in March 1971; Charles Appleton Meyer to the press in July 1971; and President Nixon to the press in April 1971 and January 1972.

45. *Granma Weekly Review*, 26 December 1971, and 2 January 1972.

46. Ibid., 25 February 1973, p. 3.

47. Ibid., 19 December 1971, pp. 10–13; and George Natanson, "Nixon Doesn't Represent World Realities–Castro," *The Times of the Americas*, 13 May 1972, p.2.

48. *Granma Weekly Review*, 4 June 1972, p. 6. Two weeks later the Cuban press mentioned conditions 3 and 4 ignoring the first two. In October, Castro mentioned conditions 1 and 2 ignoring the last two. In December he ignored condition 1 (the end of the war in Vietnam was in sight) and seemed willing to yield on condition 4. In May 1973 he definitely dropped condition 1, reiterated 2 and 3 (although changing their order, therefore giving priority to a domestic matter over an inter-American issue) and said that condition 4 was still on but had a lower priority.

49. F. Castro, "Speech on the 19th Anniversary of the Attack on the Moncada Garrison," *Granma Weekly Review*, 6 August 1972, p. 6.

50. "Bienvenido Brezhnev," *Time*, 11 February 1974, pp. 37–38.

51. In late 1973 the Soviet press clearly indicated that a Cuban rapprochement with the United States would be welcome: "Even in the United States, sober voices of politicians and public figures are raised increasingly about the need to reexamine U.S. relations with Cuba. . . .Cuba's peace-loving foreign policy is convincing proof of its desire to live in peace and friendship with all peoples, above all with the peoples of Latin America." *Izvestia*, 8 September 1973, as quoted by George Volsky, "Cuba Fifteen Years Later," *Current History* 66 (1974): 14, 35. Reviewing Brezhnev's visit to Cuba in 1974, TASS stated: "Many observers hold the view that the visit will bring about a thaw in the political climate of the Western Hemisphere." Quoted by *Latin America* (8 February 1974): 47.

52. *The New York Times*, 21 and 25 February 1974, pp. C-14 and C-3.

53. Some of these problems were briefly explained by F. Castro, "Speech at the Main Event," p. 6.

54. Cuban military involvement in Africa has not been limited to Angola; the presence of Cuban military advisors, guerrilla trainers, and technicians has been reported by the U.S. press in Somalia, Mozambique, Congo, Guinea, Guinea-Bissau, Tanzania, Ethiopia, South Yemen, etc. (See as an example *The Miami Herald*, 26 November 1975.) In 1977, Castro triumphantly toured eight African countries for five weeks, often meeting with Cuban troops, advisors, and technicians.

55. See David Binder, "U.S.-Cubans Discussed Links in Talks in 1975," *The New York Times*, 29 March 1977, pp. 1, 8.

56. "Ford Says Angola Acts Hurt Detente, Cuba Tie," ibid., 21 December 1975.

57. Most of the following information in the text is taken from Carmelo Mesa-Lago, "Chronology of U.S.-Cuban Rapprochement: 1977, *Cuban Studies* 8 (1978).

58. Details on the agreement were not released until one month later, by *Bohemia*, 25 May 1977, and *The New York Times*, 27 May 1977.

59. *Granma*, 3 June 1977.

60. Quoted by James Nelson Goodsell, "Raul Castro Sees Cuba, U.S. Building Peace Bridge," *Christain Science Monitor*, 11 April 1977.

61. For a full discussion of what the U.S. strategy should be in future negotiations see my "The Economics of U.S.-Cuban Rapprochement," in Blasier and Mesa-Lago, eds., *Cuba in the World*.

Chapter 5

1. I used a primitive version of such a model, for the first time, in the final chapter of the book I edited, *Revolutionary Change in Cuba*, pp. 510–24, to describe and analyze the feasibility of alternative paths thjt were open to Cuba in 1970. My prediction that Cuba would probably follow the Economic-Reform Soviet system has been confirmed by recent history and documented in this book. An improved version of my model was published as "A Continuum Model to Compare Socialist Systems Globally," *Economic Development and Cultural Change* 21 (1973): 573–90. This work stimulated me to organize in Pittsburgh in 1972–73 an international seminar on the "Methodology to Compare Socialist Systems." Papers presented in that seminar, including a substantially enlarged version of my own model appears in Carl Beck and Camelo Mesa-Lago, eds., *Comparative Socialist Systems: Essays on Politics and Economics* (Pittsburgh: University Center for International Studies, 1975).

2. For a full discussion of this hypothesis see my article "A Continuum Model to Compare Socialist Systems Globally," pp. 586–87.

3. In the remainder of this section the causes of the 1970-on Cuban movement toward the center and pole Y are analyzed. For an abstract discussion of the causes of gravitation of socialist systems toward one pole or its opposite in the continuum see my contribution to Beck and Mesa-Lago, eds., *Comparative Socialist Systems*, pp. 108–15.

4. The study was conducted by Luigi R. Einaudi (Kissinger's advisor on Latin American affairs until 1976), Edward Gonzalez, and David F. Rondfeldt. See Gonzalez, *Cuba Under Castro*, p. 226.

5. Cuba's military involvement in Angola since 1975 (variable 16 move to pole X favoring commitment to world revolution) is an exceptional departure from the gravitation of the Cuban system toward pole Y and is also opposite from Cuba's continuous movement toward peaceful relations within the Western Hemisphere. The economic costs of the Angolan adventure are high and, although there are obvious political benefits from it (i.e., partial restoration of Cuba's revolutionary image in the Third World, increased Cuban leverage vis-à-vis the U.S. and the U.S.S.R.), there have been some political disadvantages too (i.e., the 1975–76 halt in U.S.-Cuban rapprochement, the renewed fears of Cuban interference from some Latin American countries). Cuban active military involvement in Africa remains as the most serious obstacle to full normalization of relations of Cuba with the United States.

6. The continuation of Cuban dependency regardless of the change in ideology and association presents a challenge to the theory of *dependencia* developed by Latin American and North American social scientists. Helio Jaguaribe has articulated this point: "The transition of Cuba to socialism resulted in this country's independence vis-à-vis the United States but undoubtedly created a broad and noticeable dependency upon the USSR. . . . A country cannot break away from dependency through a mere change in its system [or ideology] but a feasible transformation of its structure is required ["national viability"]. Cuba lacked the conditions to undertake the latter due to the island's isolation and insufficient natural and human resources,

therefore, its dependent status has persisted." See "La América Latina ante el siglo XXI," *El Trimestre Económico* 41 (1974): 425. For more details see Helio Jaguaribe, *Political Development: A General Theory and a Latin American Case Study* (New York: Harper & Row, 1973).

Index

absenteeism, 95
acopio system, 98, 100, 101
administration, 1970 reform of, 66
agriculture: future of, 157, 158; labor
    productivity in, 39–40; production
    in, 58, 60; in state sector, 114. *See
    also* sugar; sugar industry
air force, 14
Algeria, Castro's visit to, 16
Allende, Salvador, 120
Almeida, Juan, 16
ANAP, 98, 99–101, 114
Angola, 142, 143, 144, 181 n.5
Argentina, 122–23
armed forces, 3, 14, 78, 136; dominance
    of, 68; future of, 157; modernization
    of, 77; officer corps of, 77–79;
    reorganization of, 76–79, 113
Arrufat, Antón, 107
arts, state support of, 106. *See also*
    culture
autocracy, criticism of, 63–64

Baibakov, Nikolai, 10, 11
Barbados, 122
Béjar, Héctor, 127
Bettelheim, Charles, 63–64
black market, 41, 100, 167–68 n.36
Blanco, Hugo, 127
Bolivia, 117, 119
Book Institute, 109
Boumédienne, Houari, 23
Bravo, Douglas, 117–18
Brezhnev, Leonid, 15, 23–25

Caamaño Deñó, Francisco, 130–31
Caldera, Rafael, 123–24
Cámpora, Héctor, 122
canecutting machines, 12, 14, 51–52
capital accumulation, 2, 33–34
Carter, Jimmy, 142–43

Castro, Fidel: on detente, 15, 24; on
    development of communism, 26–27,
    28–29; on economic "mistakes,"
    54–56; on exportation of revolution,
    131; at first meeting of Cuban-Soviet
    Commission, 11–12; foreign travels
    of, 10, 14–16, 128; at Fourth
    Conference of Nonaligned Nations,
    22–23; on material incentives, 45;
    military rank of, 78, 79; on OAS, 131;
    offices held by, 20, 72, 76, 79–80; on
    participation, 66–67; planning
    reforms of, 31; on rapprochement
    with United States, 137–38; on
    relations with nonrevolutionary
    nations, 126; on relations with
    U.S.S.R., 19
Castro, Raúl, 14, 77; on labor supply,
    39–40; on management, 36; military
    rank of, 78; offices held by, 72, 76,
    80; on rapprochement with United
    States, 144; on unions, 87–88
Ceausescu, Nicolae, 22
Center for National Computation and
    Applied Mathematics (CEMACC),
    33
Chile, 120, 128–29
China, Cuban criticism of, 13
Cienfuegos, Soviet submarine facility in,
    136, 139
cigarettes, 41, 42
Civil Code, 1973 reform of, 70
"collective work commitments," 96
collectivization, 5
Comecon, 10, 162 n.20; Cuban entry in,
    17; sugar supplied to, 17–18
Committees for the Defense of the
    Revolution, 5
Communist party. *See* PCC
Compulsory Military Service (SMO),
    104–5

computers, 33
Confederation of Cuban Workers. *See* CTC
Conference of Nonaligned Nations, 22–23
Congress on Education and Culture, 107, 108–10
constitution of 1976, 72–73
consumer goods: as material incentive, 47; price of, 42; supply of, 42–43
consumption, 2
Costa Rica, 123
Council for Mutual Economic Assistance. *See* Comecon
Council of Ministers, 65, 68, 76; Executive Committee of, 20, 68
Council of State, 75–76
Crombet, Jaime, 101
CTC, 40, 83, 114; congresses of, 45–47, 88–92; councils of, 93, 94
Cuban-Soviet Commission of Economic, Scientific, and Technical Collaboration, 10–14, 21–22
Cuban-Soviet economic agreements (1972), 20–21
Cuban-Soviet trade agreement (1965–70), 13
culture, 4, 106, 115; future of, 157. *See also* intellectuals
Czechoslovakia, Soviet invasion of, 8–9

decision making, concentration of, 62, 79–80
democratization, 66
dependence, economic, 153–54, 181–82 n.6
development strategy, 2
Dominican Republic, 130–31
Dorticós, Osvaldo, 10, 20, 27, 34, 35, 36, 72, 122; on labor supply, 40; on work quotas, 38–39
dropout rate, 102, 104, 106
Dumont, René, 64, 107, 108, 109

Eastern Europe, relations with, 22. *See also* Comecon
economic growth, 56–57; prospects for, 60–61, 157–58
"economic incentive fund," 48–49

Economic Management System (SGE), 36–37; future of, 158
Ecuador, 120–21
education, 102–3; compulsory, 104–5; control over, 4, 115; future of, 157; vocational, 102–3
efficiency, measurement of, 37
egalitarianism, 2
EJT, 76–77, 105
employment, 3, 40
Executive Committee, 20, 68
exportation of revolution, 4, 6, 7, 131, 139; in future, 159

farms, cooperative, 101
Fernández, Marcelo, 20
Figueres, José, 123
financing methods, 2
First National Congress on Education and Culture, 103, 105
fishing rights, 143
foco, 116, 117, 125
Ford, Gerald R., 142
Frei, Eduardo, 120

Gelbard, José, 122
GOSPLAN, 14
government: depersonalization of, 112–13; 1972 reorganization of, 19–20; separation of functions of, 113, 156
Guantánamo, 13, 15, 138, 140–41
Guevara, Ernesto "Che," 6–7, 8, 27–28; death of, 117; on planning, 31. *See also* Sino-Guevarism
Guyana, 122, 130

Hart, Armando, 111–12
hijacking, 136–37, 142, 144
"historical wages," 46
Honduras, 123
housing, 47–48
Huberman, Leo, 62
Husak, Gustav, 22

idealism, 26, 27, 28
identity cards, 94–95
illiteracy, 102
incentives, 2; material, 46–48, 158; moral, 44–45, 47

inflation, 3; control of, 41–44; growth of, 40–41

institutionalization, 9, 112–15; positive effects of, 79; Soviet influence on, 115

Integrated Revolutionary Organizations (ORI), 5

intellectuals, government attitude toward, 106–7, 111–12

"interest sections," 143

Intergovernmental Commission of Socialist Countries for the Development of Electronic Computation, 33

investment, 33–35, 37–38

Jablonsky, Henryk, 22

Jagan, Cheddi, 130

Jamaica, 121–22

Japan, imports from, 43

Jaruzelski, Wojciech, 22

JUCEPLAN, 14; 1966 reform of, 30; statistical bulletin of, 32. *See also* planning

judicial system, 1973 reform of, 70

juvenile delinquency, 105

Karol, K. S., 64, 108, 109, 125–26

Kissinger, Henry, 139, 140, 141

Kosygin, Alexei, 12–13

Krutskikn, Dimitri, 14

KTP-1, 12, 14, 51–52

KTP-2, 51–52

labor, voluntary, 50

labor norms, 38–39, 95, 158

labor productivity, 3; increases in, 39; and material incentives, 47–48

labor supply, and money supply, 44

labor unions. *See* unions

landholding, 97–98, 100

Lanusse, Alejandro, 122

Latin America, diplomatic relations with, 118, 124–25, 158. *See also specific countries*

Law No. 1035, 100

leadership councils, 93

legality, 113, 157

Libermanism, 7

literacy contests, 107, 109

loafing, law against, 95–96, 102

McDonald, Frank, 110–11

management councils, 92, 97

managers: government criticism of, 94; selection of, 3

maritime boundaries, 143

Martí, José, 111

mass organizations, 3; democratization of, 66. *See also* unions

"Maximum Leader," 67

media, 108–9

Mexico, 121, 129–30

Military Units to Aid Production (UMAP), 104, 105

militia, 5; phasing out of, 77

Ministry of Culture, 111

MIR, 128

Missile Crisis, 6, 19, 24, 139

mobilization, 4, 5; Castro on, 128–29

money supply, 41–44

Movement of the Revolutionary Left. *See* MIR

National Assembly, 75, 80

National Association of Small Farmers (ANAP), 98, 99, 114; Fourth Congress of, 99–100; Fifth Congress of, 100–101

National Direction of Mechanization (DINAME), 51

National Plenary Meeting on Labor Justice, 96

National School of Management, 36

National Union of Writers and Artists of Cuba (UNEAC), 106, 107, 112

navy, 14; officer corps of, 78; seizure of Panamanian vessels by, 136

"New Man," 6–7, 30–31

Nicaragua, 123

nickel, price of, 21

Nixon, Richard M., 13, 135, 141

Novikov, Vladimir, 11, 13

OAS, 118, 124; Castro on, 131; expulsion from, 117; future relations with, 158; and normalization of relations, 132–34

oil supplies, 19

Olivé, Raúl Alonso, 107

OPP, 73–75; future of, 157; limitations of, 80–82

Ordoqui, Joaquín, 21–22
Organization of American States. *See*
    OAS
Organization of Latin American
    Solidarity (OLAS), 118
Organs of People's Power. *See* OPP
overtime pay, 46
ownership of means of production, 2

Padilla, Heberto, 107–8, 110
Panama, 119–20, 136
PCC, 3, 8, 64, 113; future of, 157;
    membership of, 71; military control
    of, 68; 1970 reform of, 65; 1973
    reform of, 71; 1975 congress of,
    71–72; organization of, 70–71
Peña, Lázaro, 90, 91
pensions, 42
Pérez, Carlos Andrés, 124
Perón, Juan, 122
Peru, 118–19, 127; OAS motion of, 132
"Plan CTC-CI," 47
planning, 2; annual, 32–33; five-year, 33;
    future of, 157; mini, 34–35; reforms
    in, 31–33; for sugar industry, 154–55
Plaza, Galo, 132
Popular Socialist party, 5, 7, 8, 21–22
price increases, and inflation, 42
production, 57–58; 1970 reform of,
    65–66
production assemblies, 92
Provincial Management Schools, 36
PSP, 5, 7, 8, 21–22
Puerto Rico, 142
PURS. *See* United Party of the Socialist
    Revolution.

Qaddafi, Muammar el, 23

rationing, 41, 42, 43
Rebel Army, 5
research, repression of, 110–11
"Revolutionary Offensive," 8, 63
Revolution, stages of, 1, 5–10
Risquet, Jorge, 66, 83, 86, 88, 93, 94; on
    law against loafing, 95–96
Roa, Raúl, 11
Roca, Blas, 70, 72, 73, 75
Rodríguez, Carlos Rafael, 7, 10, 11, 13,
    20, 21, 27–28, 72, 121; Eastern
    European trip of, 16–17; on

personnel problems, 35–36; planning
    research of, 31–32
Rogers, William D., 142

self-financing, 38
sick pay, 42
Sihanouk, Norodom, 23
Sino-Guevarism, 6–7, 8, 9, 25, 152,
    155–56; abandonment of, 25–27
socialist emulation, 46, 47
Social Services (SS), 105
Soviet "model," acceptance of, 32
Soviet Union. *See* U.S.S.R.
Student Directorate, 5
sugar: price of, 13, 21; supply of, to
    Comecon, 17–18
sugar harvesters, 12, 14, 51–52
sugar industry: Australian system in,
    52–54; future of, 157–58; and harvest
    of 1970, 8, 9, 49; labor in, 49–50;
    mechanization of, 50–52; production
    targets for, 49; rationalization of, 54;
    yield in, 53–54
sugar workers, guaranteed wage for, 42
Sweezy, Paul, 63

taxes, 37
technical advisory councils, 93
technicians, training of, 35–36
telephone service, 42
Torrijos, Omar, 119
tourism, 61
trade: with Japan, 43; with U.S.S.R., 11,
    18, 21, 154
trade unions. *See* unions
Trinidad and Tobago, 121–22
Tulubeev, Nikita, 14
Tupamaros, 120
26th of July Movement, 5

UJC, 101–2; reorganization of, 114;
    second congress of, 103–5; third
    congress of, 106
UNEAC, 106, 107, 112
unions, 3; and administration of
    enterprises, 92, 93; decline of 82;
    democratization of, 66; elections for,
    83–86; future of, 157; government
    control of, 93–94; participation of, in
    national decisions, 91, 93;

reorganization of, 86–87; revitalization of, 113–14; role of, 87–88, 91, 96–97; and workers' rights, 90–91
United Party of the Socialist Revolution (PURS), 5–6
United States: economic sanctions by, 133–34, 140, 142; future relations with, 158–59; rapprochement with, 134–36, 139–40, 144–45, 155; reconnaissance flights of, 143
University of Havana, 105
University of Oriente, 103
Uruguay, 120
U.S.S.R.: constitution of, 72–73; and Cuban-U.S. rapprochement, 138–39; future relations with, 159–60; influence of, 5–6, 7, 9–12; military aid from, 14, 18; relations with, 4; and satellite communications, 164 n.51; trade with, 11, 18, 21, 154

vacations, 47

Vance, Cyrus, 143
Velasco Alvarado, Juan, 118
Velasco Ibarra, José María, 120–21
Venezuela, 117, 123–24; OAS motion of, 133
Verga, Roberto, 93
Vietnam, 15, 139

wage differentials, 45–46, 158
work quotas, 38–39, 95, 158

Year of Emulation, 39
Year of Institutionalization, 79
Year of Productivity, 34
Young Communist League. *See* UJC
youth: control of, 114–15; disciplinary problems among, 103, 105; neglect of, 101
Youth Army of Work (EJT), 76–77, 105
"Youth Centennial Column," 76, 104–5

Zeitlin, Maurice, 64